PRAISE FOR *ROY KEANE: RED MA*

'How many times after Roy Keane has been involved in some controversy do you see him pictured walking his dog? In a fascinating book, *Roy Keane: Red Man Walking* by Frank Worrall, the former Manchester United star's psyche is brilliantly analysed. In his numerous bust-ups over the years, Keane has never lost faith in his dogs. In the book the Celtic star says: "They don't let you down. They don't turn you over."'   – *Sunday Express*

'An intriguing picture of what makes Keane tick'
     – *News of the World*

'A great football book'   – *Daily Star on Sunday*

'A brilliant buy for football fans everywhere'   – *The Sun*

'Worrall has a nice turn of phrase and clearly cares passionately about his subject'   –   *FourFourTwo*

'I found it to be a great read'   – Aidan Cooney, *Ireland AM*

'Well worth a look – an objective book on Keane'
     – Robbie Irwin, RTE

'A new, alternative focus on the biggest name in Irish sport'   – NewsTalk 106, Dublin

'It has apparently been four years since the public were treated to a biography of Roy Keane . . . Frank Worrall has obliged with Red Man Walking'   – *Daily Telegraph*

'Worrall's book gives an insight into the psychological make-up of Keane and admires his successful years . . . an interesting opinion of events, including his altercation with Manchester City's Alf-Inge Haaland and Keane's departure from Manchester United'   – *The Scotsman*

'Definitely four stars'   – *NUTS*

Frank Worrall is a journalist who writes regularly for the *Sunday Times*, *The Sun* and *FourFourTwo*. He is also the author of *Wayne Rooney: World at His Feet*.

Roy Keane

RED MAN WALKING

FRANK WORRALL

MAINSTREAM
PUBLISHING
EDINBURGH AND LONDON

This edition, 2006

First published in Great Britain in 2006 by
MAINSTREAM PUBLISHING COMPANY (EDINBURGH) LTD
7 Albany Street
Edinburgh EH1 3UG

ISBN 1 84596 225 7

A catalogue record for this book is available from the British Library

All internal illustrations © Cleva

Typeset in Gill Sans and Stone Informal
Printed in Great Britain by
Cox & Wyman Ltd

For:
Angela,
Natalie,
Frankie Lennon,
Jude Cantona,
Frank and Barbara,
Bob and Stephen.

Not forgetting:
Georgie, the Belfast Boy, RIP.

SPECIAL THANKS
To: Alex Butler, Bill Campbell, Sharon Atherton,
Graeme Blaikie, Paul Moreton, Hugh Sleight,
Andy Bucklow, Martin Creasy and Colin Forshaw.

THANKS
To: Sam Wostear, Neil Rowlands, Jonathan Worsnop,
Adrian Baker, Lee Clayton, Dave Morgan, Nick Chapman
(ICF), Steve Waring, Alan Feltham and the boys on Sun
Sport, Kevin O'Brien, Roz Hoskinson, Steven Gordon,
Michael Patrick O'Brien, Pravina Patel, Craig Tregurtha,
Matthew Clark, Terry Ryle, Russell Forgham,
Ian Rondeau, Lee Hassall, Andy Mitten, Roy and Pat
Stone, Tom Henderson-Smith, John Fitzpatrick,
Shaun and Connor Taylor of KFM,
Paul and Karen, Chase, Debbie and Miles,
Roy Keane and Wayne Rooney.

CONTENTS

PREFACE

So just what do you give the man who has everything as a leaving present – especially, as in the case of Roy Maurice Keane, if he has been possibly the finest employee you have ever had on your books, someone who has given *you* everything, someone who has laid down his body and his career for you, someone who has put the whole lot on the line so many times for the betterment of Manchester United Football Club? How about handing him the keys to the manager's office, or at least a written promise that he can return as boss one day? How about an immediate job as a coach? How about a new deal that would let him play and coach? How about getting down on one knee and begging him to stay?

But this is no ordinary player we are talking about. This is not a man who can be bought off by fawning or beseeching. This is a man who would see right through any of that sycophancy. This is a man who will do what he wants, the way he wants and how and when he wants. So cut the crap and wait for him to tell you what he wants, what he is going to do. And certainly you would *never* think of sacking this loyal servant . . . or would you, Sir Alex?

This is a man who can truly be said to walk the walk – at least when his dog Triggs is tugging at his feet. Here is a man who has had a glittering career under two of the greatest football managers to grace the game, Brian Clough and Sir Alex Ferguson, a man who has battled his way to the top, a late starter in the big-time who had to overcome an initial height and weight problem and who has constantly battled a gnawing hole in his soul, a feeling of never being quite as big, quite as good, quite as hard. You know the one: the one that would compel him into using his every last scrap of mental and physical strength to prove that he was the best in everything.

You know what? I had always loved Roy Keane the footballer, but I'd never really warmed to Roy Keane the man – until, that is, I did the full research and talked to numerous people for this book. I shadowed Roy during the last 12 months of his Manchester United career, analysing his comments to the press, talking to former associates, players, psychologists, fans and admirers from Dublin to Manchester. Then I found something I half suspected all along: the real Roy Maurice Keane is not the man he would have us believe. The hard-man, warrior front is exactly that – a front, an illusion to keep you and me from getting too close to him and, more specifically, the truth.

Roy Keane is actually just flesh, blood and insecurities like me and you. He is not even the man portrayed in that wonderful read of an autobiography he penned four years ago. The man in that book is something of a parody, an illustration of how Roy Keane was willing to live up to his own infamy, of how he would like you to see him – the (red) devil who would wait patiently to wreak his revenge on an opponent with an attack that could put him out of the game for good, the couldn't-care-less Irishman who liked to be in your face and did not give a fuck personally if you liked it or not, the man for whom winning was everything and coming second was failure.

No, that was only the public face, the identifiable persona of this complex man. I found another Roy Keane and, surprisingly, it was one I grew fond of: a true man who, for all his European glory, his FA Cups, his Premiership titles and his awesome leadership of Manchester United, is a genuinely good guy. Roy Keane is, in my opinion, a top family man, a good, loyal person, a man who has had to learn the hard way how to overcome the addictive demons that once threatened his very life, let alone his football career. My abiding image of Roy Keane remains not his lifting of cups – although that is a powerful memory – but of the man who gave one of his Ireland shirts to a young boy who was dying of cancer in a Dublin hospital. The footballer's secret visit had brought such comfort to the boy that he'd asked to be laid in his coffin in one of Roy's shirts. That is the man I admire, not the swaggering tough guy.

This book is an appreciation, an anatomy if you will, of Roy Keane, the Manchester United legend, bringing the story of his magnificent footballing career bang up to date in 2006 and, just as importantly, attempting to get behind the façade and unmask the *real* Roy Keane.

Frank Worrall

ONE

THE NORTHSIDE

'Roy Keane is Damien, the devil incarnate off the film *The Omen*. He's evil. Even in training' – Ryan Giggs

'I got a reputation which pleased me. "He doesn't take no shit"' – Roy Keane

Craic – noun (also 'crack'). Enjoyable time spent with other people, especially when the conversation is entertaining and amusing. E.g.: The boys went driving round the town just for the craic – *Cambridge Advanced Learner's Dictionary*

Sometimes, the craic ain't all it's cracked up to be. Just because you hail from Ireland, it doesn't mean you are going to be the archetypal blarney-talking good companion the tourist board love to paint. Just ask Roy Keane if you don't believe me. A Cork lad born and bred, he was not renowned for having a laugh or enjoying a bit of amusing banter at Manchester United FC. No, the legend of Roy is one engendered in that image of an essentially solitary, usually serious figure who much preferred his own company to being in a crowd of jokers – the (red) devil incarnate, as Giggsy would have it.

But was he always like that? Well, no and yes. He has

always been driven to prove he is the best – a mission that would lead him to long periods of introversion and self-questioning – but he had periods as a lad when he *would* participate in the craic. And his final days at Nottingham Forest and early days at Old Trafford were characterised by his weakness in the presence of booze – a failing which would lead to nightclub bust-ups and reprimands from Clough and Ferguson.

So what was his youth like? Exactly what had moulded the Roy Keane who arrived in England as a raw, brash fighter of an 18 year old in 1990? Surely life couldn't have been that tough in beautiful Cork – 2005's City of Culture?

City of Culture? Roy would have accused you of having a laugh if you'd suggested it would end up that way. It certainly wasn't that way when he was growing up there. OK, maybe it was green and pretty downtown, what with the cathedral and all the history and architecture you would associate with a medieval Irish city, but driving a couple of miles up the north ring road to the Northside would have brought you face to face with the real world – the world that Roy Keane found himself growing up in.

Ireland's economy – and that of Cork city – began to recover from depression in the 1980s, as Roy Keane was learning his craft as a footballer – a learning curve that would eventually lead him to England. The transformation of Cork from its previous run-down condition would prove remarkable. New hi-tech industries would be set up in the city and giants of the electronic, computer and pharmaceutical industries – including the Apple computer corporation and Motorola – would establish factories there. Unemployment levels would start to fall and new shopping centres would open. The construction industry would boom, with the demand for new houses far exceeding the supply. The communications and transport infrastructures of the city would improve enormously and there would be a rise in the standard of living for many.

For many, but not for all. Not for those in the Northside, such as the Keane family, who lived a proud, honest life in the sprawling council-house dominated suburb of Mayfield. Life in Mayfield was no big party. The craic may have been heard loud and heartily in the rejuvenated Huguenot Quarter around French Church Street, Paul Street and Carey's Lane, but the same light-hearted manner was in much scarcer supply in Mayfield.

The Northside did not benefit anywhere near as much as the tourist traps in Cork from the so-called Celtic Tiger of economic uplift. Unemployment, which stood at a high of 26 per cent in 1986, and poverty were rife, along with alcoholism and drug abuse. Many were left sorely disappointed when companies such as Apple arrived in the early '80s, and were destined to remain so. 'Ask how many people at Apple are employed from the Northside,' said Joy, a community leader in the area, in *Johns Hopkins* magazine in 1999. 'Kids on the side of the road are taking down the names and licence numbers of the long, fancy cars that go by. They ask how come their parents don't go down that road.' As for the Celtic Tiger, Joy laughed bitterly: 'When it passed Knocknaheeny [a nearby community where unemployment would hit 60 per cent], it found the nearest tree and pissed on it.'

So this was the unequal social climate in which the young Roy Keane's personality would be moulded. His mother and father would make sure that he and his three brothers never went without the essentials. All their needs were met, but not all their wants, as Roy grew up in a poor suburb of a city enjoying increasing affluence.

He was an outsider looking in, the boy enviously eyeing the expensive toys in the shop windows at Christmas, and this environment would help frame his outlook on life. He would never accept perceived injustices or put-downs – whether they be the bullying of a friend or the fact that 'the suits' occupied first-class seats on trips abroad by aeroplane while he and the other Irish national players travelled economy class. And he would fight to the death for what he wanted and for what he believed in, whether it be a new contract at United or better training facilities for the Irish national team.

I asked a psychoanalyst friend to give a view on how Roy's early character determined his future make-up. She said, 'This was someone who was introverted as a boy and found it difficult to show his emotions. He was shy and concerned about how people saw him. It was important to him that people thought well of him when he was young. As he grew older, he would make out this was not important to him, although it actually was. He would hide his emotions and put on a false front to stop people uncovering the real person. This type of person is often a frightened person underneath it all, someone who will gloss over their fears by making themselves seem uncaring and unmoved.'

Roy Keane was born on 10 August 1971, the fourth of five children to Maurice and Marie Keane. A shy, diffident boy at school, he would excel early at football and boxing. He knew he was small but worked hard to overcome his lack of physical presence by practising for hours at heading the ball, shielding it and running to build up his stamina. The boxing was another way to grow physically, although he would eventually abandon the sport in favour of his first love, football. In his autobiography, *Keane*, he admitted boxing also served as a defensive shield. He said, 'I was still very small for my age and the techniques and disciplines learned in the boxing ring provided me with a psychological edge: I could look after myself even though I was small and shy.'

As luck had it, his family was rooted in strong Irish sporting achievement. His mother was a relation of Jack Lynch, who had won All-Ireland medals in Gaelic football, and his father Maurice, also known as 'Mossie', was a gifted footballer at amateur level in Cork.

At school, Roy was a quiet pupil, content simply to get through each day without incident. He conceded:

> I went to the local primary school, St John's. I didn't shine in the classroom. I was quiet, happy not to be noticed. For me and my friends, it was sport rather than education that really mattered in our lives. Life began when the bell rang to signal the end of the day.

His shyness helps to explain his late entry into the professional game. He would think he was good enough – he knew it – but he was held back by the fear of rejection. Better not to take a chance on trying to make the big grade in case he was turned down. A source close to Roy in Cork confirmed this: 'He was always the best player on the pitch but he was so chronically shy. It was as if he would rather stay as a big fish in a small pond than take the risk that someone at a higher level would say, "Well, you're not quite good enough." It made him look a slow developer when actually he was always the best. It was his shyness that was the problem.'

Roy was a homely lad, and he would face the problem of homesickness when he first sailed to England. Brought up in a council house with a close family and three brothers – Denis, Pat and Johnson – and a sister, Hilary, who also adored him, he was proud of his roots and his family. In later life, he would make a point of stressing, 'I am from Cork first, Ireland second,' and, 'Irish by birth: Cork by the grace of God.'

He would also claim to suffer from 'a superiority complex'. My psychoanalyst says, 'That is yet another coping mechanism, another defensive shield. A superiority complex is usually the sign of someone who will go to any lengths not to be hurt. Again, it's a case of you can't hurt me if you can't get close to me. Again, it is a sign of fear of being exposed as someone who feels they are a "not quite" – not quite good enough, not quite up to whatever it may be.'

Having said all that, Roy was also a good lad, someone whom his closest friends trusted and were loyal to. He would stick up for anyone who was getting a bad deal – again, his sense of injustice being activated. There is the story of how he stepped in to help another boy at secondary school who was being bullied. A bigger kid was pinching the boy's lunch box each day on the way to Mayfield Community School and the victim was afraid to tell his parents. Roy found out about it – the boy walked the same route to school as he did – and 'sorted out' the bigger lad with his fists. The bullying promptly came to an end.

His football career began at the age of eight when he joined Rockmount AFC instead of his local club Mayfield, where all his schoolmates played. He was swayed by the fact his brothers Johnson and Denis played for Rockmount but also because '. . . Rockmount was a very successful club . . . Because of its renown, Rockmount attracted the best young footballers from all over the Cork suburbs . . .'. Aged eight he may have been, but even then he had a calculating brain. This was a boy who knew what he wanted and how he would get it, even if he were at a disadvantage because of his shy personality. By nine, he was playing for the Under-11s, but he would not make the grade for the Irish Under-15 international team – an omission he blamed on his size and personality.

Roy struggled at school because his mind was obsessed

with a career in football. He was no genius but he was a clever lad who is the first to admit he could have done much better if he had only applied himself. He left Mayfield having failed the Inter Cert exam – the Irish school-leaving certificate – and faced what you might optimistically term an uncertain future. The economy was struggling and, as is the case in many unemployment black spots around Ireland and indeed the UK, Roy faced realising his dream to become a pro footballer or ending up with a job in a local factory or signing on. He enrolled on a course designed to bring him up to the necessary education standard for the leaving certificate and started to write to English football clubs in the hope of getting a trial. It would prove a fruitless exercise. The only glimmer of hope came when Brighton and Hove Albion offered him one, only to change their minds and cancel the trip at the last minute.

Roy is a Catholic but was probably unaware of the irony that – when all seemed lost – hope back then would come in the shape of a local carpenter. Eddie O'Rourke was also the youth team manager for Cobh Ramblers and persuaded Keane to sign, nicking him from under the noses of Cork City. Both clubs offered a future for him as a semi-pro, but Cobh and O'Rourke seemed to have the better prospects.

It would also involve more travelling for Roy to the island town ten miles from his home. That did not deter the young Keane, now 17. He knew what he wanted and was willing to put in the extra effort. It quickly proved worthwhile; he was nominated by his new club as their player to participate in a new football training scheme set up by the Irish government. Roy would spend five days a week in Dublin on the course, then turn out for the Ramblers at the weekend. In the biography *Roy Keane: Captain Fantastic*, Maurice Price, one of the directors of the course, says Keane was a winner from day one, particularly with his never-say-die attitude. Price said:

> His attitude was superb. We'd play little five-a-side and seven-a-sides and he'd be scoring goals and even in those days he had that desire to win and would never stop running, like he does now.
>
> He was always very skilful, always very professional and very good at working on the course. Keane and the other boys would get a weekly wage but it wasn't much, maybe £30 if that, and then their clubs would put something towards their travelling expenses, especially if they had a midweek game.

Roy felt homesick in Dublin and longed for the weekends and his return to Cork. He admitted that homesickness and his shyness were a problem and that he missed his parents terribly. The familiar traits that would in later life lead him to a period on the booze and then to become something of a recluse can be traced back to his childhood, his youth and his teen years. Looking at it this way – that Roy had always been at a disadvantage because of his shyness – certainly helped me warm to him as this book progressed. It became easier to accept that the tough-nut exterior was, as my psychoanalyst friend would consistently argue, a mere front. As his close friends would confirm, Roy is actually a decent man with a soft side, although he would not thank them for airing that view in public and denting his macho image.

The experience of living in Dublin toughened him up emotionally, mentally and physically. When he returned home to play for Cobh, it was noticeable that he had grown bigger and stronger and the regular detachment from his family would stand him in good stead when the time came for his departure for England.

His big break would not be long coming. Roy had subtly changed his game as he matured. From being an all-rounder – which he felt held him back when the scouts from England came to the matches – he decided to base his performances on his new hero, Bryan Robson. True, Glenn Hoddle had long been his idol but our Roy was a realist. He knew he could not perform the tricks of the Spurs man, nor did he have his skills. But Robbo? Well, that was a different story.

Roy himself was proving just as much a powerhouse figure on the Irish semi-pro circuit and, inevitably, he was eventually spotted by a scout from an English club, Nottingham Forest. The exact day was 18 February 1990. Cobh Ramblers travelled to Dublin to play Belvedere Boys, a well-respected outfit, in the National Under-18 Cup. Belvedere had held Ramblers to a 1–1 draw at Cobh a few days earlier and were expected to wrap up the tie in the replay – which they did, thrashing them 4–0. But they had their work cut out containing the emerging force that was Roy Keane. As Keane, in his best macho autobiographical voice, would later admit:

> I played for myself. Even when the game was lost, I kept going. I'd show those Dublin bastards that I could fucking play . . . I was like a man possessed – by that strange compound of anger, frustration and personal pride.

The last phrase just about summed up the demons that would drive Roy Keane throughout his professional footballing career in England, demons that he would describe as a raw 18 year old as 'strange' – as in puzzling – yet that he would ultimately come to understand. The anger, the frustration and the personal pride were the base ingredients of a mighty brew that would lead him close to the edge and sometimes – as in the case of the dreadful sequence of events involving Alfie Haaland – over it. It was a brew that he could neither control nor make sense of as an 18 year old and one that would continue to haunt him for the rest of his playing career in England.

As my psychoanalyst friend adds, 'You have got to understand that someone who is motivated by resentments and anger is going to push himself to the limit – and others, too. It is not a matter of them being "bad"; they just have to be the best to make up for that underlying feeling of insecurity and never being quite good enough. They can only lose these demons when they confront them, and for that to happen, many people need help.'

Bearing those words in mind, my search for a 'warmer' Roy again gathers pace – in a sense, he was not to blame for some of his more unpleasant indiscretions. In fact, and this may sound crazy, he was actually the victim of those demons.

Noel McCabe was the man who will go down in history as unearthing the player who would go on to become one of the world's greatest ever exponents of the midfield craft. By June 1990, the Forest employee had arranged for Keane to travel for a trial to Nottingham. The boy was asked to turn out for Forest reserves against Tranmere in a Midland League game. Now the stakes were at their highest: flunk it and obscurity beckoned; pass the test – in front of Liam O'Kane and chief scout Alan Hill – and a golden future could be had. Keane took to his biggest stage with the butterflies rumbling in his belly but that potent brew of rebellious defiance – from the years of anger, frustration and personal pride – beating loud within his heart.

Young Roy Keane was to sign for the first of two managerial legends who would shape his professional career. Given Roy's dislike for anything that was half-cocked, half-baked, half-hearted or simply not perfect, it was provident that Brian Clough would become his first boss in the pro game and that his second would be Alex Ferguson. Here was a boy-man with his own strongly held opinions: two lesser men than Clough and Ferguson may well have struggled to cope with the fire within.

Clough – affectionately known as Old Big 'Ead – made his presence felt within minutes of meeting the nervy young Irishman. Walking in on the deal being brokered by Ronnie Fenton, he told his assistant to wrap it up quickly after Fenton had confirmed the good news that Roy 'can play a bit, boss'. Forest paid Cobh Ramblers £47,000 for Keane's services and signed the boy on a £250-a-week three-year contract. Roy would return to Cork for the summer, spending time enjoying the craic with his friends, drinking and socialising. He had crossed the line from relative poverty to sudden minor riches – and felt he deserved to bask in his good fortune.

Roy Keane had made the first steps on a trail that would lead to worldwide fame, acclaim and money beyond his wildest dreams. Yet, while you could take the boy out of Cork, you could never take Cork out of the boy. He remained at heart staunchly loyal to his upbringing, his family and the so-called rebel county in which he had been moulded. He would take all his character defects and feelings of insecurity and inadequacy with him to Nottingham and, subsequently, Manchester, and hide them beneath a tough-guy façade. But he would remain a symbol of hope and a hero in his native Cork.

Just before the World Cup of 2002, he would receive an honorary doctorate from University College, Cork. About the presentation day, still modestly shy, Keane would later say, 'I was in UCC last week and it was a huge honour for me and my family, but a day like that takes its toll on me. I don't feel comfortable in places like that. I'm grateful, but give me my kids and walking the dog any day.'

When, in July 2004, he returned to play football in the city for the first time in 14 years, he was greeted like a returning king. The Manchester United skipper proved to be as popular in his home city as he was in his adopted city of Manchester – despite his controversial return home from the 2002 World Cup. Roy proudly led a young United reserve side into a fund-raising match for his old Cobh Ramblers club – and, once it had been confirmed he would be playing, the match had to be switched from Cobh's tiny home to the bigger Cork City stadium. The capacity crowd gave Keane a rapturous welcome as he led United to a 2–1 win. When he was substituted on the hour, the applause was deafening. This meant everything to the local boy who had done good: the same shy, uncertain boy who had grown up within the tough environment that was now gleefully celebrating his return.

His cake was iced just a year later when he received the freedom of his home city. An audience of 850 was at the Cork City Hall to see their famous footballing son receive the honour, together with athlete Sonia O'Sullivan. Keane, watched by his wife Theresa and three of their children, plus mother Marie and father Mossie, said, 'I am tremendously proud more than anything else to be honoured in my home town and I am deeply moved by the occasion.'

The Lord Mayor Sean Martin spoke of United's skipper as 'a role model and a cultural icon' and added that walking away from the World Cup following the bust-up with the then Republic of Ireland boss Mick McCarthy was his 'most courageous performance'. Irish singer Conn O'Driscoll wrote a special song about the 33 year old, and a framed copy of the words to the 'Ballad of Roy Keane' was presented to the player.

Not bad, hey, for a boy who had been variously described as not tall enough, not big enough, not good enough.

Sometimes the demons that would destroy us can also propel us towards greatness. The latter was certainly true in the case of Roy Keane. In 1990, this awkward, stubborn and prideful son of Cork, this fiery product of the Northside would sail across the Irish Sea and go on to become the best player of his generation, the captain of Manchester United and possibly the greatest midfielder ever to pull on the club's red shirt. But the 18 year old's first stop would be Nottingham, where he would come of age under that old rascal and motivational genius Brian Clough.

TWO

YOUNG BIG 'EAD

'You get it, you pass it to another player in a red shirt' – Brian Clough to Roy Keane, August 1990

'Cloughie is the greatest English manager ever. Sir Alf Ramsey won the World Cup but what Clough did was more impressive' – former Forest star Kenny Burns

'Wherever you go in the world, the city of Nottingham has become synonymous with Robin Hood and Brian Clough and there is no doubt he has touched the lives of so many people in the area' – Nottingham Forest chairman Nigel Doughty's tribute after Clough's death, September 2004

'In Keane's early days at the City Ground, we thought about bringing in an interpreter. His Irish brogue was so pronounced and rich that, for a second or two, I thought we'd landed someone from the Continent' – Brian Clough

If Old Trafford was to be the theatre in which Roy Keane would emerge as a truly world-class player, the City Ground proved to be a fine rehearsal room on the road to fame and fortune. Keane was blessed indeed to have the two best managerial motivators of his generation as mentors. His talent developed from a brilliantly raw potential to pure genius. These two managers were, in their own idiosyncratic ways, all he could have hoped for to guide him to greatness.

Old Big 'Ead certainly touched Keane's life and helped his development. Keane had spent the summer of 1990 celebrating his move to Forest before finally joining them in August. In his own mind, he was in the big-time – he had made it at the age of 18, a relative latecomer in the big league, maybe, but, finally, here he was. Clough would take an interest in him from the start, but often through his coaches. He would get reserve-team coach Archie Gemmill to push 'the Irishman', as he liked to address Keane, to the limit. Clough made it one of his first jobs when Keane arrived from Ireland to improve his fitness. It would not be easy – Roy had not left his days of excess behind in the Republic. He still enjoyed his late nights out 'on the lash'. It was no way for a young footballer to look after himself. Roy was also still suffering from that ingrained shyness. A drink or two, or three, allowed him to relax; he could 'be himself' and socialise more easily. In reality, of course, he was hiding behind the drink. As my psychoanalyst friend says, 'It is typical behaviour of someone who is beguiled by self-doubt and chronic shyness. The person uses a crutch to get by – in this case, alcohol, rather than addressing the main problem behind the feelings of discomfort. The alcohol eventually becomes the only way some people can function after a period of time – they need the crutch permanently. It is their main form of solace.'

Roy found many places of solace in Nottingham. In many ways, it was similar to Cork. It had also suffered from economic decline and the social problems inherent in many poorer inner cities. Like Cork, it also possessed places of great beauty on its borders – Sherwood Forest being the obvious example. The major difference for Roy Keane in 1990 was that, while in Cork he was the poor boy looking in, he was now well on the way to becoming the rich boy looking out. He could afford to live in relative luxury and have the comforts and excesses that a pro footballer's money would bring.

Clough, himself not averse to a good booze-up, saw the temptations bestriding his new boy and did his best to 'keep him on the straight and narrow', even suggesting he should get married and settle down. That did not appeal to the Irishman, still in his late teens.

In these politically correct days, Clough would probably have been brought to book for his constant niggling of Keane by referring to him as the Irishman. He rarely called him by his name; it was part of Clough's own eccentric pattern of control. He liked to make it clear he was *the* man. Any upstarts were soon put in their place.

He managed to get Keane in digs with a family and worked hard to protect him from the media. 'Cloughie did a great job keeping the press at bay,' says one Forest insider. 'He told them Roy was one for the future and that they should concentrate on the first team. He saw that Roy was terribly shy and tried to shield him for as long as he could.'

Clough also allowed Keane frequent returns to his family in Cork, understanding that he was homesick and that it could affect his development if it became too big an issue. A grateful Keane would later admit, 'Brian Clough understood I was a lot younger and obviously homesick at the time and he was very understanding.'

Clough was also a marvellous motivator on the football pitch. He had a Midas touch, and Keane listened to him and learned. Keane knew the man was a winner, and that was a trait he would value throughout his career. If a manager had produced the goods – like Clough and

Ferguson – Keane would knuckle down without question. If the boss could not show his medals – as was the case with Ireland manager Mick McCarthy – Roy could prove argumentative and, as McCarthy would claim at the World Cup finals in 2002, even disruptive.

Clough's pedigree was beyond debate; Keane knew he was joining arguably the greatest club manager ever. He had transformed Nottingham Forest's fortunes during an amazing spell of success from 1978, when they won the old First Division championship. Forest then went on to win the European Cup twice in succession; they also won the European Super Cup, which was then held between the winners of the European Champions' Cup and the European Cup-Winners' Cup. During the same period, the club also won four League Cups.

This club was no Manchester United. It had been a run-down outfit in the East Midlands when Clough first arrived. With limited resources, he turned Forest into one of football's biggest names, his work arguably outstripping the success of Sir Alex Ferguson at Manchester United. While Fergie's club had tradition, cash and a massive fan base, Forest had none of those three assets to build upon when Clough arrived at the City Ground in 1975. True, with his reputation, he would be able to attract players – he had already won the League title twice at Derby County, another unfashionable footballing outpost. But they would initially be players on a budget. Signing glittering names for big fees, like Trevor Francis for £999,999, would not happen until four years into Clough's Forest reign.

When Keane arrived in 1990, the great glory days seemed over. Forest had won the League Cup during the summer but the biggest prizes now appeared beyond their reach. It was an ideal situation for the Irishman. He would quickly snatch a place in the first team and then be in a position to try to bring back the days of wine and roses.

Keane was fortunate in another sense: the team was not as good as that of 1978 or 1979, but then again it was hardly a line-up of duffers. As colleagues, he would have the likes of Stuart Pearce, Des Walker and Nigel Clough, son of Brian.

But first he had to prove himself in the reserves, under the eye of that old Scottish grappler Archie Gemmill. Roy refused to accept that he was already at a disadvantage in the imminent battle with the other squad players for a first-team role. OK, he was a late starter, but, the way he saw it, that could actually be to his advantage. It was an attitude that would pay dividends – and surprisingly quickly. Clough was taking an interest in the Irishman and decided to take a look himself when Forest reserves lined up at Sutton-in-Ashfield. To his surprise, Keane was on the bench, with Gemmil's son Scott in Keane's favoured position – but not for long. Clough told Gemmill to 'get your son off and get the Irishman on'. Roy played the last 20 minutes and obviously impressed Clough. Two more reserves matches and then the shocker – at Anfield on 28 August 1990. Keane had arrived at the City Ground for training that morning to learn that Steve Hodge and Stuart Pearce were unfit and would not be travelling to play against champions Liverpool. He and striker Phil Starbuck were told to get on the coach to make up the numbers.

Keane was helping get the kit ready in the dressing-room when Clough pulled him to one side. 'Irishman,' he said, 'what you doing?'

'Helping get the kit ready, boss,' Keane replied.

In Daniel Taylor's fine book on Forest, *Deep into the Forest*, Brian Laws, one of Roy's teammates that night, takes up the story:

[In the dressing-room] we started laughing, thinking Cloughie was taking the mickey out of this kid. Cloughie said, 'No, he's playing – Lawsy, look after him, he's playing right midfield.'

But there was no fear in him. John Barnes was playing left-wing for Liverpool and Roy kicked seven bells out of him. Barnes turned to Roy and said, 'Who do you think you are?'

'Fuck off,' said Keane.

Years later, Roy would admit that nerves never affected him in his career – and that it probably stemmed back to that day at Anfield, when Clough had brilliantly dropped him into the boiling pot of top-class football. Roy told the BBC, 'If you've done your preparations and looked after yourself all week, there's no need to be nervous. I think players tend to get anxious if they've not really done things properly – like eating, resting or training. If you're fully prepared, you've got nothing to worry about – it's just a game of football.

'Brian Clough brought me over from Ireland, gave me my debut after only a few weeks at the club and looked after me well away from football. With top managers like Clough and Ferguson, the advice and the way they train is very simple. People might think there's some magic science to it, but there isn't – they just keep it nice and simple. Brian Clough's advice to me before most games was: "you get it, you pass it to another player in a red shirt". That's really all I've tried to do at Forest and United – pass and move – and I've made a career out of it.'

Keane did well enough against the English champions – although a depleted Forest went down 2–0 to goals from Peter Beardsley and Ian Rush – and Clough rewarded him the next day in his own typically bizarre fashion: by getting him to clean his muddy shoes. Clough had a lot of time for the Irishman – he said he was 'thrilled to bits with him' after the Liverpool match. In his autobiography, *Cloughie: Walking on Water*, he added:

> Shy off the field, on the pitch the boy was a revelation . . . He improved quickly after that nice, comfortable debut I gave him – against Liverpool at Anfield! Keane had that aggressive streak that is so important to players in his position, providing they can control it. We made sure he could control it but I'm not certain he found himself quite so restricted when he moved to Old Trafford. I got fed up seeing him sent off . . . I became incensed at those close-ups of him ranting and raving at the referee or a linesman . . . he wouldn't have got away with any of that when he worked for me and he knows it. But I'll let it pass because Roy Keane is – and was for me – the genuine article.

Quite a tribute from a man like Clough – and after Keane's debut in front of the Kop, Old Big 'Ead would keep him in the team for the next encounter, an away game at Coventry, then for his home debut the following week, when Southampton were the visitors. Keane's driving performance in midfield against the Saints propelled Forest to their first win of the season. Clough brought him off ten minutes from the end of the 3–1 triumph and the crowd gave him a standing ovation. A little embarrassed, Roy headed for the dressing-room. Clough then hauled him back out and, in the public glare, gave him a kiss on the cheek!

It was the start of a wondrous career in English football – and, ironically, Manchester United were also there at the start of it all. Sitting in the Anfield stands that debut night in August 1990 was United scout Les Kershaw, who reported back to his boss Alex Ferguson that he had seen the future, and that the future was from Ireland. From that night onwards, Ferguson would receive regular updates on Keane's progress.

Back at the City Ground, it was clear that Keane respected Clough: he was his sort of man. He had the medals, the T-shirts to say he had been there and done that, and, perhaps most of all, the inspiring man-management that would make you walk over hot coals for him.

Keane became a regular item in the first team and Clough would privately boast about his Irishman. In their biography on Keane, Stafford Hildred and Tim Ewbank report the time an excited Clough said, 'The Irishman has everything he needs to go all the way. He can tackle, he can pass, he can head the ball, and he can score. And he can do it all with the impression he has plenty of time, which is always the indication of a top-class player. You didn't have to be a genius to see that he had something going for him – even my wife could have spotted it. He is one of the best headers of the ball I have ever come across. Blow me, I've not seen anyone jump so well since Red Rum called it a day.'

Keane scored his first goal for Forest in the 4–1 Rumbelows (League) Cup victory over Burnley at the City Ground on 26 September 1990. He had to wait until December for his first League goal at Sheffield United. Soon he was handed the keys to a club car – a brand-new Ford Orion – but he felt another side of Clough when Forest drew 2–2 in an FA Cup replay against Crystal Palace at the City Ground in the New Year. He made a mess of a back-pass to keeper Mark Crossley, allowing John Salako to make it 2–2. Clough's response in the dressing-room was to punch Keane in the face. As his career progressed, it was something that many infuriated opponents – Alan Shearer among them – would have loved to have done. But Clough was probably the only man in football who could have got away with it. In fact, you sense Keane almost felt he deserved the bullying assault. It is hard to imagine the shaven-headed hard man who would patrol the Manchester United midfield in the late '90s taking such a philosophical stance.

By the middle of 1991, Keane would be appearing in the FA Cup final against Tottenham Hotspur at Wembley, in his first season in the top flight and as a result, in no mean part, to his own committed performances in the Forest engine room. His team had finished eighth in the old First Division and Roy had scored eight goals in thirty-five games.

The FA Cup final was to be the day when, to all intents and purposes, Paul Gascoigne ended his glittering career. Gazza would be taken off on a stretcher after a crazy tackle on Forest full-back Gary Charles and would never be the same player again, despite brave attempts to recover from the crippling cruciate ligaments injury he suffered. The star of Italia '90 had fallen out of the sky.

Keane was also struggling with injury in the final – an ankle problem that he later admitted affected his usual all-running, powerhouse performance. Stuart Pearce put Forest ahead just after Gazza was carried off, but Spurs wrecked Roy's day and kept Clough still awaiting his first FA Cup final victory parade. Terry Venables's team regrouped following Gazza's demise and in extra-time emerged as 2–1 winners, courtesy of a Nayim equaliser and a Des Walker own goal. It was a crushing blow, bringing Roy down to earth after the events of the previous nine months, beginning with that unexpected debut at Anfield. Keane would admit, 'The day flew by me. People say you should take it in, but I didn't. I was only a young player at the time. I was very disappointed and I don't think I was 100 per cent fit.'

His life away from the game was also becoming brutal – a consequence of that short-fuse temper and the insecurity we talked about in Chapter One. The summer following the Cup final defeat he spent partying in Cork, with inevitable consequences. His name started appearing in the newspapers for reasons other than football – a problem that would continue right up to his middle years at Manchester United. Roy initially refused to change; in his own mind, he was a rebel without a pause, his own man. It was an attitude that would bring him all kinds of aggro over the years, until he finally learned to walk away from the bigmouths and those who would claim their five minutes of fame at his expense. The drink was fuelling his inner demons. It was the petrol he poured liberally to quell his anger and frustrations, but it would end up doing the exact opposite, actually bringing them to the fore, and he would take it out on some punk in a pub or a club. During the booze binges at Forest, he would be arrested after rowdy scenes outside a Nottingham nightclub and released without charge in 1992. And just a year later he would be thrown out of another nightclub after being caught up in a brawl.

Larry Lloyd, that bull of a Forest defender, once barred him from his pub in Nottingham. He said, 'Keane was jumping up and down on the tables, shouting his mouth off and acting the fool. I had to pull him down by his coat. He was horrible when he had a drink. I gave him short shrift at my place but he used to get in all sorts of trouble elsewhere . . . But it seemed to me that he was looking for trouble rather than it finding him.'

Roy himself would admit, 'I've obviously got involved in one or two scrapes over the years but I wouldn't change a thing. If someone is going to have a go at me, then usually I'll have a go back. You know it's a fault but that's the way it goes.'

In an illuminating interview with *The Observer*'s Sean O'Hagan in September 2002, Roy went some way to admitting that he understood he once had a booze problem and that he also was beginning to comprehend why. When asked if he would be up for a scrap on one of his frequent journeys home from Nottingham, he replied, 'Oh aye. The amount of fights I've had in Cork that I haven't even mentioned. That,' he says, laughing, 'would probably be another book. I mean, people go on about my problems off the field, but they don't even know the half of it. My uncles used to say to me, "Why don't you go and have a drink in a hotel – Jury's or the Metropole, nice hotels like that?" But I would say, "No. No. I don't want to drink in a hotel. I don't want to sit in a hotel with the shirts and ties when I'm 20. I'd rather take me chances in the bars in Cork."'

But O'Hagan delves deeper and gets to the very roots of the character traits that would continue to make life difficult for Roy Keane – the chronic shyness and hopelessness that made him throw up a defensive shield. O'Hagan says:

> Early on, his drinking was linked to loneliness and an inability to fit in socially with his fellow players. I read him back one of his book's most honest passages. 'I found it very difficult to cope with the kind of fame that accompanied my status as a footballer. I wanted to be alone. Stupidity and pride meant that I would never dream of making the first move to initiate a friendship. I was my own worst enemy. My pride stopped me saying, "I wouldn't mind going for a meal with one of yous."'

And there you have it: a gentle, melancholic insight into the man who is often made out to be some sort of monster.

In actual fact, he was a man who was doing the best with the social and psychological information at his disposal at the time. Again, it warms me towards him, and confirms my belief that the macho Roy Keane is a defence mechanism, a public caricature which he plays up to.

Keane's second season at Forest saw his wages rise dramatically – from £250 a week to £700 a week – and Brian Clough, as promised, handed him a £15,000 signing-on fee. It also saw him twice travel to Wembley – for the Zenith Data Systems (ZDS) Cup final and the Rumbelows Cup final. The exotically named ZDS final brought Roy his first medal as a pro, as Forest beat Southampton 3–2. It was a nothing competition for the big English clubs, but Roy still got a buzz picking up his medal.

The League Cup final would bring only disappointment as Forest lost 1–0 to . . . Manchester United – Brian McClair's goal settling the match. Roy had grabbed the winning goal in the semi-final against Spurs and had been sure that would be a good omen at Wembley. Forest once again finished eighth in the League – but Keane and the fans had their fears for next season, the one which would give birth to the Premiership. Could Clough take them any further? Or had the old Midas touch deserted him for good? By October of the 1992–93 season, they had a good idea of the answer. Forest were rock bottom of the newly formed Premiership. Keane, who still had 18 months of his contract to run, became the subject of newspaper speculation and Blackburn are believed to have enquired whether £3 million would be enough for his services. Then there were rumours that Clough would call it a day if the nightmare of relegation came to pass.

Roy took it all in his stride and simply got on with playing his normal game – a role that would bring him the club's Player of the Year award at the end of what turned out to be a tough season. Clough spun the roulette wheel for a final time when he paid Manchester United £750,000 for his old favourite Neil Webb. But Webby was, by now, overweight and out of condition – nowhere near as effective as the player who had left the City Ground in 1989 to join Alex Ferguson's troops. In January 1993, Clough took time away from his side's relegation battle to once again urge Keane to settle down. He said, 'The best thing that Keaney can do is get himself a steady girlfriend, have a courtship and think of settling down to married life.' Incredible, really, when you think about it: Clough was himself a man on the brink, wheeling towards the end of a glorious footballing career and here he was taking time out for the lad who had become his final favourite footballer. Clough would later admit that, along with the likes of Kenny Burns and Peter Shilton, Keane had been one of his best buys.

Keane rewarded Clough's loyalty by signing a new three-and-a-half-year contract at the start of 1993. He was carrying Forest and was disheartened that some had questioned his loyalty over the delay in signing the new deal. Afterwards he said, 'I'm just glad it's all sorted out. I've always said if I was offered the right sort of deal I would stay.' Neither he nor the club mentioned the fact that the contract contained a get-out clause should Forest be relegated. When it did leak out a month later, he felt duty bound to defend himself: 'The bottom line is that I am under contract here. Forest released the fact that I had an escape clause built into it. That was up to them . . . It's a business; it's an industry. If the club does go down, it will be up to myself where I go. Money is not the be all and end all of it. What is important is that I make the best career move I can.'

Clearly, the writing was on the wall. On 26 April, with Forest teetering on the brink of the drop, Brian Clough announced his resignation. It was a shock and it was not a shock. I can remember on the one hand thinking, well, yes, we've expected it, then on the other not quite being able to come to terms with the fact that Old Big 'Ead was actually going to carry out his threat. Keane was also stunned, but he put it like this: 'somehow the energy and belief that Brian Clough at his best had instilled in his teams had been sucked out of the club'. He added: 'He was the one who gave me the chance in the first place and I was banking on him being with us for quite a bit longer.'

The final game of Clough's reign was the 2–0 home defeat by Sheffield United – when the home fans cheered him off the pitch amid their own tears. Roy Keane was also on his way. He was too good to play in League One and he was too ambitious. As Clough remarked, 'Roy Keane shone like a beacon through all the gloom of that desolate season.' He had given Forest good service for that £47,000 fee, playing in a total of 154 games and scoring 33 goals. The second part of his footballing education – under the tutelage of the brilliant but eccentric Clough – was now complete. The door to Old Trafford had always been ajar for the Irishman, but now it was opened wide with a hearty welcome from Alex Ferguson.

THREE

OFF TO SEE THE WIZARD

'I'm not sure whom he [Sir Alex Ferguson] regards as his best-ever signing at Old Trafford but there can't have been one better than Keano' – Steve Bruce

'The game kicked off, the ball went back to Bryan Robson and Roy absolutely creamed him. I thought: Bloody cheek of him – how dare he come to Old Trafford and tackle Robbo like that! I made a mental note there and then that we had to get this boy to Old Trafford' – Sir Alex Ferguson in *Managing My Life*

'He [Keane] left, of course – like all Forest's best players seem to. But, parochialism aside, who could really say he should have hugged the shores when the high seas offered so many new adventures?' – Daniel Taylor, author of *Deep into the Forest*

The story goes like this: when Roy Keane was 16, he wrote to every club in England for a trial. Every one, that is, except Manchester United. And this is where we come in. The reason he did not write to United was simple: he did not think he was good enough. There it was again, that old insecurity floating up to the surface, linked to his shyness, that pervading helplessness.

When he finally decided to leave Forest in that summer

of 1993, the route to Old Trafford would be tricky and treacherous. Keane initially agreed a deal with Kenny Dalglish, then manager of Blackburn. The two men shook hands upon it and Keane travelled back to Cork to let his family and friends know the good news. He liked Dalglish and knew that Rovers had big ideas under mega-rich owner Jack Walker. Keane fully intended to honour his handshake with the Scot and to return to Blackburn on the Monday to put pen to paper on the contract that would eventually make him a multimillionaire.

But that all changed when Alex Ferguson intervened on the Saturday of Keane's longest weekend. Ferguson had become known as The Wizard to the Stretford End, because of the magical times he had brought to the club after the wilderness years. Now he would need to perform some of those skills on Keane if he was not to lose out on the Irishman's talents. Ferguson was distressed to learn that Keane – the man he had for three years earmarked as Bryan Robson's eventual replacement – had been pinched from under his very nose by Dalglish, a man he had little time for. Their vendettas were already the stuff of legend. In 1988, Fergie had walked down the tunnel at Anfield after a game complaining to the referee about a penalty decision. Kop boss Dalglish was nearby cradling his daughter in his arms. With a wry smile, he told newsmen, 'You'd get more sense out of my baby.'

Now Dalglish had trumped Ferguson with an ace card – and the United boss was not happy. In desperation, he called Keane in Cork and asked him why he had not considered coming to Old Trafford. It was then that Keane dropped the bombshell that would alter his future irrevocably and leave Ferguson dancing a private jig of joy. He had not known United would be in for him, he said, but hey, he would be happy enough to fly over and see Ferguson. After all, he had not yet signed forms with

Dalglish. The two men were to spend several hours at Ferguson's Cheshire home and the meeting would lead to Keane joining Manchester United. Ferguson would later admit that he had not even talked money with the man who was to become his skipper. He had simply stressed to him that he saw him as the missing link in his team and that he could expect to replace Bryan Robson as United's engine. The United boss had also spoken about the history of Manchester United and what it meant to be a player at the world's most famous football club.

Keane had not taken much persuading – his family were all United followers and Old Trafford would always have been his number one preferred destination if he had only believed he was good enough. Was this a man of dishonour? In this case, if we look at the stark facts without any emotion, I think we have to say yes, he was. He had verbally agreed a deal with Dalglish and shaken on it, and now he had gone back on his word. On the other hand – and this was the beginning of a love-in with United fans that would never be broken – he had shown how much playing for the Red Devils had meant to him by double-crossing Dalglish. Keane is a genuinely honest man but he was prepared to go back on his decision for something he strongly believed in.

He had been a big fish in a small pond at Forest, but now he was a small one in a massive lake. He had left a relegated team and joined the champions of England – a team with stars like Bryan Robson, Paul Ince, Mark Hughes, Andrei Kanchelskis, Ryan Giggs and so on. United had won their first championship since 1957 – a 26-year wait – and on 3 May 1993 Bryan Robson had jointly lifted the trophy with Steve Bruce in their final home Premiership game of the season, a 3–1 win over Blackburn.

Ferguson, ever the perfectionist, had celebrated with his team but knew Robson was on the last lap of a glorious career. The former England captain had made just five starts in the League all season and Ferguson had been planning a move for Keane when news of the Blackburn deal broke. Keane finally arrived after a fee of £3.75 million – a new British transfer record – was agreed at the end of July. The player, still only 21, would receive a basic wage of £8,000 a week.

Arsenal had also tried an eleventh-hour manoeuvre to lure him to Highbury, with the pledge of even bigger wages and a £4 million fee for Forest, but Keane was now set on a career at United and explained his decision this way: 'I signed for Manchester United because they have got the best stadium, the best team and the greatest supporters in the country. Blackburn Rovers made me a fabulous offer but as soon as United declared an interest there was only one outcome. This is a career move. To come to a club of this size is a good thing for my future. I just want to be a part of it all. Now the new demand for me is to get into the United team. That will be hard enough – they have some fabulous players.'

He wasn't wrong in that last analysis. Some of the United stars would not have been exactly overcome with delight when Keane arrived – Paul Ince probably being the best example. He and Keane had had several exchanges of opinion when they had faced each other for United and Forest over the previous two years and it was rumoured that the self-styled 'Guvnor' did not like him. Still, Keane's Irish international roommate Denis Irwin was awaiting his arrival with a warm welcome and a smile, and Keane was mentally strong enough, and stubborn enough, to stand his ground should the need arise. He had always been able to put on that tough front when needed. Eventually, he would take Bryan Robson's place *and* see off the challenge of Ince for undisputed leader of the pack when the Londoner was sold to Inter Milan.

Keane's first game for United was in the Charity Shield contest against Arsenal on 7 August 1993. He also won his first silverware for the club as United triumphed on penalties after the match had ended all square at 1–1. The Irishman's first game 'proper' was in the League at Norwich City on 15 August 1993. He played a key part in the Reds' 2–0 win, setting up the opening goal for Ryan Giggs with a splendid cross and making sure United stayed solid in the centre of midfield as Bryan Robson surged forward to make it 2–0.

If Keane was a rookie for United that day, there was another man also learning his trade and heading for the big-time in the press box. Colin Forshaw would later go on to make his name on the *Mail on Sunday*, but on Roy Keane's debut day he was honing his craft on the sports desk of the *Eastern Daily Press* in Norwich. Forshaw saw enough in Keane's powerhouse show to convince him he had glimpsed the future of Manchester United. He told me, 'There was a bit of a buzz in the press box that day – what with Keane making his debut and being the most expensive player in British football. The United boys in the press box had told us that Roy had been buzzing in training the week before the match – and that they reckoned he would take over from Bryan Robson as the key man in the side sooner rather than later.

'There was also talk that he and Incey didn't get on that well and that they were competing with each other to show who was the best. The game kicked off and Keane came in with a crunching tackle and it quickly became clear that he was a player who could stand his own ground. He wasn't in the least afraid of letting Ince or Robson know if he felt they had messed up or not gone in hard enough. You could tell there was a friction between him and Ince, but I remember Keane being the one who came out on top – the one who dictated the play rather than Ince.

'Robson was clearly the captain but he was getting on a bit – and Keane and Ince were his legs. It was a bit like United and Keane in 2005 – where young Darren Fletcher and Rooney did the running for Keane as his legs went, only Keane was the one doing it back then. Keane set up the first goal for Giggs and helped United keep their shape when Norwich occasionally threatened. At the end the United lads in the press box were phoning their reports through saying that Keane had been their man of the match. He certainly wasn't in the least compromised by the occasion. There was no disgrace for City losing to United in this form – any team would have struggled – in Keane, they had found a gem of a player.'

Keane made his home debut on Wednesday, 18 August 1993 in the 3–0 win over Sheffield United. In a scene straight out of 'Roy of the Rovers', he scored twice, the first set up by Giggs, the second by Mark Hughes, who grabbed the other goal. It was some introduction to the Old Trafford faithful, who took him to their hearts that night – a mutual appreciation society that would last for another 12 years. Keane then went on to score another brace in the 3–2 Champions League win over Honved in Budapest the following month.

His star was rising on the pitch and off it. He was slowly starting to put his life together. Still abrasive, shy and defensive, he showed a more caring, human side when he started dating his first steady girlfriend, Theresa Doyle, the Irish lass who would become his wife. He bought himself a £600,000 home in the stockbroker belt of Bowden in Cheshire and enjoyed all the luxuries a millionaire could hope for. The readies were certainly rolling in, what with his wages and a £200,000 boot deal he had signed with Diadora.

His first season would be crowned on the pitch as United stormed to the double – winning the Premiership for the second successive year and beating Chelsea 4–0 to lift the FA Cup at Wembley. Three other events would stand out in his footballing life during that first season. He would play the game of his life as United won 3–2 at local rivals City, scoring the winner in his first derby, a result that propelled United on to another championship-winning run. If that was the height of ecstasy, Keane also felt sadness in January when the legendary Sir Matt Busby died. Busby was the initial creator of the club that would become the biggest name in world football, the man who had the courage to not only dream the dream but actually make it happen. The third watershed came at the end of that triumphant season when Bryan Robson left the club to join Middlesbrough as player–manager. He had made 345 appearances for the club, scoring 74 goals. With his departure, Keane would be thrust into the limelight, vying with Ince to become Robson's natural replacement in midfield and also as club captain. But the first season without Robbo would be a disappointment, with United heading off for their summer holidays trophy-less. They surrendered their Premiership title to Blackburn, crashed out of the Champions League at the group stage and lost the FA Cup final 1–0 to Everton at Wembley.

It was time for Alex Ferguson to begin the process of creating the second great team of his reign at Old Trafford. He shocked the fans by flogging three key players: Ince was sold to Inter Milan, Kanchelskis to Everton and Hughes to Chelsea. There were protests outside Old Trafford by supporters who were convinced Ferguson had finally lost his marbles, and after an opening League defeat at Aston Villa it looked as though Ferguson would be fighting for his job. BBC pundit Alan Hansen famously put the boot in on the United boss by pronouncing, 'You'll never win anything with kids' on *Match of the Day*. Hansen was to be left with egg on his face at the end of the season.

Ferguson had not been suffering from a mid-life crisis. No, he had been secretly planning the revolution for some time. Youth team coach Eric Harrison had told him he had the best batch of youngsters he had ever known – the likes of the Neville brothers, Paul Scholes, David Beckham and Nicky Butt – and Ferguson had seen the proof of it with his own eyes. He also believed that Keane was a better player than Ince and that he could do without Kanchelskis and Hughes. Plus he had the inspirational Cantona back as his club captain after his ban for that karate kick at Crystal Palace – and Ferguson reckoned he would be fired up to lead the new generation forward.

The gaffer was to be proved right on every one of his hunches. His decisions were arguably the most important – and the best – of a glittering managerial career. United would overtake Newcastle during the season to win back their Premiership crown. Famously, Ferguson would also out-psyche the volatile Kevin Keegan as the tension reached its highest point. Keegan's Toon army had beaten Leeds 1–0 to build a ten-point Premiership lead over Ferguson's side. Keegan claimed that Ferguson had implied Leeds would roll over against Newcastle – a catalyst for Keegan's now infamous rant on Sky TV: 'Things which have been said over the last few days been almost slanderous. I think you will have to send a tape of the game to Alex Ferguson, don't you . . . isn't that what he wants? You just don't say what he said about Leeds . . . I would love it if we could beat them. Love it. He's gone down in my estimation. Manchester United haven't won this yet; I'd love it if we beat them.' Yes, indeed: if introducing the kids was Ferguson's bravest – and ultimately most personally satisfying – decision, then sparking Keegan to meltdown was probably the highlight of all his mind-game wars over the years.

Keane's personal high point in that 1995–96 season

would come at Wembley on 11 May 1996. With impeccable discipline in a holding midfield role, he proved he had indeed become Robson's rightful heir with a fine performance in the 1–0 FA Cup final win over Liverpool. The victory brought United another Double, and both the fans and Ferguson were quick to acclaim the impact the determined Irishman had had on the team's fortunes. Ferguson embraced Keane after the final whistle and lauded his achievement in bolting the door at the back. He said, 'For all their possession, they didn't open us up once. Keane must take the credit for that. He carried out our tactical plan to perfection. Roy is capable of doing that because he understands the game as well as anyone. We made sure [Steve] McManaman had no room to damage us. Keane protected our space.'

Keane's reward was a new four-year deal from United. The deal, signed on 20 August 1996, saw his wage increase from £8,000 a week to £20,000 a week, enabling him to buy his parents a new luxury home on the edge of Cork's Northside. The deal would keep him at Old Trafford until he was at least 28 and the United hordes took him closer to their hearts because he had turned down opportunities to move abroad that would have made him a much wealthier young man. His allegiance to 'the badge' truly touched the Old Trafford loyalists: he was already approaching legendary status among those on the terraces.

The 1996–97 season was a bit of a downer for Keane and United after the Double glory of the previous campaign. Early season he was blighted by injury: first a problem with his knee that kept him out for a month, then a leg injury that sidelined him for a further four weeks. United did win the League again, but were knocked out of the FA Cup by Wimbledon and enjoyed little success in the Champions League.

On 11 May 1997, Eric Cantona, as United's captain,

lifted the Premiership trophy aloft at Old Trafford after the 2–0 win over West Ham, then walked out of Old Trafford for good. Eric 'the King' explained in a prepared statement that he wanted to do things outside football. He said, 'I have played professional football for 13 years, which is a long time. I now wish to do other things. I have always planned to retire when I was at the top and at Manchester United I have reached the pinnacle of my career.

'In the last four and a half years, I have enjoyed my best football and had a wonderful time. I have had a marvellous relationship with the manager, coach, staff and players and not least the fans. I wish Manchester United even more success in the future.' Inside sources claimed the decision was also made because Cantona had become disillusioned with the financial aspect of the game.

Cantona's decision to leave had taken the club by surprise. The news was announced by chairman Martin Edwards at a hastily convened news conference. Ferguson was also present, but Cantona had returned to France. Edwards said, 'Eric Cantona has indicated his wish to retire from the game. He is away on holiday with his family at the moment. It is not our intention to get involved in speculation about other players at the moment. Eric has been a marvellous servant to United. He came to see me on Thursday and told me of his intentions.'

Ferguson added, 'It's a sad day for United. He has been a fantastic player for the club and we have won six trophies in his time with us. Eric has had a huge impact on the development of our younger players. He has been a model professional in the way he conducted himself and has been a joy to manage. He is certainly one of the most gifted and dedicated players that I have ever had the pleasure of working with. Whenever fans discuss United's greatest ever side, you can be sure that for many Eric's name will be very high up on the list. He leaves with our best wishes and will always be welcome at Old Trafford. He has given us so many wonderful memories.'

Cantona's departure had left Ferguson dismayed and with a problem to wrestle with during the summer break. Just who would he appoint as the Frenchman's replacement as captain? The final team-sheet of the King's reign had read like this: Peter Schmeichel, Denis Irwin, David May, Eric Cantona, Nicky Butt, David Beckham, Phil Neville, Karel Poborsky, Paul Scholes, Ronny Johnsen and Ole Gunnar Solskjaer. Looking at that line-up, the only name that immediately sprung out as a potential team captain was that of Schmeichel. The other two candidates in Ferguson's eyes were his two injured men: Keane and Gary Neville.

Ferguson did not fancy the idea of a goalkeeper leading the team and, in his opinion, Gary Neville was a possible leader of the future. He announced Roy Keane as his new skipper at the start of the 1997–98 season. He knew Keane would not let the troops slack – on the contrary, he would drive them on with the same fire that sparked his own particular brand of passion play.

Keane was 26 on 10 August 1997 and was looking forward to the biggest season of his career. He would lead United through the season and then embark on what promised to be an exciting World Cup campaign with the Republic of Ireland. That, at least, was the plan on paper, and the celebrations had been long and hard back in Cork when he announced what, for his family at least, was the ultimate honour.

The dream survived a mere 48 days. It collapsed into tears and acrimony at Elland Road, Leeds, on 27 September, in a rough-and-tumble Premiership derby clash. Leeds triumphed with a goal from big defender David Wetherall ten minutes before half-time. Keane suffered a dreaded cruciate ligaments injury in a clash with

Alf-Inge Haaland. Some claim Keane deliberately tripped the Norwegian and fell from the alleged foul. Either way, it was Keane who came out of it worst with the injury that would wreck his season. It was an incident that would still have consequences years later. Keane would never forget how Haaland had stood over him hissing and shouting, claiming he was a cheat as he lay injured on the pitch, his season in tatters. It was the beginning of a destructive connection between the two men: one that would mar both of their careers.

Keane would be the initial and, some would claim, the ultimate loser in the vendetta. Afterwards, he said he knew immediately the injury was a bad one: 'I actually heard the ligament snap as I went down and I told our physio Dave Fevre it was bad.' Remarkably, Keane had played on, hobbling around Elland Road for the final ten minutes of the match because United had used up all their substitutes. The United skipper left Leeds on crutches and with the sombre words of Fevre ringing in his ears: 'The knee's knackered, Roy.'

As he lay in his hospital bed in autumn 1997, he inevitably felt sorry for himself – but then the determination kicked in. Ruptured cruciate ligament damage had been known to end the careers of some players, but Roy had beaten the odds before; why not again? He would recover from this and emerge a stronger, better player. It would take a lot of work both mentally and physically to recover, and long hours of torturous remedial training.

The club announced the news the fans had dreaded on 2 October, the day after United minus Keane had still managed to beat Juventus 3–2 in a thrilling Champions League encounter at Old Trafford. Goals from Teddy Sheringham, Paul Scholes and Ryan Giggs had seen off the Italian champions in a group match. This result was no mean achievement; even with Keane, United would have been pleased to win. Juve replied through Zinedine Zidane and Alessandro Del Piero, but fate seemed to smile on United that night. After 65 minutes, midfield grafter Didier Deschamps was sent off, helping balance the teams in the absence of the influential Keane.

United fans were still celebrating the excellent win when the club's stark statement filtered through. It said, 'Roy Keane had an exploratory operation on Monday. A small piece of cartilage was removed and it was also discovered that he would require a cruciate ligaments operation. That will be performed in approximately four weeks when the swelling has gone down. He will be out for the rest of the season.' It was a crushing blow for player, club and fans.

Keane would be joined on his journey of recovery by United youngster Terry Cooke. The promising winger had suffered a similar setback and his presence helped Keane buckle down and lose any lingering self-pity. The sight of the young hopeful also suffering was enough to get Roy going all-out for a full recovery. The way he saw it, he had to push hard and keep his spirits up, if only to help young Terry. Having said that, the road was long, narrow and lonely. On the DVD *Roy Keane: As I See It*, the United skipper was honest enough to share the demons that threatened to engulf him during that desperate season – how he felt depressed and as if he would never recover, how a similar injury had wrecked Paul Gascoigne's career and might ruin his own, how grateful he was to physio Dave Fevre, the man who would push and nurse him back to fitness. Roy said, 'I know it's going to be hard but if anyone can get me back, I know it will be Dave and United. It looks as if I will miss an exciting year on the club and international front but that's life. There's nothing I can do about it and there's no point in dwelling on it.'

On a lighter note, Keane did have something to smile

about in late 1997 when the singer and Manchester United supporter Morrissey released a song called 'Roy's Keen' about a window cleaner that is seemingly a tribute to Keane. The lyrics painted the window cleaner as sharing the same perfectionist characteristics as the United skipper. The song would hit No. 42 in the UK singles chart and was featured on the album *Maladjusted*. Eight years later, Keane would receive more cultural plaudits when, in February 2005, the comedy musical *I, Keano* opened in the Olympia Theatre, Dublin. The comedy show told the story of Keane's exit from the 2002 Irish World Cup squad in the form of a Greek epic, with characters like Keano (Roy Keane), General Macartacus (Mick McCarthy), Fergi the Scottish Dolphin God (Alex Ferguson) and tap-dancing wood nymph Dunphia (Eamon Dunphy, the Irish broadcaster).

Back in 1997, while still recovering from his career-threatening injury, Keane had been in no mood for laughter. He would explain how the injury had made him see life differently – that he had come to understand that football was only a temporal fixture, how lucky he was to have a lovely wife and soulmate in Theresa, and how important his children were to him. He admitted, 'When you get an injury like this, you realise how important your family are to you. Before it was football, football, football, but over the last few months I spent a lot of time with my two girls.'

During the lay-off, he would rarely venture to Old Trafford on match days – his working week did not include weekends. His place of employment became United's Carrington training complex rather than the Theatre of Dreams. He later said, 'It was harder for my wife Theresa than for anybody else, with me hanging around the place at weekends. I couldn't say I'm the easiest person to live with.'

By November, he had been in a hospital theatre for the

operation on his cruciate ligaments: it went well and he even had dreams of playing again before the end of the season. It was typical Roy Keane exuberance. Boss Ferguson warned him to take it easy, to do as Fevre told him and not to take chances or overdo it in the gym.

Keane would also admit that he was unhappy with some of the press coverage after the incident at Elland Road. Some critics had quickly rounded on him, saying it was karmic forces that were at work, that Keane had got what he deserved after his own aggression on other players, not just Haaland. The Irishman was quick to respond in public: 'I don't think I deserved the injury because I nearly lost my career for trying to trip a bloke up. Obviously there are a lot of people who were happy to see me injured but they just keep me going. Their attitude just makes me hungry to get better.' There it was again – the hard-man façade, masking the essentially decent, somewhat fearful man behind it. This was a typical Roy Keane public response when he was cornered.

Later he would emerge bare, without the 'don't fuck with me' front, and admit he was scared and lonely, just a normal guy: 'I haven't forgotten how low I was at times at home. I tried to put on a brave face to the press but there were times when it was so hard.' He would also put on a philosophical face – one you certainly would not associate with Roy Keane the warrior – when asked what he thought in retrospect about the injury and the effect it had had upon him. He said, 'Things happen for a reason. I believe a lot in fate and I know for a fact that what's happened to me has made me appreciate the game more. I hope I'm that little bit wiser.'

In his absence, Nicky Butt had partnered Paul Scholes in central midfield. Butt was a terrier: he would run all day and battle for you as if his very life depended upon it. However, he was no Roy Keane – few were, few are. To my mind, he did not possess that instinctive vision that enabled Keane not only to break up play, but also dictate it. United lost the title as Arsenal raced past them with a superb run of ten consecutive Premiership-match wins. The Red Devils ended the season without a trophy, but there was hope amid the gloom.

Ferguson and the fans knew the skipper would be fit and back in business at the start of the new season, and, at the end of July 1998, Keane successfully came through two friendly matches on United's pre-season tour in Scandinavia. Far from being spent forces, the 1998–99 season would prove to be Keane's and United's greatest season ever – as the recovered skipper and his troops entered the history books as the first English team to win the Treble.

FOUR

THE MIRACLE OF TURIN

'The minute he was booked and out of the final, he seemed to redouble his efforts to get the team there. It was the most emphatic display of selflessness I have ever seen on a football field' – Sir Alex Ferguson, from *Managing My Life*, on Roy Keane's masterful display at Juventus, 1999

'Keane ... is the most important player in the recent history of Manchester United' – Hugh McIlvanney after United's 3–2 victory at Juventus in 1999

In many ways, Roy Keane's destiny during Manchester United's season of wonder summed up the dichotomy of this immensely contradictory man. In 1999, he would virtually single-handedly drag the Red Devils into their first European Cup final since 1968, only to earn the booking that would rule him out of that remarkable night in Barcelona's Camp Nou stadium. Even his consolation prize – a place in United's FA Cup-final-winning team a few days earlier – was tinged with regret and frustration, as he lasted just eight minutes before bowing out with injury.

The United skipper certainly knew what the word frustration meant. He had led United out at Wembley for the Charity Shield against Arsenal in August 1998 eager to blow away the remaining cobwebs and get some of that pent-up energy out of his system. He looked a different man, a different player to the one who had been injured at Leeds the previous season. Shaven-headed, leaner, fitter, this was Roy Keane in his majesty; this was Roy Keane at the peak of his career. What a tragedy that his *annus mirabilis* would be associated with personal sadness – that is, from not wanting to accept his European Champions Cup winner's medal because he hadn't played in the final and felt he didn't deserve it.

Ridiculous logic, really. The final couldn't have been won without the matches that went before it, and Keane had contributed decisively in those. Sadly, though, his demons drove him into conveniently forgetting the part he had played in actually getting United to the European Cup final in Barcelona. Typical of the man: that ingrained perfection again blocking him off from the sunlight of joy from his club's achievement, telling him he was not part of it, that he was only a failure. What utter crap, Roy. You were as important as the rest of them. You *did* deserve that bloody medal. Stop beating yourself up, and one day tell your grandkids the part you played in the miracles of Turin *and* Barcelona.

Funnily enough, for the first couple of months of the season, as Keane eased himself back in like a car with a new engine running carefully for the first 1,000 miles, the critics got it terribly wrong, claiming he was finished, that the injury had slowed him down, that he was afraid to get stuck into a tackle in case the problem flared up again. By November, he was back in business. United had lost just twice – once in the Charity Shield and once in the Premiership, both 3–0 setbacks against Arsenal – and Keane was running around like the Rolls-Royce we knew him to be, rather than the clapped-out Skoda some of the press boys had claimed he had become.

While the year would be one of Keane's best, it would also prove to be one of Ferguson's. The United boss knew his home-grown kids would never let him down and now he stacked the cards superbly well, buying the excellent 'one-man defence' Jaap Stam and the ebullient Dwight Yorke. Stam, a £10.75 million capture from PSV Eindhoven, was arguably one of United's greatest ever centre-backs: it still remains a mystery why Ferguson would later get rid of him. OK, he was a little critical about Gary Neville in his autobiography and alleged in the same book that Ferguson had tapped him up at PSV, but doesn't the United boss regularly knock players in his own bestselling books? No, a United insider suggested to me that the real reason Stam left was that Ferguson believed he was past his best, that he was turned too quickly by speed merchants. I cannot subscribe to that notion: if Ferguson had kept Stam and bought Edwin van der Sar to replace Peter Schmeichel when he retired in 1999, United could well have retained the European Champions Cup.

Like United, Ferguson seemed to falter after the Treble. During it, he could do little wrong. Dwight Yorke, a £12-million snip from Aston Villa, was a master buy. Not only did he contribute goals and flair, he made Andy Cole smile! With the ever-grinning Yorke by his side, Cole appeared free at last from a prison of his own making: one in which, to me, he looked frightened, even like a snared animal. Yorke brought the introverted Cole out of his shell, and they struck up a fine partnership on the march to the Treble.

Ferguson also bought Swedish winger Jesper Blomqvist. He never set United alight – he was no replica of the marvellous Jesper Olsen, who thrived at Old Trafford in the 1980s – but he played his part in the Treble, particularly in the European Champions Cup final, when he was called upon because of the bans that meant Paul Scholes and

Keane would miss United's biggest party night for 31 years.

United fans had been talking cautiously about the idea of the Treble from April. The team were going great guns in the Premiership and when they beat Arsenal at Villa Park in the FA Cup semi-final, the impossible dream started to appear attainable. The Reds had fought a goalless draw in the semi – with Keane having a legitimate goal ruled out by his nemesis referee David Elleray, the Eton housemaster with a niggling penchant for sending our Roy off. On this occasion, he did not give him his marching orders but disallowed his goal on the debatable ruling that Dwight Yorke was in an offside position when Roy's volley flew into the net.

Elleray was chosen to officiate in the replay at Villa Park, and this time he did send Keane off, for two yellow-card offences. In the cauldron of a tremendous midfield battle – Keane and Butt for United taking on Patrick Vieira and Emmanuel Petit for the Gunners – a referee might have allowed some inevitable argy-bargy. Not Mr Elleray: when Keane brought down Marc Overmars 15 minutes from time, he was off.

A point worth making here: in United's Treble season, the games that mattered – in Turin, Barcelona and even, to an extent, the FA Cup final against Newcastle – were also exceptional for their drama and entertainment. This semi-final was to be no different. After Keane's red card, there were two more moments that will forever live in the memory: a Dennis Bergkamp penalty-kick save by Peter Schmeichel and the Ryan Giggs wonder goal. The Welsh rare bit snatched a 2–1 victory eighteen minutes into extra-time, dazzling like Georgie Best in his prime, beating four defenders and hammering the ball high into the net beyond David Seaman's despairing grasp.

Next up for United, a week later, was Juventus away – and arguably Keane's greatest ever display in the club's red shirt. Having drawn the first leg of the European Champions Cup semi-final 1–1 at Old Trafford (thanks to another Giggs goal, this time a last-minute lifesaver) and beaten Arsenal in the FA Cup semi, the team headed for Turin in a hopeful mood, although Giggs would sit out the encounter injured. That quickly transformed into a mood of despair as United went 2–0 down in 11 minutes. This was no functional, average Juve: it was a class outfit containing players like the legendary Zinedine Zidane, Filippo Inzaghi, Edgar Davids and Didier Deschamps. Inzaghi was the man who broke United hearts after six and eleven minutes, much to the satisfaction of those critics who had written off United and said Juve merely had to turn up to confirm their place in the Camp Nou final.

But by the end of a momentous night, it would be the 6,000 United fans who would be celebrating, silencing the fireworks and taunts of the Old Lady's Ultra fanatics. If Inzaghi's first goal was a cracker as he latched on to a Zidane cross to fire home from eight yards, his second was lucky. The Italian striker beat Stam and tried another shot. It freakishly powered off Stam's leg and over Peter Schmeichel.

To every neutral, it now looked like mission impossible. Juve were 3–1 up on aggregate and were regulars at this stage of the competition – indeed, this was their fourth successive semi-final and victory would bring them their fourth consecutive appearance in the final itself. It was an understatement to claim that United, who were in the last four for the second time in three seasons, had a mountain to climb.

But, as they say, cometh the hour, cometh the man. From a David Beckham corner on 25 minutes, skipper Roy Keane rose superbly to head home for United, the precision and power of his effort giving keeper Peruzzi no chance. It was Keane's third goal of the current European campaign and it gave them hope: from no chance they now had a chance.

Then calamity struck: Keane received a yellow card on 33 minutes for catching Zidane with a tackle. It would rule him out of the final, should United get there. Panic temporarily reigned as everyone associated with the Reds wondered whether it was a booking that would disrupt Keane's flow and command, and ultimately allow Juve to walk the tie. But this was no Paul Gascoigne: this was a man who could keep his emotions in check, who would unselfishly sacrifice all for the badge. This was a man born to lead Manchester United into their ultimate triumph.

Ironically enough, it was in the same Stadio Delle Alpi that Gazza had also paid the price for a booking nine years previously. Playing for England against the Germans, he had burst into tears when it dawned upon him that the booking would rule him out of the World Cup final should England get there. Vivid images of Gary Lineker signalling to the bench that Gazza's 'head had gone' and that he should be substituted remain with England's army of fans to this day.

Keane's attitude was typical of the man: he was more annoyed with himself than concerned at his misfortune. He simply shrugged his shoulders and pulled himself together. If anything, his performance was even more inspired after the booking. He drove on his troops relentlessly and covered every blade of grass, determined that United would not throw away their big chance just because he had thrown away his. Only after the match would it sink in that he would miss the final – then the darkness would descend upon him and be difficult to shift. In his own mind, he had failed himself and his team. In fact, it was he who had arguably done the most to get United to the final in the first place.

He would also admit that he would forever be unforgiving to himself for picking up the first of his two bookings – for dissent at home to Inter Milan in the previous round. He said to the press, 'I don't mind so much getting booked for making a tackle but to get one for dissent or arguing is a bit of a nightmare. I was annoyed with myself because what really cost me was the booking I got against Inter Milan in the quarter-final. Coley or Yorkie was arguing with Simeone and I ended up, believe it or not, trying to break it up. Then Zamorano came over and we started having an argument and the referee came over and booked the two of us.' If that booking was certainly avoidable, the one against Zidane was contentious.

Before the Juve semi-final, Keane had insisted he would not abandon his normal game to keep out of the referee's notebook. He had said, 'I can't afford to sit back and hope we get through the game and that I will be OK for the final. That's the wrong attitude and if you go out with that attitude, I know for a fact that it would backfire. If I tried to tiptoe through the game, I would end up not doing myself or the team justice. Manchester United come first and if we get through to the final that is the most important thing. If I happen to pick up a booking and the team get through, I would obviously be disappointed, but that would just be one of those things.'

Two minutes after Keane's booking at the Stadio Delle Alpi, the first miracle happened, as Dwight Yorke put United level on the night but ahead on the away-goals ruling. The Trinidad and Tobago international had failed to find the net in seven games – but he more than made amends with a diving header in the same corner as Keane's opener. The Irishman had bawled and yelled at his team after scoring. He had refused to lie down and surrender and was damned well sure he would not let his teammates falter either.

Now United heads were held high and the 6,000 fans drowned out their Juve opposite numbers. All of a sudden, the traditional smoke bombs and sirens from the Ultras were being fired off in rage, rather than celebration. Juve continued to come at United but Schmeichel and Stam were magnificent in marshalling a defensive rearguard action. Six minutes from time, all Alex Ferguson's birthdays came at once, as Andy Cole grabbed United's third of the night and sent them into the final at Barcelona. Yorke swept around the desperate Peruzzi, who pulled him down for what would have been a penalty. There was no need for it: Cole picked up the loose ball and slotted it home. The Red Devils were now on their way to Barcelona and a further re-match with the German club Bayern Munich, with whom they had drawn twice in the earlier group stages of the competition.

Keane led United off a proud man: a warrior who had inspired his troops, the man you would always want at your side in the trenches. The accolades for his inspired performance immediately poured in. Probably the biggest – and the only one that would have truly mattered as far as the Irishman was concerned – came from his manager, Ferguson, in his book, *Managing My Life*:

> I didn't think I could have a higher opinion of any footballer than I already had of the Irishman but he rose even higher in my estimation in the Stadio Delle Alpi . . . Pounding over every blade of grass, competing as if he would rather die of exhaustion than lose, he inspired all around him. I felt it was an honour to be associated with such a player.
>
> I have been privileged in my time as a manager to work with some individuals who had no need of Alex Ferguson, players with such inner resources that they don't have to draw any strength from a manager. Willie Miller at Aberdeen was like that, and Bryan Robson in my earlier years at Old Trafford. Roy

Keane is certainly in their category. As you develop a team, you try to get your drive and ambition and the playing principles you believe in to enter into their personalities. You hope they will soak up your values, as if through their pores. But, if you are lucky, you encounter one or two men who are natural mirrors of your commitment, who are such out-and-out winners that you consider it an honour to be compared with them. That's how I see Roy Keane.

A few days later, Roberto Bettega, a Juventus giant of yesteryear, would add his own words of respect to the achievement of Keane and his United teammates, telling Alex Ferguson simply, 'Congratulations – you outclassed us.'

On Sunday, 16 May 1999, Keane and United completed the first of the three-piece jigsaw that represented winning the Treble. They won the Premiership title for the fifth time in seven seasons with a 2–1 win over Tottenham at Old Trafford. The triumph was all the sweeter for boss Ferguson, who at the final whistle rushed onto the pitch to embrace and publicly thank Keane for his efforts in securing the trophy. Ferguson could now continue to shout down the claims of his biggest rival, Arsene Wenger, that Arsenal were also becoming the stuff of legends. As Ferguson would say time and again, you cannot be considered legends if you have never successfully defended a Premiership title – as his United boys had done. The victory over Spurs meant defending champions Arsenal – and Wenger – would once again be left licking their wounds.

The Gunners had played their part in an exciting season and, at the same time as United were taking on Spurs, had defeated Aston Villa 1–0 at Highbury. It was not enough – goals from David Beckham and Andy Cole cancelled out Les Ferdinand's for Spurs and left United on seventy-nine points, one ahead of the despairing Gunners. Ferguson's five titles now equalled the benchmark set by Sir Matt Busby. It was also Fergie's tenth major prize since arriving at Old Trafford thirteen years previously. This was already two more than Sir Matt, but most of all the man from Govan desperately wanted to equal Sir Matt's lifting of the European Champions Cup.

That dream would have to be put on ice for ten days. Next up was the battle to complete the Double, with Keane again a certain starter in the FA Cup final against Newcastle at Wembley on Saturday, 22 May 1999. The Reds were now unbeaten in 32 games, and goals from Teddy Sheringham and Paul Scholes ensured that record would continue. For Scholes, the match would prove a personal landmark. Like Keane, he would miss the European Champions Cup final because he had picked up two yellow cards. Unlike Keane, he would play a major part in winning the FA Cup final, with his goal and general creative play.

The final was a record tenth win for the Reds and gave Alex Ferguson's side its third League and Cup Double of the decade to go with 1994 and 1996. Keane's role, however, was limited to an eight-minute cameo. He was the victim of an illegal tackle by the over-eager Gary Speed after just two minutes and, although he bravely tried to continue, he limped off with an injury to his right ankle and was replaced by Teddy Sheringham. The applause from the United hordes was deafening, as was the relief felt in the stands occupied by the Toon army. By a quirk of fate, I was sitting in the Newcastle VIP section that day, chaperoning for *The Sun* newspaper a Geordie fan who had won a competition for a free VIP trip to the FA Cup final. In front of me sat Bryan Ferry, of Roxy Music fame, and those young TV buddies Ant and Dec, while two seats to my left was Sting. When Keane left the pitch, the privileged few I was among reacted as if the Toon had actually just won the Cup.

Their joy was short-lived. Even without Keane and Nicky Butt, who was left out to ensure he would be fit to face Bayern, Manchester had too much in reserve and too much class for Newcastle. The constant crowd chants of 'You can stick your fuckin' Treble up yer arse' were soon drowned out by the roar from the Manchester fans as the Reds took a vital step towards the second part of the Treble dream with a slick goal from Sheringham, just two minutes after he had emerged as substitute for Keane. Sheringham slipped the ball through the legs of Toon goalkeeper Steve Harper after being set up by passes from Scholes and Andy Cole.

Ten minutes after the interval, Scholes settled it with a low shot from 20 yards. Sheringham had again been involved, this time returning the favour to Scholes by setting him up for the shot. At the final whistle, a hobbling Keane led United up to collect the FA Cup from Prince Charles. Ruud Gullit's Newcastle, without a domestic trophy since 1955 and a mid-table team that season, had been outclassed and Ferguson was delighted. He said, 'That's fantastic – three Doubles in five years. The boys were marvellous. This has been a tremendous season and once again the players produced it when it mattered.'

It was a night of celebration, but not a full-scale one: the most important work remained to be carried out at the Camp Nou. As Dwight Yorke said, 'It has been a tremendous season – the lads were fantastic again. We've got two trophies now so we can go all-out for the third.'

His partner in crime up front, Andy Cole, summed it all up: 'The hunger is still there for Wednesday and the Champions Cup final. It's another big game but this final hasn't taken anything out of the lads. Roll on Wednesday.'

Wednesday at the Barcelona ground was a watershed moment for Manchester United. It was arguably the moment when Ferguson and his team reached their peak – a mighty peak from which the only way was down. The victory over Bayern Munich was Peter Schmeichel's final match for United, and the likes of Jaap Stam would also soon be gone. According to a Manchester United insider, there seemed to be a feeling among those that remained after the triumph – Keane being the honourable exception – that they had now made it, that there was nothing left to achieve. The mindset of winners – of which Keane is clearly one – would have been that we start again from scratch and win another European Cup. This is the mindset ingrained within the great teams of footballing history, such as Real Madrid and AC Milan.

It was not to be that sort of future in Europe for Manchester United, but at least they won the ultimate club trophy that amazing night in Barcelona. Yes, they were lucky winners, for the most part being outfought and outplayed by the hungrier Bayern. But if fate was to shine on anyone that night, it was only fair it should beam down on the faces of Ferguson and Keane, the two warriors who had arguably done more than anyone else to bring United to the exalted Treble.

In the dressing-room before the Champions Cup final, it finally hit home with Keane what he was missing as he walked around in his grey club suit. Keane – one of United's greatest-ever servants – was distraught, but he managed to hide his own feelings, his own wretched personal disappointment, as he tried to help Ferguson drum it into the men who would play that they were unbeatable, that they certainly had the measure of this efficient, but hardly world-beating, German machine.

It was all very well to say that United could get by without Keane, but few people were crazy enough to believe that the Reds would put up a better showing in Barcelona without his mighty presence. His absence meant boss Ferguson had to shuffle his midfield. David Beckham, much to his personal delight, would be given the creative role in the additional absence of Paul Scholes, while Nicky Butt would play alongside him in the Keane role in central midfield.

That doyen of sports writers, the brilliant Hugh McIlvanney of the *Sunday Times*, summed up the task facing Ferguson in typically sparkling prose:

> Manchester United are entitled to feel like a high-jumper who has just done a personal best and is then asked to clear the raised bar with lead in his shoes. Whatever they do in Barcelona on 26 May is unlikely to be more dramatic or admirable than their feat of coming from two goals behind to beat Juventus last Wednesday, but there should be no doubt that the handicaps they carry into the European Cup final create a challenge even more daunting than anything they faced at kick-off time in Turin. Anybody who objects to such an assessment should answer one simple question: would that unforgettable night in northern Italy have taken the shape it did without the contribution of Roy Keane?

That United did triumph was a credit to their own determination never to give in and to the effect Ferguson and Keane had on keeping their spirits high both before and during the match. The stoppage-time goals from Teddy Sheringham and Ole Gunnar Solskjaer – which cancelled out Mario Basler's opener – ensured this team, with Keane as their skipper, a special niche in football history.

The Miracle of Barcelona – following so swiftly on from that other miracle in Turin – meant the Reds had become only the fourth side in history to win both their domestic league and cup competitions and Europe's premier club tournament in the same season. Only Celtic (1967), Ajax Amsterdam (1972) and PSV Eindhoven (1988) had ever done it before.

Out of sixty-two competitive games in the Treble season, United won thirty-six, drew twenty-two and lost only four – three matches in the League to Arsenal, Sheffield Wednesday and Middlesbrough, and one in the League Cup, when the club's reserves crashed out to Spurs. United scored a total of one hundred and twenty-eight goals, conceding sixty, and the club remained unbeaten in all thirteen European matches, winning six and drawing seven. The Reds' thirty-one European goals put them in second place on the all-time scoring list in a season, behind AC Milan, who scored thirty-three in 1962–63.

The win was also good news for the prestige of the English game, which had been in the European doldrums since 1984, the last year when an English club had won the Champions Cup. That season, Liverpool had beaten AS Roma on penalties in Rome. The following year, a riot by Liverpool supporters led to the deaths of 39 Italian fans at the Heysel Stadium in Brussels before the European Cup final against Juventus, leading to a five-year ban from European competition for English clubs.

So, although United had not played well on that hot May night in Barcelona, their will to win and self-belief – characteristics most often identified with their indefatigable skipper Keane – had served them and English football well in the great man's absence. Keane would join in the celebrations in the dressing-room and was forced out for a lap of honour on the pitch when it became clear that around 40,000 United fans were refusing to leave the ground until they had given him the acclaim he deserved. But, when finally settled on the plane home, he would sit alone with his thoughts and personal recriminations. The greatest night in the club's history had, regrettably, become one of the most difficult, darkest nights of the skipper's life. As Roy would later sum up his feelings, 'Football is a very selfish game. No matter how many people tell me I deserve that Champions League medal, I know I don't.'

FIVE

REBEL WITHOUT A PAUSE

'This is the age of the disposable player. Roy Keane is a task-oriented leader. In the movie *Gladiator*, Maximus is very much a task-oriented general that has the love and loyalty of his troops. Keane does as well. He is a warrior on the field! ... Roy Keane is a magnificent player with a fiery temper' – Bill Beswick, sports psychologist

'The only thing that goes with the flow is dead fish' – Roy Keane

'Unfortunately, one of my character defects is that I make very rash decisions on and off the pitch' – Roy Keane

Keane seemed to be a prime contender for the 1998–99 Player of the Year award. However, his brilliance for United was not reflected when the results of the annual gongs of the Professional Footballers' Association (PFA) and Football Writers' Association (FWA) were handed out. Instead, both revered bodies would plump for Tottenham's David Ginola as their man. No argument that the Frenchman was a marvellous winger, but, in my opinion, he could be complacent as to where and when he chose to display his undoubted skills. He was not a man I would want with me in the trenches, or even the rain and snow, when the going and the grounds got tough. Keane, on the other hand, was that sort of man: he turned it on week in, week out. As a consolation, the United hard man snatched both awards the following season – a fair reward for another fine campaign for the Cork warrior.

The 1999–2000 season would also be remembered as the one in which Keane would take United to the very brink in his demands for a much-improved new contract. He was now 28 and the following June would have been available on a Bosman free to the likes of Juventus or Bayern Munich (the only two teams he admitted he would have seriously considered joining). That meant United would have had to cough up at least £10 million for a replacement, who would always struggle to be as influential around Old Trafford as the massive Keane. In real terms, it also meant that Keane was on a winner. Given the situation, how could United not cave in to their skipper? With Ferguson backing him, the board eventually did just that, increasing his wage to £2.5 million a year (£52,000 a week) in a four-year contract signed in December 1999.

What strikes me about the deal is how it contrasts sharply with the saga over Rio Ferdinand's demands in 2005. In Keane's case, both the fans and the board made it clear they wanted their man to stay; in laid-back Rio's, there was no such loyal clamour. The man the fans dubbed 'The Peckham Penguin' had lost their support because of his own disloyalty. His plea for 30,000 more readies a week when he was already drawing £70,000 did not go down well after United had stuck by him during his eight-month absence over a missed drugs test. He had forgotten to stay behind for the test, but there was no such memory lapse from him and his agent when it came to discussing his contract.

It came to a head at the fag-end of the 2004–05 season, when Ferdinand was verbally abused by United fans during the 4–0 victory at Charlton. Some visiting supporters chanted 'Chelsea rent boy' – a reference to Ferdinand's clandestine meeting with Chelsea supremo Peter Kenyon a couple of months earlier. The abuse continued during United's pre-season friendlies, with regular chants of 'Sign the fuckin' deal, Rio'. United's loyal fans had clearly lost patience.

Even boss Ferguson made a mistake as tempers frayed, effectively telling the men in the street who paid his own and the players' inflated wages that they had no right to have a say or an opinion on the matter. During a press conference, Alex Ferguson said, 'I'm not entirely happy with the reaction of the fans. Players who go on the field and hear their own fans booing them is not encouraging at all. We don't want to make a monster out of this thing. You can maybe push players into these things and you can make it worse. He [Ferdinand] knows we want him to sign and that's important and he knows the fans want him to sign, so we don't want to be shoving the lad into something he is not sure about. If he's not sure, then he should take his time.'

When Keano held out for his extra readies in 1999, there was no such furore, only backing, although club secretary Ken Merrett dropped a bollock that would send Keane ballistic. When sending out renewal forms for season tickets, he tried to 'persuade' the fans that, although prices were rising, they were still getting a good deal – especially as they would continue to see Keane in United's colours for at least the next three seasons. Merrett's letter read:

> There was a huge collective sigh of relief when Roy Keane agreed to a new contract which will ensure he remains a Manchester United player for at least a further three years. In making this commitment to Roy, the directors believe they are also making a commitment to the supporters. Manchester United

fans have grown accustomed to the best. It is our duty to ensure that we remain in a position to be able to provide the best. Price increases are never popular but we are sure the supporters will recognise the importance that we place on staying competitive and being able to compete not only in the transfer market but in our endeavours to retain our existing players.

As far as retaining the loyalty of your best employee, it was hardly the best ploy from the United board. I am told Keane stormed in to see Merrett and give him a piece of his mind. Despite the fallout, Keane would go on to lead United to their sixth Premiership title in eight years by May 2000, scoring, by his standards, a record-breaking twelve goals, with half of them coming in Europe. Ironically, failure by the team in Europe would be the only other blot on his personal landscape, although even Keane would concede that going out 3–2 to eventual champions Real Madrid in the last eight was no disgrace. It certainly didn't help, though, that he had scored an own goal against the Spanish giants and missed an easy chance – an open goal – later in the game. He later admitted that he was distraught about the own goal.

In the Premiership, Keane led United to a record-breaking achievement of 97 goals scored and a record 11 consecutive victories. Their final winning margin was 18 points – beating Everton's previous record 13-point lead in 1985.

In November 1999, Keane had also inspired United to become the first British team to lift the Intercontinental World Club Cup. It was Keane who grabbed the winner as they overcame Palmeiras 1–0 in Tokyo.

January 2000 would not be remembered with as much nostalgia by United fans. For the first time, Keane went on record to reveal that he would like to finish his career at Glasgow Celtic, and United flopped in the inaugural World Club Tournament in Brazil – the competition for which they had abandoned their hold on the FA Cup. In public, Ferguson would claim that United were still committed to fighting for the legendary old trophy in future years, but Keane's private comments can be traced as the first rumblings that the domestic giants of the game – such as United and Arsenal – no longer saw winning the FA Cup as a priority mission. Keane admitted that the competition had lost its relevance and glitter for him.

The following season, Keane would lead United to a seventh Premiership title, their third in a row, which put them in the illustrious company of the record-breakers from Arsenal, Huddersfield and Liverpool, the only other three teams to notch up the hat-trick. Keane, naturally enough, was more interested in working on the present than glorying in the past. According to a source at United, he nodded his approval at Ferguson's two big buys – men who would offer competition for places and help to snuff out the complacency Keane believed had descended upon the squad since they had won the Treble.

More than anything, given his own inner search for perfection, Roy despised those who felt they had 'made it'. The arrival of French World Cup-winning goalkeeper Fabien Barthez at the start of the season and the planned advance purchase of £19 million Dutch striker Ruud van Nistelrooy for the start of the next season pleased Keane greatly. Barthez would have a fine first season at United, which temporarily helped to dispel the hold that the now departed Peter Schmeichel had held over the United goal. Ruud would prove to be an inspired buy: an instant hit who would eventually go on to beat United's record European goals tally set by the phenomenal Denis Law.

It was Teddy Sheringham whose place would eventually

come under threat from the arrival of van Nistelrooy. During the 2000–01 season, though, Sheringham was United's attacking star. The popular Cockney topped United's goalscoring charts with 21 goals and won both the PFA and FWA 2001 Player of the Year awards. Van Nistelrooy himself would go on to win the FWA gong when he got down to business the following year.

In a season of exhilarating football for the Reds in the Premiership, two particular games stood out for Keane. On 25 February 2001, the skipper led United to a remarkable 6–1 thumping of Arsenal at Old Trafford. The superb win meant the Premiership title race was over for another year – and Keane got on the score-sheet with a 25th-minute goal. The match was over bar the shouting by the interval, with United 5–1 ahead thanks also to a Dwight Yorke hat-trick and a screamer from Ole Gunnar Solskjaer. Keane set up Yorke's second goal with a measured pass on seventeen minutes and grabbed one himself with a fine volley after the Trinidad and Tobago centre-forward returned the compliment with an accurate cross. Teddy Sheringham compounded Arsenal's misery with a last-minute shot that David Seaman was powerless to stop. Thierry Henry had grabbed the Gunners' consolation goal after 15 minutes – but it was scant compensation in the overall context of the League.

It was one of Keane's best-ever games for United. The Reds had thrashed their closest rivals and opened up a sixteen-point gap at the top of the Premiership and a virtually unassailable lead with just over two months of the season remaining. Afterwards, even the normally cautious Ferguson said, 'If we had lost or drawn today, Arsenal would still have had thoughts of catching us. But 16 points clear, and with the goal difference we have, makes it impossible for them to catch us.'

The other game that stood out for Keane in the

Premiership – but for all the wrong reasons – was that end-of-season clash with Manchester City when he hit new depths in his personal conduct with *that* disgraceful sending off for his revenge tackle against Alfie Haaland in April 2001, but more of that in a later chapter.

United had another disappointing season in Europe, which prompted Keane to bemoan the performances of his colleagues and the lack of fervour among the fans at Old Trafford on European nights. The Reds had again crashed out of the competition, this time 3–1 on aggregate to Bayern Munich in the quarter-finals. Keane accused United's corporate fans of being more interested in eating prawn sandwiches than getting behind the team in the 1–0 first-leg loss at Old Trafford and said his team were 'no better than average' after their collapse to the Germans.

At least at the start of the 2001–02 season, United would be able to parade their two big summer signings in the team – a bolstering of the side that Keane had demanded as part of his outburst the previous term. Ruud van Nistelrooy would finally make his big-time United debut in the FA Charity Shield 2–1 loss to Liverpool on 12 August 2001, while Juan Sebastian Veron would have to wait just a week longer, finally pulling on the famous red shirt for his first big match in the 3–2 home win over Fulham. It would be ten days further down the road before the 'Little Witch' would link up with Keane in the heart of United's midfield, the two men joining forces in the 2–2 draw at Blackburn.

Unfortunately, the introduction of the £28.1 million former Lazio midfielder would not have the impact Ferguson or Keane had hoped for. Keane would admit a liking and admiration for the little Argentine – indeed, he would make it clear that Veron was not one of the players he felt disdain for this particular season – and Ferguson would go to extraordinary lengths to defend the player, dismissing all criticism of him in the press. But the truth was that Veron never shone for United; he had the air of a heartbroken lover who could never truly settle with his new suitor. His heart remained in Italy and, but for a legal wrangle over his passport, he would probably never have moved from Lazio. The most expensive player in British football when he signed, he would move to Chelsea for £15 million in 2003 and return to Italy a year later after a similarly disappointing spell at Stamford Bridge.

His effect at Old Trafford during the 2001–02 season was largely to disrupt the rhythm of the United side. With Ferguson constantly chopping and changing to ensure Veron's inclusion, United finished the Premiership season in third spot and exited from the Champions League in the most disappointing fashion. Ferguson had seemed determined to prove Veron's signing had been a master stroke; he reckoned that the little bald warrior would help United reclaim the European Champions Cup. Winning it again had become Ferguson's holy grail – and at the end of this particular season, as if to give the mission an even more enhanced edge, the final would be in Ferguson's native Glasgow at Hampden Park. In the event, Veron's arrival, far from providing the alchemy that would take Ferguson to his nirvana, proved to be the making of his own undoing.

David Beckham, the man upon whom Ferguson could rely as a regular match-winner with his brand of magical free-kicks and corners, suffered most for Ferguson's bid to prove he had not dropped a bollock by signing Veron. During the season, Beckham would be sporadically dropped to accommodate Veron, causing United to stutter like a blocked exhaust on a motorbike.

But it was only truly brought home as to who was the more important to United's fortunes when Beckham broke his left foot in the 3–2 Champions League quarter-final win over Deportivo La Coruna on 10 April 2002. It meant Beckham would be out for eight weeks, and would miss United's semi-final clashes against Bayer Leverkusen. These were two matches that United should have won. Keane and Ferguson have both gone on the record agreeing that this was United's best-ever chance of reaching the Champions Cup final again during their time at Old Trafford. Bayer were no world-beaters. In fact, apart from the brilliant Michael Ballack, they were a fairly average outfit, as Real Madrid would prove by steamrolling them in the final in Glasgow.

Yet, without the guile and craft of Beckham, United's dream crashed again. The first leg at Old Trafford on 24 April 2002 ended 2–2. In the return match in Germany a fortnight later, United could only draw 1–1, going out of the tournament on the away-goals ruling.

It was a devastating blow for Ferguson – and Keane. The United boss's dream of recapturing the Cup in Glasgow was dead, and Keane's long sulk over his own failure to appear in a Champions League final was destined to linger. Without a second European Cup final appearance, both men would continue to feel unfulfilled and cheated of their destiny. In the press conference after the defeat, Keane spoke about it as 'a disaster'. He said, 'It is very hard to win the European Cup if you give goals away like we did in the semi-finals. This club deserves to win European Cup finals and we blew it; it is as simple as that. We had a great opportunity and these sort of chances don't come around very often. The club belongs in the European Cup final and it is a disaster.

'It was very disappointing. I am more disappointed for the manager, the staff and the fans because I think they deserve better than that. It was probably not the standard we expected of ourselves over the two games. If we had gone in at half-time 1–0 up, we'd have been pretty confident. But scoring just before half-time gave them a lift. I thought we had control of the match at that point and they cleared one or two off the line. Their heads dropped a little bit but then they scored. We just couldn't get that killer goal.'

Keane would not let go of the bone. He was bitterly disappointed and along with the fallout with Mick McCarthy and Ireland in Saipan during the summer – which will be discussed in depth further down the line – this was probably, after the injury-hit campaign of 1998, the lowest season of his career. His rage flared up again before the crunch Premiership match against Arsenal in May 2002 – a match that would see United surrender their League crown to the Gunners in a 1–0 setback. Just prior to the make-or-break showdown, Keane ranted, 'There are a lot of cover-ups sometimes and players need to stand up and be counted. I'm not sure that happens a lot at this club. That's the least we should do. We shouldn't have to demand it from the players – they should be proud to play and give 100 per cent. We're not asking for miracles. We're asking them to do what they should be doing. When players don't do that, it's bloody frustrating. We're going to find it hard to win the League and if we end up with no trophies there's something wrong.' Prophetic words, as United did indeed end that season empty-handed.

In his autobiography, Keane would wind the book up at the end of the next season (2002–03) with the following rather sombre and ominous words:

> Success in the Champions League is the yardstick for all Manchester United teams. We are no closer to that goal than we were a year ago . . . So season 2002–03 can only be regarded as a qualified success.

United would regain their Premiership crown, but that, for

Keane at least, would not be good enough. It highlighted the enormous pressure the Irishman put upon himself in that almost demented search for perfection, that aching will-to-win whatever the cost to satisfy the raging demons within.

His autobiography would play a key part in determining the outcome of his early season in August 2002. Let's get one thing straight right here: the book is a footballing classic, one of the best ever, with Keane almost tripping over himself in his efforts to tell the truth. Whether that truth is actually 'real' is debatable, as we have suggested in this book. In it, the picture he paints of himself is one that could almost parody the public perception of 'Keano': the footballing nutter who is always up for a row and a punch-up, with shaven head and veins bulging in a fierce neck. As I have suggested, the *real* Roy is not so mono-dimensional. Away from his public persona, he can be decent, caring and thoughtful. These were my 'shock findings' as I moved on with this book and delved beneath the man's outer image.

Part of Keane's autobiography – the stuff about cropping Alfie Haaland – would land him in deep trouble with the FA and curtail his influence on the club he loved as autumn turned to winter in 2002. His privacy was already almost non-existent after the fallout with Mick McCarthy and Ireland in Saipan; now there would be no hiding place as *Keane: The Autobiography* hit the streets in August.

Keane played in just three games for Manchester United before being sidelined until December. On 31 August, he took the bait when Jason McAteer – one of the Irish teammates he had fallen out with – wound him up at the Stadium of Light. Keane elbowed him in the final minute and was promptly sent off. Keane had already been booked in for a hip operation the following week and was out longer than expected because the surgery turned out to be more serious than initially anticipated. By October, he was still convalescing and the FA did not help his recovery. On 15 October, they announced that the United skipper would serve a five-match domestic ban and be fined a record £150,000 after being found guilty on two charges of bringing the game into disrepute.

The first charge related to his tackle on Haaland, which the three-man FA disciplinary panel confirmed had been 'improperly motivated by an element of revenge'. The second charge criticised Keane for telling the story of the run-in for financial gain in his autobiography. Keane's suspension would start on 4 November and he and boss Ferguson decided not to appeal as the ban would run while he was working towards full fitness through that month and into December 2002.

Opinions were highly charged among football fans as to whether Roy had been badly treated or had actually got off lightly, as illustrated by these four writers to the footballing website, Soccernet:

> Nope, the FA did not get this one right. Compare the case of Paolo Di Canio, who pushed a referee and was suspended for 11 games, with Roy Keane, who intentionally wished to bring a colleague's career to an end, celebrated the act and also cashed in on it.
>
> The punishment is just not commensurate with the offence. It should have been not less than eight games and a £250,000 fine. Then a personal apology to Haaland for this cruel act.
>
> Sam

> I think the FA got Roy Keane's punishment spot on. Anyone who deliberately sets out to injure another player and then has the audacity (or stupidity) to brag about it and make money out of the incident

deserves everything the FA can throw at them. The evidence was there in black and white. I think the only people that will disagree with the punishment will be anybody connected with Manchester United.

Martin Patmore

I'm convinced that this punishment was prepared even before the hearing. How on earth can you be punished twice for one offence?

The first charge I can understand, but telling the truth does not make any crime worse. All those shouting 'crucify him' have all at one time or the other carried out revenge on another person. I respect him for telling the truth, at least.

After all is said and done, he should serve the ban, get his act together and devote the rest of his career to doing what he does best: playing football.

Dennar Kelechi

I am disappointed with the FA's decision. This is a clear case of restriction of an individual's right to freely express his thoughts on a matter that should have been dealt with at that instantaneous moment.

The FA has set a precedent that all future revelations by soccer players in a written medium are likely to be subjected to FA hearings. Maybe the FA has too little work to do during the Premiership season!

Anthony D'Cruz

I intend to examine the ins and outs of the Haaland incident later in this book, but let me say now I thought it was a disgraceful, totally indefensible act of revenge by Keane. He lost his head and will always be condemned and remembered for such a career-threatening tackle whenever his legacy to the beautiful game is evaluated. Keane served his time on the sidelines for the outrage, but was undoubtedly lucky that the ban would coincide with his recovery from an operation.

A surprise spin-off from his sending off was that on-field discipline undoubtedly improved at Old Trafford that season – no other player was red-carded after Keane's 31 August indiscretion. Keane would be back in business by Boxing Day – and the 3–1 defeat at Middlesbrough. Ryan Giggs's consolation goal hardly lifted Keane's festive spirits, but at least he avoided any run-ins with referee Graham Barber. Indeed, many critics would, for the next few weeks at least, question whether the Keane of old – that fire-breathing hard man – had gone for good, such was the more measured calmness of his displays. With Keane back in the fray, though, United would embark upon an 11-game unbeaten run stretching into February and ending only on the 15th of the month, when Arsenal won 2–0 at Old Trafford in the FA Cup fifth round. In the Premiership, they would be even more impressive, remaining unbeaten from the Middlesbrough match until the end of the season – a remarkable 18-game run. Highlights of that run included a 4–0 win over arch rivals Liverpool at Old Trafford on 5 April 2003 and a superb 6–2 win at Newcastle seven days later.

Keane would not be on the score-sheet in those two games, but the long line of excellent results confirmed how much United relied upon their spiritual leader. The Reds after 26 December were a different proposition to the United team 'marshalled' by Juan Sebastian Veron and Phil Neville in Keane's absence.

The superb run took United to their eighth Premiership title. The fight ended on the penultimate weekend of the season as the Reds defeated Charlton while Arsenal lost. However, as mentioned earlier, that achievement still left

Keane unhappy. He had wanted to lift the Champions Cup but that particular dream was wrecked by the might of Real Madrid. United again headed out of the competition in the quarter-finals, losing 3–1 in the Bernabeu and going out 6–5 on aggregate in a thrilling encounter at Old Trafford that saw United triumph 4–3. Thrilling maybe, but that was also no consolation to Keane. The FA even chose the two-leg battle between the teams as their matches of the season, with the following summary on their website:

> Both games showed just what football can be like when played by two teams playing at their maximum capacity. Real were never in trouble in the match but the joy of the tie was the amount of skill that was displayed by the likes of Zidane, Ronaldo, van Nistelrooy, Beckham, Scholes and Raul. Let's hope that one day they meet in the final.

This dream was shared by Roy Keane, but would it ever be achieved? Could United ever dominate Europe again, as they had in 1999? Or would the pursuit of that particular dream eventually weigh down even a character as strong as Keane, leaving him feeling unfulfilled, bitter and resentful at the very end of his career?

SIX

BITTERSWEET FA

'Please God don't interview me in 30 years' time and talk about Juventus in 1999. I hope in the next 30 years I might achieve something else in my life' – Roy Keane to *United We Stand*

'I've got two or three good years left in me yet' – Roy Keane reassuring United fans in 2003

By August 2003, Roy Keane had been sulking for the best part of three years about United's inability to win the European Champions Cup for a third time and was still moaning about the failure to anyone who would listen. Little did he realise that he should have been grateful for small mercies (and smaller trophies). Three months earlier, in May 2003, he and Sir Alex Ferguson had won what would be their final Premiership title together. Yet that triumph in itself still did not assuage the frustrations burning within both men since May 1999.

Keane's story at United is inextricably intertwined with Ferguson's – the fierce mentor and the student with fire in his belly. So it is no real surprise that the glory of Barcelona 1999 would also lead to the unfulfilled holy grail that would ultimately derail and define both men. The quest and failure would eventually bring about their downfall, as both men outstayed their shelf-life at the Theatre of Dreams.

Sure, United ended a 31-year wait in the Catalan capital with that second European Champions Cup triumph, and, sure, Keane was awarded a winner's medal. But in his own eyes he had won it by default, and it meant nothing to him. He needed to win it again to stave off those familiar demons of impatience, frustration and perfection – those old 'mates' who continually threatened his very health and emotional sanity. Similarly, Ferguson would never believe he had achieved as much as he could/should have done with just that single European Champions Cup victory. Both would rage at themselves for failing to win it a second time. They both stayed at Old Trafford in the mistaken belief they could put the record straight, when both would have been better off quitting the Theatre of Dreams when they won the Premiership again in May 2003.

Roy Keane's loyalty to United and belief that United would rise again kept him at Old Trafford in the summer of 2003 when, with the benefit of hindsight, it is clear that a move to, say, Juventus, Madrid or Milan could actually have brought him the medal he so craved. By then, United were already finished as *the* force in British football, let alone European. Arsenal had made up ground and the ever-blossoming Abramovich cash-tree would propel Chelsea beyond both the Reds and the Gunners within 12 months.

Boss Ferguson's big-name signings – like Juan Sebastian Veron – had not worked out and Keane's despair was justified. Yet while Keane was perceptive enough to see all was not well at Old Trafford in 2003, Ferguson did not see the warning signs. Lifting the Premiership title for the eighth time in eleven campaigns a few months earlier had seemingly persuaded him that a new era of success was on the horizon for United when, in reality, it had merely been a false dawn before what would become a host of dark nights.

In August 2003, on the eve of the new season, the United boss had proclaimed: 'The best thing that could have happened to the players last season was winning the League. It brought back exactly where they were as a football team. It reinvigorated them. They got excited about it. Their form from Christmas was phenomenal and it is true what they say about people's character always being on the pitch and you saw that last season. It was fantastic for them.'

Yet the 2003–04 season would prove a major disappointment, with only the winning of the FA Cup to shout about – and that, as Keane had previously stated, was no big deal or consolation prize any more. Unbeknown to Keane (and Ferguson), that FA Cup win would be the final honour they would share together at United. Maybe they would have celebrated its winning with more relish if they had known that the United of the new era would become the Liverpool of Gerard Houllier – a stumbling, bumbling outfit grateful for any Cup wins to decorate their trophy room.

Where did it all go wrong? Well, by August 2003, Keane's 32-year-old body was creaking as the injuries and full-throttle efforts of former years finally came home to roost. He had played 393 games for the club, scoring 46 goals. It was no secret that the Irishman would need a hip replacement by the age of 45. Back in 2003, he was already taking more time to recuperate from the excesses of individual matches. Keane had started tailoring his game to fit in with the realistic coping abilities of his strained limbs.

Of course, that game had developed technically in the ten years since his arrival at Old Trafford. When Keane first arrived, he was a raw diamond. He had little discipline in his positional play; he would roam from box to box seemingly without contemplating, for instance, whether it left the United defence exposed. He loved to be the marauding hero, the man who might grab the winning goal after another dashing run. It was in part thanks to Bryan Robson that he began to become the player we will remember him as. Robson told him he needed to develop the defensive and positional strength of his game, as he himself had done, that he had to become more of a holding midfielder if he wanted to dictate the game, rather than flit in and out of it. Roy buckled down and, when Robson left, he moved into the vacated role.

By August 2003, Keane was, out of necessity, stuck in that holding role. His legs were going but he still had the genius and intelligence to break up play and spray passes around. Youngsters like Darren Fletcher would become his legs. Ferguson understood the nature of the beast. He still wanted his captain out there to direct operations and dictate the game and he helped out by playing youth around him. To Keane's consternation, given his competitive appetite, Ferguson rested him for a number of games throughout the season. Keane would still suffer minor injuries, but the rest-and-play routine enforced by Ferguson would at least bring him a fourth – and final – FA Cup winner's medal.

If Ferguson is to be praised for his handling of Keane in the 2003–04 season, his transfer-market dealings must bring damnation. Getting rid of David Beckham in the summer of 2003 was a poor decision, one clouded in rancour and a personality clash rather than the wider interests of Manchester United Football Club. Ferguson might as well also have sent Ruud van Nistelrooy on his way, because, without the ammunition supplied from Beckham's mercurial crosses, the Dutchman would never be the same player, certainly never the same goalscorer.

Ferguson would replace Beckham with the brilliant potential of Cristiano Ronaldo, but in the twilight of their days at Old Trafford, both the manager and his captain did not have time on their hands. Ronaldo would become a world-class winger, but no way did he replicate the work ethic or the pinpoint crosses that had become Beckham's trademark. Indeed, the most common sight in Ronaldo's first two seasons at Old Trafford was that of van Nistelrooy clasping his head in despair as Ronaldo wasted another cross or ran into trouble after some intricate dribbling shows.

In an interview at the time in the *Sports Illustrated* magazine, published in New York, Ferguson conceded that Beckham had been a dedicated professional at Old Trafford. But then he went some way towards explaining why he had decided to sell him for £25 million to Real Madrid – and it was not because of any declining footballing powers. No, the United manager admitted for the first time in public that the reason Beckham had to go was because he had become a celebrity footballer. Ferguson said:

> He [Beckham] was blessed with great stamina, the best of all the players I've had here. After training, he'd always be practising, practising, practising. But his life changed when he met his wife. She's in pop and David got another image. He's developed this 'fashion thing'. I saw his transition to a different person.

Alex Ferguson's interpretation of his functions did not include bowing to the needs and demands of what he saw as a problem child – despite his acceptance that Beckham was still the perfect pro. By the time Beckham left, he and Ferguson were barely speaking. All interested parties –

United and consequently Keane and Ferguson, van Nistelrooy and Beckham – suffered as a consequence. There were no winners from the distasteful affair.

Ferguson could have bit his lip in the wider interests of United, but felt he could no longer work with Beckham – and so what was the point? Writing in the *Daily Telegraph* on 16 June 2003, the distinguished journalist Mihir Bose highlighted the unwillingness of United to keep their star player, an unwillingness that would cost them dear. Bose wrote:

> David Beckham was offered a new contract by Manchester United on 14 May – three days after the England captain celebrated winning his sixth Premiership title with the club he joined on his fourteenth birthday. . . . But Beckham did not see this contract until Sunday, having spent the last month either with England or in the United States.
>
> By then, it was irrelevant . . . this time there was no disguising the end of their [Ferguson and Beckham's] surrogate father/adopted son relationship.

Beckham had his own circle and had replaced all his old advisers with those supplied by his wife, Victoria, apart from his adviser Tony Stephens. His VIP treatment by England also seemed to put Beckham on a pedestal far removed from the collectivist team philosophy Ferguson espouses.

With Beckham gone, Ferguson entered the transfer market once again, rolling the dice he hoped would bring himself and Keane a final flurry of trophies. Ronaldo would prove to be a fine signing after taking three seasons to settle in. The 18 year old – whose full name was Cristiano Ronaldo dos Santos Aveiro – was signed for £12.24 million from Sporting Lisbon on a five-year contract and was convinced he was joining a team that would win trophies galore. He said, 'I am very happy to be signing for the best team in the world, and especially proud to be the first Portuguese player to join Manchester United. I look forward to helping the team achieve even more success in the years to come.' By the time this book had gone to the publishers in April 2006, the Portuguese international had won only the FA Cup at Old Trafford.

But back in 2003, United boss Ferguson was also convinced that glory days were still part of the club's imminent prospects, and he was gushing about how Ronaldo could take the club to a higher level. He said, 'We have been negotiating for Cristiano for quite some time, but the interest in him from other clubs accelerated in the last few weeks so we had to move quickly to get him. It was only through our association with Sporting that they honoured our agreement of months ago.

'He is an extremely talented footballer, a two-footed attacker who can play anywhere up front: right, left or through the middle. After we played Sporting [in a pre-season friendly in Lisbon] last week, the lads in the dressing-room talked about him constantly, and on the plane back from the game they urged me to sign him – that's how highly they rated him. He is one of the most exciting young players I've ever seen.'

True as that may be, the boy could not be expected to turn it on straight away. By August 2003, United had gone backwards from the team that had won the Premiership three months earlier. The remainder of Ferguson's buys that summer were simply disastrous. Whatever you may think about the United boss's transfer dealings over the years, it is surely undeniable that he either gets it wonderfully right – with the likes of Peter Schmeichel, Denis Irwin and Eric Cantona – or dreadfully, horribly wrong – as with the purchase of the likes of Juan Sebastian

Veron and the flogging of Beckham. There seems to be no in-between, grey area for Ferguson in this particular department.

That summer – Ronaldo apart – the boss played an absolute stinker. In came the 'talents' of Cameroon midfielder Eric Djemba-Djemba, French striker David Bellion, US goalkeeper Tim Howard and Brazilian midfielder Kleberson. Eric 2DJ, as the fans initially called Djemba-Djemba with an affection that would drift away over the months, and Kleberson had been drafted in to learn from Keane and eventually take over from him. At least, that's how the plot went. Both men were a disaster and both were eventually taken away under cover of the night to Aston Villa and Besiktas (in Turkey), respectively. Eric 2DJ was almost a candidate for the men in white coats rather than the boys in claret and blue when, in his goodbye speech, he ridiculously claimed that, but for Roy Keane being in his way, he would have had a bright future at Old Trafford. This from a man who was one of the most ineffectual players ever to 'grace' the famous red shirt of Manchester United.

As for Kleberson, who had helped Brazil win their fifth World Cup in 2002, the big question was: just how did he get into that Brazil side? He too was a major disappointment: unfit to even lace Keane's boots, let alone replace him as the king of Old Trafford. To be fair to Ferguson, he was not to know that the men he was bringing in would be so poor. Indeed, he had voiced great hopes for them, saying, 'The 22–23 age group is important. Having experience in the squad is obviously vital. In the past, we've had some great experience with players in their 30s like Laurent Blanc, Denis Irwin and Teddy Sheringham. If you look after yourself, there is no telling what age you can play to. We don't have that many in their 30s now, only Roy Keane, Fabien Barthez, Ryan Giggs and Ole

Gunnar Solskjaer. But there is a group below them as well with great experience.

'When you are thinking about the future, it is easier to construct your model with younger players, so we had to look at that 22–23 age group. Eric Djemba-Djemba can go in there and challenge now. That's what you want and I think the boy is like that. He's broken into the Cameroon team and played all their games and he is only 22. He has a long future in front of him but he is very much the present also.

'Kleberson is young and we certainly think he is one of the most progressive young players in Brazil at the moment. He is athletic, creative and quick. Roy Keane is 32 and Butt and Scholes are 29 in the winter, so Eric and Kleberson give us support for the experienced players.'

These words would come back to haunt the United boss in a season of ups and downs. OK, by the end of term, United had won the FA Cup for a record eleventh time, but their failings in the League and the Champions League drowned out any triumphalism. No, this was a season where joy was in short supply, a season that felt as if the very foundations that Ferguson and Keane had laid under Old Trafford were slowly beginning to crack. United would trail home in third place in the Premiership behind the resurgent Chelsea and the champions of Arsenal. The success of the Gunners, in particular, was a bitter pill for Keane and Ferguson to swallow, the former having to play second fiddle to Patrick Vieira, the latter losing out to his own nemesis, Arsene Wenger. And in Europe, Keane would have a disastrous season, being sent off at a vital time: a time which would see United fail to make the last eight.

In the League, it all started to go pear-shaped when Rio Ferdinand failed to attend a drugs test and was banned for eight months from January. It would cost him a place at Euro 2004 but, as far as United were concerned, the cost was much worse. Their League season – and their pursuit of the so-called Invincibles of Arsenal – fell apart, with shock defeats to the likes of Wolves and Middlesbrough.

The Ferdinand ban was a particular blow to Keane and Ferguson's hopes of regaining the European Champions Cup. The defender had played a big part in United's battle with Arsenal at the top of the Premiership in the autumn and early winter of 2003. The grim news arrived on Friday, 19 December when the FA found Ferdinand guilty of misconduct after he failed to take the drug test on 23 September and handed out the ban, which would come into force on 12 January, and a £50,000 fine. Speaking for the club and with Ferdinand at his side, United director Maurice Watkins said, 'We are extremely disappointed by the result in this case. It is a particularly savage and unprecedented sentence.'

The judgment had come 86 days after Ferdinand failed to take a test at United's Carrington training headquarters. Ferdinand had claimed he had forgotten about the appointment and then contacted the club to offer to take the test, but was told it was too late. It was hard to feel sorry for Ferdinand. His actions had let down the club and his teammates and would end any dream of United gunning down the Highbury Invincibles. The independent commission did not have much choice other than to hand out an eight-month ban. Any less and it would have encouraged those who had taken drugs to claim they had forgotten to take a test. As a yardstick for the length of the punishment, former United keeper Mark Bosnich had received a nine-month suspension from the game after failing a drugs test for cocaine. World Anti-Doping Agency president Dick Pound said, 'The sentence is a third of the theoretical maximum he could have got so he's done pretty well from his perspective.'

At the start of the season, Keane had lifted the Charity

Shield for United when they beat Arsenal 4–3 on penalties at Cardiff's Millennium Stadium. The match had ended all square at 1–1, with goals from Mikael Silvestre and Thierry Henry. Keane had enjoyed his customary battle with Patrick Vieira in the centre of midfield but had avoided any major run-ins.

Six weeks later, Keane would play an unusual role: that of peacekeeper, as Vieira lost his rag with Ruud van Nistelrooy in the 0–0 draw at Old Trafford. Images of Keane pulling his French rival away from the Dutchman to try to help him escape a red card were unusual – the normal portfolio of pictures had them grappling with each other or standing eyeball to eyeball. Keane's efforts that day were to no avail – Vieira was sent off nine minutes from time for a second yellow-card offence after kicking out at van Nistelrooy following a challenge from the big Dutchman.

United could not capitalise on their one-man advantage and van Nistelrooy went on to miss an injury-time penalty, firing his spot-kick against the bar after Martin Keown was adjudged to have fouled Diego Forlan. That, in turn, brought recriminations from Keown and other Arsenal players at the final whistle. Who can ever forget the images of Keown, once known as a model pro, pushing and shoving the Dutchman, his hands raised aloft in glee at the penalty miss?

From Keane's point of view, the result had been a failure, but the fact that he had come through the whole 90 minutes – after hurting his ankle a week earlier at Charlton – was encouraging news for the season ahead. Boss Ferguson had also been positive about his skipper's prospects for the season before the Arsenal match, saying, 'I made the point last year that it [Keane's hip operation] was not an easy operation and there is no question about that. It took Freddie Ljungberg, who is five or six years younger than Roy, virtually a whole season to get over it.

We gave him a week off during the recent two-week break and he prepared himself for the Charlton match but unfortunately he got an ankle knock.

'We'll gauge the right things to do with Roy. He won't play every game this season, there is no doubt about that. I will be leaving him out of a lot of games because the important thing is to have him when it really matters. If I can't do that, then there is something wrong with my squad. It isn't a matter of him taking it, he will just have to accept it. There isn't going to be a halfway house where I am going to have to go to Roy and get him to pass the verdict whether he is playing; I am going to make the decision, because it is going to be for his benefit. If I can get him playing in the important games in May, then we will know we were right.'

Sir Alex admitted that the likes of Keane and Vieira were a rare breed, with their all-out aggression and commitment, but felt confident someone else would come along one day to replace his skipper – just as Keane had arrived to take Bryan Robson's place. Ferguson said, 'Somebody comes along and surprises you. I don't think they are a dying breed. People are born with a certain determination and it never leaves them and they get better with it. When you go into sport, you get people like John McEnroe, for instance, and people like that and you can't avoid it. Winning is in people's nature and that never leaves them.'

But things were changing at Old Trafford, and Keane's all-action-hero role of the past was one of them, as was United's claim to be the undisputed kings of the ring. A couple of weeks after the Arsenal encounter, United would lose 2–1 in the Champions League group stage to Stuttgart. And three weeks after that, Fulham left Old Trafford with a 3–1 win on a day when the hapless Eric Djemba-Djemba stood in for Keane in central midfield. At the same time, it was revealed that an American investor by the name of Malcolm Glazer had acquired a three per cent stake in the club. United were certainly changing with the times – but not for the better. According to the Glazer family foundation's website, he was a 'true American success story'. He started his working life in his father's watch-parts business at the age of eight and, at fifteen, took over the business when his father died. He bought the struggling Tampa Bay Buccaneers in 1995 and the team won the Super Bowl in 2003. But surely his ambition to own the Buccaneers *and* United was nothing but a dream?

Yet the times certainly were a-changin' . . . and a cold wind was blowing into Old Trafford as Keane's reign at the Theatre of Dreams began to wane. By December 2003, another setback in the Premiership at Chelsea had Arsenal fans crowing that the skipper and United were truly finished as a major force. The Gunners were still unbeaten in the Premiership by Christmas and would stay unbeaten all season – a remarkable achievement. The 0–0 draw at Old Trafford that September had given Arsenal the belief that they could claw out points even when they were not playing well. The result was arguably their most important that season, coming after their 3–0 Champions League thrashing by Inter Milan at Highbury four days earlier.

They would go from strength to strength after the fortitude, resilience and no little mischief they had shown at the Theatre of Dreams. As Alex Flynn and Kevin Whitcher point out in the entertaining *The Glorious Game: Extra Time*:

> the point Arsenal earned was probably as significant as any they would win all season. Not only had they prevented the title-holders from inflicting further psychological damage after galloping past them in the previous season's title run-in, but they had

shown the kind of fighting spirit their supporters love to see.

Additionally, they had proved themselves to be a far more resolute defensive unit than when they had attempted to retain their League crown . . . Moreover, in the heat of the moment, Arsenal fans cheered to see their nemesis – a man who had replaced Teddy Sheringham as their favourite hate figure [van Nistelrooy] getting roughed up . . .

Going unbeaten for 38 games in the Premiership in the 2003–04 season meant, of course, that Arsenal would strip United of the title and enter the record books. In the modern era, only two other teams have won their leagues in Europe and stayed unbeaten in their League programme: Milan in 1991–92 and Ajax in 1994–95.

United's consolation was that they would still trump the Gunners on three counts during their unbeaten season – in the Charity Shield, in the FA Cup and in signing the bubbling skills of Ronaldo. Yes, the Portuguese wonder-kid had been watched many times by Wenger's spies, only for Ferguson to sneak in with a killer punch just days before the Frenchman was about to bid for Ronaldo.

The FA Cup semi-final win over the Gunners was one of Keane's most satisfying outings and results of that season. He led United out at Villa Park in a match most pundits believed would be beyond them. A Paul Scholes goal on the half-hour settled matters, sending United to another FA Cup final. It was a result that would salvage Keane's season, but in terms of the broader picture, it only papered over the cracks of what was a declining empire at Old Trafford.

Another consolation for Keane and, indeed, all concerned with United was that Scholes's winner meant Arsenal now could not emulate United by winning the

Treble and that the Gunners would not win the FA Cup for a third successive year.

Keane's season ultimately swivelled around two matches: the Champions League clash with Porto and the FA Cup final against Millwall. He would miss the vital second leg at Old Trafford against the Portuguese champions after being sent off in the first match. Without him, United would crash out of the competition in the last 16. The red card was the 11th of his Manchester United career – in his 11th year at the club.

United had taken the lead on 15 minutes when Quinton Fortune sneaked in to score after keeper Vitor Baia dropped the ball from a Paul Scholes free-kick. Porto equalised on the half-hour when Fortune's South African international teammate Beni McCarthy volleyed Dmitri Alenichev's cross past Tim Howard. McCarthy won the match 12 minutes from time with a fine header.

United boss Ferguson could accept the setback – he knew United could still turn things around in the second leg at Old Trafford – but he was unhappy with Keane's sending off. The United skipper stamped on the Porto keeper, Baia, with three minutes remaining – a foolish and callous indiscretion that meant he would automatically be suspended from the second leg. Yet, rather than lambast Keane, Ferguson turned his wrath onto the injured Baia. He said, 'There was no malice in the incident; it is not Roy's style to do anything like that. The goalkeeper made more of it than he should have done. Certainly he stood on the lad but I don't know whether he could have got out of the way. I can understand why the linesman flagged but the keeper made a meal of it.'

Maybe Gareth Southgate – who felt Keane's studs in 1995 in the United v Crystal Palace FA Cup semi-final replay – would disagree with those sentiments on Roy's style. One man who did feel Ferguson was being slightly tunnel-visioned was the Porto manager, a certain Jose Mourinho. This would be the first clash between Ferguson and the man who would go on to win the European Champions Cup with Porto and the Premiership with Chelsea. As the teams left the pitch, the United boss confronted Mourinho over Baia's part in the sending off. But Mourinho said, 'I understand why he is a bit emotional. You would be sad if your team gets as clearly dominated by opponents who have been built on 10 per cent of the budget. Ferguson told me in the tunnel that he thought Vitor had made the most of it. I said I wanted to see it on television before I would make a comment but if he was right, I would apologise.

'However, if he has no reason to make the claim, he can apologise to me. Vitor told me he was diving for the ball, Keane left his foot in and he felt a bit of pain with the contact. I understand why he is a bit emotional. He has some top players in the world and they should be doing a lot better than that.'

In the return leg, United, without their banned skipper, could only draw 1–1. Ferguson had gambled on Djemba-Djemba to replace Keane. It was a gamble that failed. Scholes again scored the United goal, heading home after 30 minutes, but a Tim Howard blunder in the last minute cost United dearly. The American goalkeeper could only parry a simple free-kick from McCarthy into the path of Francisco Costinha, who gratefully hammered the ball home. It meant United had failed to reach the quarter-finals of the Champions League for the first time in eight seasons, another statistic highlighting the way the club's powers were slowly but surely ebbing away.

A kind of redemption would come with the FA Cup semi-final win over Arsenal and the final win over Millwall, but it was not enough for perfection-seekers like Keane and his mentor. Ruud van Nistelrooy knocked the stuffing out of the battling south Londoners with a brace after the dazzling skills of Ronaldo, climaxing in a goal on the brink of half-time for the Portuguese, had sent them dizzy.

It was the 17th trophy of Ferguson's reign, and skipper Keane had set a post-war record of six FA Cup final appearances. Afterwards, Keane said, 'It is always nice to win – the last one is always the nicest. All credit to Millwall; I thought they were outstanding. The goal before half-time was very important as Millwall had grown in confidence. Millwall had nothing to lose and we were on a hiding to nothing. It was about being patient and hoping that quality would tell, which it did.'

Keane would need much patience as his final two seasons at United loomed – and he was hardly noted as a man who could muster up any at the best of times. How would he cope, and was he right in his belief that United still had the 'quality' which 'would tell'? Indeed, would he have celebrated at all on Saturday, 22 May 2004 if he had known that this win over First Division Millwall in an FA Cup final in Cardiff was actually about as good as it would get in the latter days of his glittering Old Trafford career?

SEVEN

THE PARTY'S OVER

'When you are talking about Manchester United 30 or 500 years from now, Roy Keane will still be regarded as one of the greatest players ever at this club' – Sir Alex Ferguson, February 2005

Hopes were high as Keane and United burst into their stride for the 2004–05 season with a Community Shield opener against Arsenal. In retrospect, the signs that the cracks in the team's make-up had merely been papered over by that FA Cup win over Millwall were there for all to see in the charity showpiece at Cardiff's Millennium Stadium. United were a team in decline; Keane was a player in decline, although that season he would make 42 appearances for the senior side, maintaining his role as its mainstay and leader.

The Gunners would roll over United 3–1 with goals from Silva, Reyes and an own goal by Silvestre, United's reply coming from Alan Smith. Funnily enough, in the final domestic game of the season, the two teams would meet again at the same stadium – with Arsenal winning the FA Cup, albeit luckily. The United team in the Community Shield would give some clues as to why Keane's penultimate season would be yet another dismal let-down.

The names David Bellion and Eric Djemba-Djemba in the starting line-up and those of Liam Miller and Kleberson on the sidelines were probably not ones Keane would have advocated laying out cash for.

The manager's buys for that midfield area had, frankly, been a disaster for some time. Juan Sebastian Veron had flopped, and the triumvirate of mediocrity, Miller, Kleberson and Djemba-Djemba, would go the same way. They were not players of the standard required by Manchester United.

On the plus side, Ferguson snapped up the boy who could lay claim to be the best player to grace Old Trafford since Keane in his prime. At £27 million, Wayne Rooney was a bullish, brutish genius of a striker. Like Keane, he would not give an inch: he had the same 'Who the fuck are you?' mentality. He was, simply, the best English player since Paul Gascoigne and a marvellous buy. Ferguson had also brought in the 'madman' of Argentine football, Gabriel Heinze: he has a sneer and a smile akin to that of Jack Nicholson on the poster accompanying the movie *The Shining*. He was another great buy, but would arrive late for the season's start, along with Cristiano Ronaldo. Both men were playing football for their country in the Olympics: Ronaldo with Portugal and Heinze for the eventual winners in that sport.

The excellence of these men and the mediocrity of the likes of Bellion and Djemba-Djemba increased Keane's irritation with his manager from 1999 onwards. According to a source, the Irishman would tell Ferguson on numerous occasions in private that his midfield buys were duds. Yet this was the same manager who could pluck the likes of Ronaldo out of the blue and unveil a star in the making. It was always said that Ferguson was more tuned in to attacking players because he was a centre-forward himself – maybe that had something to do with some of the flops in midfield and defence he purchased – but then it does not explain how he also brought in the likes of the superb Heinze.

By the end of the season, United had won nothing – it was two years since the Premiership trophy had been at Old Trafford and the fans despaired that they might not see it again for some time. At least Keane had played in 17 more competitive matches than the previous campaign. That was essentially down to two reasons. The first, as Ferguson took time out to explain, was that he had not used his captain enough the previous season. He would not make the same mistake again, saying the title race in 2003–04 would have been much closer if Keane had played more than 25 games. Ferguson admitted, 'I'm not sure I did the right thing with Roy. I overprotected him. You can underestimate Roy Keane. We had a chat last summer and obviously we discussed his situation. There were some problems, but it was his first year back after major hip surgery.

'What I said to Roy at the start of the season was, "We'll monitor the situation; we'll talk before games. Certain games, we won't play you." What happens? The ones I left him out of, we lost the points. Fulham, Middlesbrough, Leeds – three games. We got one point. If we'd won those games, we'd have eight points more.'

Ferguson was adamant that Keane still had a major role to play at Old Trafford and remained a unique influence on the pitch and the dressing-room. Asked if the Cork man would be leaving the club to help United rebuild, the United boss said, 'I don't see the need for that. Not at all. The big players who have left here, apart from Bryan Robson, who went into management, they never had that Keane factor. Nobody had that Keane factor.'

He added, 'What we're going to do with Roy this season, now he's had a good rest this summer, followed by a good pre-season, we're going to work on the basis of how he feels. Roy's 33, but there's some players that are playing at 36 and 37 and doing well. There is nobody more respected than Roy Keane in this place, and I mean by the players. Because he will do a lot for them. If they have a case to fight, he will fight it for them.

'He is an unusual person. He is a different breed of person to your normal footballer of today.'

Fine words of support and encouragement from the United boss for his veteran star as the season got under way. The second reason Keane managed so many games in 2004–05 was that Ferguson had also decided to continue the new tactical plan he had introduced fleetingly the previous season, the much maligned 4–5–1 formation, which allowed the likes of Darren Fletcher to do Keane's running. It was a success sometimes; at others it inhibited United and held back the fast-flowing, attacking football that generations of Red Devils fans had been brought up on.

I remember joking in my last book, *Wayne Rooney: Simply Red* (which followed Rooney's first campaign at Old Trafford in the year we are now discussing), that Keane would eventually be brought out onto the pitch in a wheelchair with Fletcher at the helm. That bit of fun apparently did not go down too well with Mr Keane! The fact remained that with Keane in the side, United ground out better results, although it might not always be pretty to watch. He was like an omnipotent emperor positioned just behind the midfield and just in front of the back four, dictating play from his kingmaker role.

Just before the season got under way, Keane, in that typically contrary way of his, would give a major interview, but not to the nationals – instead to *United We Stand*. The chat was conducted by Andy Mitten, editor of that excellent fanzine. Here are some extracts:

Are you optimistic about this season?

Always. I always am at the start of the season and after my injuries I see every season as a bonus. If we've been successful or have to come back from disappointment like last season, I'm always the same. I always hope for the best . . . Personally, I really get a buzz out of pre-season training. I really do. I never take my place in the team for granted and really enjoy working with Mickey Phelan, Carlos and the gaffer. Working with players like young Fletcher too. I try not to harp on about a player but he impressed me from the very first moment I saw him. He has got the potential to be outstanding. He's got unbelievable talent but he's got a good head on him and that's what I like about Fletch. He could be up there.

Do you think this will be a successful season for United?

It's a great challenge to try and get our championship back because if things don't go well this year, all of a sudden we could be like Liverpool – 14 or 15 years without winning the championship. It happens.

How does age affect your performance?

I don't think it does, although injuries can affect you more and your recovery times increase. I've got two years left at United and I really hope I can finish those two years. Realistically you have to say that that will probably be it.

Interesting – in the light of developments further down the road, particularly the banned MUTV tape – that Keane admitted admiration at the time for Queiroz and Darren Fletcher. Also, he was very perceptive in his analysis that United could struggle for years to win the League again if they didn't bring it home in the 2004–05 season.

The United skipper had expressed his admiration for

Rooney – as well as Fletcher – in another part of the interview. He was, he would later admit, 'delighted' when the prodigy finally arrived at Old Trafford. Keane had earlier said, 'There are only two English players from the last 15 years I would pay to watch. One of them is Paul Gascoigne; the other is Wayne Rooney.' Rooney would make his debut for United in that unforgettable 6–2 thrashing of Fenerbahce in the European Champions League – a match in which the sometimes unfathomable Ferguson decided not to play his main men, such as Keane. Instead, Rooney, like some modern-day Maradona, would inspire a team containing Kleberson, Eric 2DJ and Bellion to play above themselves for one night only, much as the Argentine legend had inspired a mundane national team to World Cup glory and an even worse Napoli to the Italian Scudetto.

Rooney and Keane lined up together for the first time five days later in the 1–1 home draw with Middlesbrough. Rooney looked shattered after his efforts against the Turks; Keane tried to drive on his troops but only picked up a booking for his efforts as United struggled after an early goal from Stewart Downing. Only Alan Smith's equaliser nine minutes from time saved Rooney from being a loser on his debut.

The great pity of it all was that Rooney would never play with Keane the world-beater. He would never know what it was like to have that whirlwind at his back, egging him on, pushing him to the limit, providing the ammunition upon which he would have thrived. The Keane Rooney played with for a season and a bit was an imitation of the real thing. Yet what Keane did bring to Rooney was the knowledge that it was OK to be passionate about the game. The Irishman took time out to encourage Wayne to maintain his natural love and aggression for the game, whatever the critics might say.

Ferguson had admitted he wanted Keane and Paul Scholes to be the youngster's minders on the pitch. It was a rather ironic, not to say unusual, twist of fate for the Irishman. Few people would have regarded the combustible midfielder to have the necessary traits to teach someone else how to control their temper! But bodyguard to Rooney he did become on the pitch, often rushing forward to save the Scouse kid from an early bath. One thing Keane definitely did have for the role was the T-shirt to prove he had been there himself.

Keane would also be ordered to look after Rooney's co-partner-in-crime, the bubbly Ronaldo. Keane and Ryan Giggs were selected by Ferguson to make sure he stayed clear of major problems on the pitch. Giggs admitted, 'I can see similarities in how the manager handled me to the way he is handling Cristiano. Every time he has a good game, he wants to play again, the fans want him to play and deep down the manager probably wants him to as well. But you have to look at the bigger picture. To get the best out of Cristiano, he needs rest and help at the right points. It's not just physical; it's mental as well. There were times the manager did it with me.'

Unfortunately for Keane, an injury meant he would miss the titanic battle with Arsenal at Old Trafford in October – Phil Neville would take his place – but he would later admit to much pride as he watched Rooney and Ronaldo dismantle the Gunners' bid to make it 50 matches unbeaten. The heavyweight showdown saw United 2–0 winners to end the champions' run one short of the half-century. A controversial 73rd-minute penalty by Ruud van Nistelrooy and an injury-time breakaway by Wayne Rooney – who had earned the penalty – secured the victory.

It was Arsenal's first defeat since losing 3–2 to Leeds United in May 2003. Yet they remained top of the League on 25 points. United manager Ferguson said, 'It was an important victory. It's a great boost. We've been drawing too many games and hopefully we can get on a run now because we need wins to get alongside Arsenal.'

Keane also felt it could be a 'turning point' but both men were to end up disappointed. While United kept their sights on the Gunners, Jose Mourinho, the new kid on the block, emerged from the shadows to steal both their glories with his powerful Chelsea team. The Blues, who had beaten Keane and United 1–0 in the first match of the season at Stamford Bridge, proved simply too strong, with a squad backed up by Russian Roman Abramovich's millions.

My three personal favourite memories of Keane in the 2004–05 season came in the matches against Bolton, at home, Arsenal, away, and Birmingham at home. The Bolton match saw Old Trafford covered in snow and frost on Boxing Day 2004. It was my six-year-old son Frankie's first visit to the Theatre of Dreams and he was well cued up for the big event. Naturally, he had come to see Rooney, but he also knew all about Roy and what he had done for the club. Roon should have been sent off after he pushed Trotters defender Ben Haim in the face; but my little boy was impressed at how Keane defused the situation.

'I thought he was a bad man, Dad,' he said to me.

'No,' I replied. 'He is really one of the good guys – he just likes to act the bad man to keep people at a distance.'

Keane drove United on, leading them to a 2–0 win over their Lancashire neighbours – no mean feat given the almost miraculous improvements Wanderers had made under Sam Allardyce. I particularly liked it when Roy brought down the unpleasant El Hadji Diouf when the Senegal striker threatened to give him the runaround. The former Liverpool player had become renowned for his constant spitting attacks on players and fans. Trust old Roy to sort him. If anyone could, hey? Big Sam would eventually take him off after 50 minutes, such was the successful shackling job Keane carried out that cold day in M16.

The game at Arsenal that heralded in February 2005 was another cracker. Keane's performance off the pitch, in the tunnel before kick-off, easily matched his intimidating show in the 4–2 win for the Reds that followed in terms of pure drama and intensity. Who will ever forget the United skipper's snarling attack on his Gunners counterpart, Patrick Vieira?

Keane clashed with the Frenchman after Vieira had had a go at United defender Gary Neville, who had rowed with Vieira before the match. Afterwards, Keane said, 'I'd had enough of Vieira's behaviour and I would do what I did again tomorrow if I had to.' Referee Graham Poll had to keep Keane away from poor Vieira when, eyes and veins in his neck bulging, he pointed at the big Frenchman and threatened to sort him out.

Later, Keane admitted that Neville may also have been at fault over the incident, which added further ill-feeling to an already tense atmosphere. 'It takes two to tango. Maybe Gary deserves to be chased up a tunnel every now and then – there would be a queue for him, probably. But you have to draw a line eventually.'

Keane said the trouble between Vieira and Neville was more serious than mere name-calling. 'I'm usually first out in the tunnel but I had a problem with my shorts and I was maybe fourth or fifth out and by the time I got down I saw Vieira getting right into Gary Neville again,' he said. 'I mean physically as well now. I don't mean verbally.'

Later, Vieira would claim Keane had wound him up in the tunnel by condemning him for playing for France when he was born in Senegal. Vieira would hit back by saying, 'For someone who leaves his team in the World Cup – he should keep the remark to himself. He does not know my background and I do not want him to make a comment like that because he is not in a good position to say something like that.

'I will not say I intimidated Neville. I would say I tried to make a point. Keane reacted the way I would react if somebody came to talk to one of the Arsenal players – that's what I would expect.

'It did not surprise me at all. It was a captain's, a leader's, reaction. I have big respect for him and all the Manchester United players. No doubt about it.'

It was great entertainment – a tasty appetiser for the main course as Keane and United went about their business in a brisk, no-holds-barred style, completing the domestic Double over the team who had been dubbed 'The Invincibles' just three months earlier. Vieira enjoyed a brief moment of glory over Keane when he scored Arsenal's opener, but it was the United captain who had the last laugh as his inspired display and a brace from Cristiano Ronaldo ended the Frenchman's lofty ambition of retaining the Premiership crown.

After the match, Keane could not resist rubbing it in, repeating his criticism of Vieira: 'It makes me laugh, players going on about how they are saving this country and saving that country but when they have the opportunity to play . . . well, it's probably none of my business.' To be fair, it was unnecessary – and Keane's comment at the back end of that interview suggested he himself realised his gloating was out of order.

Four days later, Keane grabbed his 50th goal for United, after a 53-game drought, in the 2–0 home win over Birmingham City. The Reds had been struggling to break down a stubborn Brum back line, and it was Keano who came to the rescue. Another inspirational display was capped by the opening goal to set his team on their way to the triumph. Cristiano Ronaldo set up United's first early in the second half and Wayne Rooney's late lob sealed an eighth win in nine League games.

The milestone goal earned praise from boss Ferguson. He said, 'When you are talking about Manchester United 30 or 500 years from now, Roy Keane will still be regarded as one of the greatest players ever at this club.

'Some people are capable of revisiting old times and he is one of them. That was the Roy Keane of ten years ago out there this afternoon. When we needed some urgency and someone to open them up, he provided it. It was a fantastic goal and the fact it was his 50th for the club just made it more special.

'He was everywhere – fighting for possession, winning tackles, pounding forward. That was a truly great performance. I just hope someone invents something that can keep him going. Until then, we just pray!'

Typically, Keane initially preferred to talk about what the result meant to United's title chances than reflect upon his 50th goal for the club. He said, 'It was a job professionally well done. After the decent result in the week, we would have been disappointed if we'd dropped any points, especially at home.

'We made a mistake a few months ago by getting beaten at Portsmouth after beating Arsenal, so it was important not to do that again. The manager made one or two changes and freshened things up, but it was all about keeping the momentum going.

'We had to be patient but we opened them up a bit in the second half. Credit to Birmingham – they had a game plan and made it hard for us. At half-time, we felt we had been down this road many times before. I am sure the fans were a bit impatient, but you have to be professional and get the win. It was quiet in the first half and our passing wasn't quick enough. We improved that in the second half.'

Finally, he smiled and talked about the goal that had

been coming for 15 months – his last being against Portsmouth in November 2003. He said, 'It was about time I got my 50th. I just shut my eyes and went for it!

'It was a nice bit of skill by Cristiano to set me up, but I thought my run made it easier for him! It was a decent move and, before I knew it, it was opening up for me. You just hit and hope.'

The victory kept United on the tails of Chelsea at the top, but the gap in points and class would be too much to fill for Keane and Co. The new Stamford Bridge outfit, modelled in the spirit of their disciplined top-notch boss Mourinho, were rapidly proving to be the new force in British football. United's time as champions on the pitch seemed over as Lampard, Terry and Co. prepared to take their crown.

Off the pitch, officials and fans had been in a sombre mood as the threatened takeover by American Malcolm Glazer moved a step closer. The times they were a-changin' at the Theatre of Dreams – and not for the better. The Glazers were not the same sort of proposition as Abramovich had been at Chelsea. While the Blues' new owner brought cash galore and the prospect of shopping at Harrods, the Glazers' deal would hit United with unprecedented debt and force Ferguson to rustle around in the bargain bins at the corner store for any fresh purchases. And how would they look at any new deal for Keane, who would be pushing 35 and not nearly as influential on the pitch when his contract expired in May 2006?

Keane's big ally in the national press, Tom Humphries, the chief sports feature writer of the *Irish Times*, weighed in during the week of Keane's 50th goal and the shadow of the Glazers' takeover with a typically staunch defence of the man who was a potential early victim of any cutbacks enforced by the Americans. Humphries, speaking in *The Observer*, said:

Last Tuesday night at Highbury was stuff for the career highlight reel. A long drum roll of hyped animosity between the hosts and their guests fed Keane's passion before he stepped in and seized the moment.

At 33, Keane remains one of the few players capable of taking a top-class fixture by the scruff of the neck and annexing all three points to his team. He remains the only player capable of dissolving solid matter with a single glare. There have been signs of his waning, but Keane has banished them before anybody plucked up the courage to ask him about them. His style has evolved in a way that suggests his intelligence has bought him a new lease on excellence.

United and their fans were largely in agreement with Humphries – and anyway, they had enough on their plate at the time trying to see off Glazer. It soon became apparent they were fighting a losing battle: Glazer had found the £800 million needed to buy the club through funding from bankers JP Morgan. He was now in a position to put in a formal bid. Before the Birmingham game, fans action group Shareholders United had handed out cards begging fans to back their anti-Glazer stance. They featured pictures of manager Sir Alex Ferguson and two of their all-time favourite players, Eric Cantona and Ole Gunnar Solskjaer, under the heading: 'These three great men have taken a stand. Will you stand with them?'

Cantona had said, 'If Glazer were to come here, we would lose everything,' while Ferguson urged United fans to join the campaign. He said, 'We don't want the club to be in anyone else's hands. Groups like Shareholders United can only be good for the game and I'd like fans to get involved.' Keane backed Ferguson's stance on the takeover.

In many ways he is a traditionalist; he also did not want United's, and consequently his own, future in the hands of people who did not have red and white running through their veins.

Solskjaer stood up in public for the battle against the Glazers, becoming the first current player from the Reds to join Shareholders United. 'I think it is important that the club remains in the right hands,' said the man who scored the winning goal in the team's 1999 Champions League victory. 'I am honoured,' added Solskjaer. 'I am absolutely on the supporters' side and think the club is in very good hands as it is today. I am a United fan myself and only want what is best for the future.'

By the end of the season, United would be in the hands of the Glazers, and the club's future – and that of older players like Keane and Giggs – would be unclear. To sustain and finance the debt the American family had taken on to gain control, they would need to cut their costs. The farming out of players on loan to reduce the wages bill was just on the horizon, and, in Keane's case, the future looked a lot less optimistic.

On the field, things were getting worse too. United would finish third in the Premiership, behind champions Chelsea and runners-up Arsenal, and lose an FA Cup final to the Gunners that they should have won. United outplayed their bitter rivals at the Millennium Stadium in Cardiff but could not break down their resistance. It would end 0–0 after extra-time, but the Gunners would lift the Cup after winning 5–4 on penalties. Ferguson had left Ryan Giggs on the bench in order to accommodate Darren Fletcher to do Keane's leg work. This time, it paid off, as Keane put in a strident skipper's performance.

Afterwards, Keane said, 'We played quite well and had plenty of chances but it's about putting the ball in the back of the net, and we didn't quite manage it. It's small consolation to say that we had all the chances. We dominated, but I'm sure the Arsenal players won't be too bothered about that – they've got the winners' medals and the Cup and we haven't.' It was typical Keane: brash, honest and in no mood to accept patronising platitudes when he had lost.

Then he walked around the field consoling his men like a defeated general. This proud man waved to the United fans packing two sides of the Millennium Stadium, then walked down the tunnel with his head bowed, deep in thought. Maybe at that moment he knew the party was finally over at Old Trafford. If he did, his instincts would certainly be proved correct in pre-season, as he and Ferguson fell out for the first time in public – but that is a story for slightly later.

EIGHT

STABBED IN THE FRONT

Dear Mr McCarthy,

Excuse me for writing out of the blue. I am a journalist who writes on football for, among others, the *Sunday Times* and I have just completed a biography on Wayne Rooney, called *Simply Red*, which is just out.

I am now working on another commissioned football book, which will be out this time next year on Roy Keane and what could be his last season at Manchester United. It is a tribute-style book and I was wondering if you would perhaps like to add some comments about his overall contribution, where you see his position among the greatest stars at Old Trafford, and how you feel now about the incidents of the 2002 World Cup. This could be an opportunity to let bygones be bygones – or to put your side of the story once and for all?

Once again, many thanks for your help and time, Mr McCarthy. I am very grateful to you.

All the best,

Frank Worrall

The consensus in Ireland after the Saipan incident of 2002 was that you were either for Roy Keane or against him. The end of his World Cup dream either proved he was a hothead who could not see beyond the red mist on his nose or a man of principle who would not take shit from someone when he felt he did not deserve it. If you believed he was a Mr Angry who was not worth the hassle he caused any more, your opinion would arguably be vindicated three years down the line when his bust-up with Ferguson and Queiroz cost him his job at Manchester United. Here, you could say, was a man incapable of managing his own emotions, a man who was kicked out of both country and club because of a bad attitude. Or you could argue – again with a certain conviction – that on the contrary Keane was the victim of both pieces, that he only had a go at McCarthy and Ferguson because things were not right in the Irish and Man United set-ups, and that as skipper it was his moral duty to be the one who spoke out.

My view is that there's an element of truth in both arguments – that Keane was right to speak out about the nightmare training facilities for the Irish camp in the 2002 World Cup and that he was also right to let Ferguson and Queiroz know how he felt about the steady decline at United, due to poor tactics, poor buys and poor decisions. Yet, of course, he was wrong and juvenile to blow up like some spoilt kid: surely by 2002 and 2005 he should have grown up enough to be able to make a convincing case without throwing his dummy out of the pram? He was skipper of his club and country – an ambassador for both – not some loud-mouthed thug, for God's sake.

Again a case could be made that the problem linked back to his childhood. It seemed that the sulky, shy boy from Cork had never grown up properly, had never learned social graces or how to manage his anger. When threatened, according to my psychoanalyst pal, he would still bark back – it was his coping mechanism, his defensive shield. He still seemed emotionally immature.

Having said all that, I must say my sympathy lies with Keane on both occasions. Let's leave the hectic 2005 happenings at United as Keane's finale at Old Trafford loomed for now and examine his contribution to the Irish cause. First, I must make another admission: Mick McCarthy is not one of my favourite people in football. I don't like the way he tries to engender his persona as the gruff, tough but likeable Yorkshireman, the honest broker who is one of the lads but also the boss. The by-now Sunderland manager was one of the few people not to bother responding when I sent off my letters for this book in September 2005 (the one addressed to him is the one that starts this chapter).

The letter was a genuine attempt to give Mick McCarthy a chance to present his side of the story, maybe even for him to proffer a forgiving, generous arm to Roy. Surely the gruff, tough but likeable McCarthy would be big enough to do that? The months idled by and no reply, so I thought, 'Well, maybe he ain't got the letter.' I rang the Stadium of Light and asked to speak to him. I was told it was not possible that day, but if I would explain why I wanted to speak to him and ring back, he would perhaps be able to talk for a couple of minutes. I explained that I was doing a book on Keane and wanted him to say a few words, and was asked to phone back a week later.

When I phoned back, the man on the other end of the line did not mince words: 'He's got enough on his plate with keeping this club in the Premiership to be messing about with niceties about Keane. Don't bother ringing back.' And with that, the line went dead.

Without the benefit of getting McCarthy's own view, my feeling remained that he had goaded his skipper in Saipan in 2002, that he knew Keane would blow up if he pushed the right buttons and that the bust-up had been coming for many years. The sad fact is that Keane's exit, plus his booking in Turin in 1999, meant he had missed out on what should have been the two highlights of his career: the 1999 European Cup final and the 2002 World Cup. He would never get another chance to play in either competition for Manchester United or Ireland – and that was a real tragedy. Arguably the greatest warrior for club and country would never be able to live out the biggest moments, the moments that should have held the fondest memories in his old age.

Keane would win sixty-six caps for Ireland, spanning fourteen years and three managers. He was handed his first cap in May 1991 by Jack Charlton in the Republic's 1–1 draw against Chile in Dublin. The midfielder scored nine goals for the national team, including two in the Republic's 4–0 win over Cyprus in March 2001 – the match that marked his fiftieth cap. His last game for his country was the 1–0 defeat against France at Lansdowne Road in September 2005. He announced his retirement after missing the crucial World Cup qualifiers against Cyprus and Switzerland in October 2005 due to a foot injury. Without his influence, the Irish would miss out on the 2006 World Cup.

Keane enjoyed two major highlights as an international player. The first came when he was named Ireland's player of the tournament at the 1994 World Cup in the USA. Then, in 2001, inspired by captain Keane, the Irish went undefeated against Portugal and the Netherlands in their World Cup 2002 qualifying group, famously knocking out the Dutch to make the finals in Japan and Korea. Also worth mentioning – and worth bearing in mind given the combustible nature of his relationship with McCarthy – was that he would get onto Big Mick's bad side twice in 1996.

First, in March, he would be sent off on his 30th appearance for the Republic against Russia in McCarthy's debut match as manager. Then, in May, he would fail to report for both McCarthy's testimonial match and Republic of Ireland training after going on holiday to Italy – a failure that would temporarily cost him the Republic captaincy and lead to him being left out for six matches by the national boss.

McCarthy was not the only one of the three Ireland managers who selected Keane to feel the sharp end of his tongue. Only Brian Kerr, who treated Roy more as a grown-up and an equal, would enjoy a period of relative calm with the forthright midfielder.

In October 1990, Keane's first taste of the international scene came when he was picked for the Irish Under-21 team to play Turkey in Dublin. He did not like the look of Jack Charlton from the very start. In his autobiography, he says:

> Unfortunately, the Irish set-up was a bit of a joke. Jack Charlton was God in Ireland. Maurice Setters, his right-hand man, was in charge of the Under-21 side. Apart from a few clichés about 'having a go' and 'putting 'em under pressure', Setters had very little to say. The set-up didn't impress me. I smelt bullshit.

One famous incident concerning Charlton came in 1991 when Keane, even as a teenager, showed he was not afraid to stand up for himself. Following a friendly against the United States in Boston, the Republic lads enjoyed a night out. This was the time when Keane was not the sullen loner: he was one of the boys, keen to enjoy himself with the craic and a beer (or two). Typically during this period, his night went on rather longer than the other lads' in the squad and he found it hard to raise himself the next morning after a few hours of restless kip. The team bus was due off at 7.30 a.m., with Keane finally ambling aboard half an hour late. A furious Jack Charlton bollocked him with the words: 'Nineteen years old, your first trip. Do you have any idea how long we have been waiting?'

A couldn't-care-less, forceful Keane replied, 'I didn't ask you to wait, did I?' He then shrugged his shoulders and walked to his seat, past the disbelieving, shell-shocked Charlton.

Later in his Ireland career, teammate Jason McAteer would explain how the squad learned to accept Roy as he was, knowing they would never be able to change him and simply being grateful for his presence. McAteer said, 'Roy is very, very professional and nothing gets in the way of football. Football is the thing, right? That's a great attitude to have and our relationship cooled at one point because he thought it wasn't the same for me. But I've got back to a level where we know where we're coming from. I know how to handle him now. I know when not to talk to Roy and when I can have a chat. But no one gets really close to him. In spite of what people think, he's a good character to have around.'

Charlton felt much the same – he didn't particularly admire Keane as a person but was certainly glad to have him in his team. Keane's quibbles with Charlton were essentially the same ones that would lead him into war with McCarthy. That fierce determination to win and competitive edge meant the Cork man simply could not accept the idea of Ireland being a team that was just in it for the craic. He had no time for the notion that 'good old Ireland' could be relied upon to put on a show for the fans, and who cared if they didn't even make the knockout stages of the World Cup, wasn't it enough that they had simply qualified? For Keane, the answer was a resounding 'no'. It wasn't enough just to be there and be part of it. The World Cup was not just an excuse for the fans to have a wild time.

Keane expected Ireland to be run along the same lines as

Manchester United: a powerful, professional set-up where winning was all that mattered. This led to disagreements with Charlton and McCarthy over training facilities and lack of preparation. Training facilities were to be a major source of irritation for Keane. In 2001, he had a go at the Football Association of Ireland (FAI) for treating the players in a second-class way. He said, 'Where we trained last Monday, in Clonshaugh, was abysmal and it has been for as long as I've known it. I was fairly critical about our seating arrangements on the flight out here, when the officials were sitting in the first-class seats and the players were sitting behind.' And it was the initial row over the quality of a training pitch in 2002 that sparked the ultimate row with McCarthy that would lead to Keane being sent home from Saipan. Even afterwards, Keane was adamant that the players had received a raw deal, that they had hardly been treated with the reverence of teams that were expected to go a long way in the competition. He growled, 'You've seen the training pitch and I'm not being a prima donna. Training pitch, travel arrangements, getting through the airport when we were leaving: it's the combination of things. I would never say "That's the reason or this is the reason," but enough is enough.'

Keane did not get along with Charlton and his assistant Maurice Setters. He felt Charlton patronised the Irish, that he saw the job as being a walk in the park, that Ireland were lucky to get his services. After all, he was a World Cup winner with England in '66, wasn't he? Keane would claim that tactics from the duo were non-existent, that the players were told to kick the ball high up and not to mess about with it in midfield or defence. To a top player like Keane, such sentiments were anathema. In hindsight, it could be said that in the early days of Charlton's reign, Keane's beef was as much with his countrymen as with the man known as 'the giraffe' in his playing days. Charlton would bring relative success, but Keane would argue that the Irish should not be satisfied with being good losers.

Charlton ruled Irish football for ten years, from 1986 to 1996, with Keane accompanying him for the last five. Charlton's first game in '86 would end in a 1–0 defeat against Wales, but he soon won plaudits from the Irish nation by guiding Ireland to victory in the Icelandic tournament against Czechoslovakia and the host nation. It was the first tournament Ireland had ever won.

He then led the country to qualification for the 1988 European Championships – their first-ever major finals. A sixth-minute goal from Ray Houghton gave Ireland an opening-game victory over England and this was followed by a 1–1 draw with the Soviet Union. In the final group match against Holland, Ireland only needed a draw to progress to the semi-finals, but a late Wim Kieft winning goal meant the Irish returned home.

What happened next is the sort of thing that would grate with Keane, as more than 200,000 people lined the streets of Dublin to welcome back Charlton, Setters and the players as returning heroes. In Keane's mind, they had failed.

However, Charlton could do no wrong with the Irish public, taking the nation to the last eight of the 1990 World Cup tournament in Italy. After drawing all three of their opening group matches, against England – with Kevin Sheedy scoring Ireland's first-ever goal at a World Cup finals – Egypt and Holland, Ireland beat Romania in a penalty shoot-out in the second round, before going out 1–0 to hosts Italy in the quarter-finals. Keane gritted his teeth again as Charlton *et al.* once again returned to Ireland as heroes.

Despite not losing a game in the qualifiers for the 1992 European Championships, Ireland only finished second in their group, and their campaign ended there. It was England who travelled to Sweden as the group winners.

By now, Keane was a major player in the team, and he helped them to qualify for their second World Cup finals in succession in 1994. On Sunday, 19 June, Keane played in his first World Cup match for his country – the celebrated 1–0 win over the Italians in Giants Stadium, New York. Charlton's team were knackered by the end of the 90 minutes, having delivered the goods for him. He had asked them to block out the creative genius of Roberto Baggio by maintaining their discipline in a 4–5–1 system. It meant lots of defensive running for Keane and Houghton in midfield, and a definite curbing of their attacking instincts, as they provided back-up for Paul McGrath and Phil Babb in the heart of the Irish defence. A defeat by Mexico was followed by a goalless draw with Norway – which was enough for Ireland to progress to the second phase, where they were beaten 2–0 by Holland.

The Charlton era was drawing to a close – much to the relief of Keane. He was sick of the Englishman's tactics and the way he drew the applause of the Irish nation. In his autobiography, he would later explain his reasons for disliking Charlton:

> I'd watched Jack Charlton's teams in Euro '88 and Italia '90 as a fan, so I knew the style was pretty basic and difficult to come to terms with for someone coming from my Forest background, where we played a passing game.

There you have it: a pivotal elementary difference in style marked the two men down as chalk and cheese. Keane would never come to terms with having to hoof the ball up-front, and he disliked having to adapt his game to the Charlton method of 'Don't give the fucking ball away . . .'.

Yet other comments made by Keane about Charlton suggest that he did have some good times with him, that it wasn't all one big downer over tactics and Big Jack's hero persona. After Ireland's exit from the 1994 World Cup, some had demanded that Charlton step down. Keane was not among them. In fact, in public at least, he was one of his staunchest backers. Keane said at the time that he could not visualise the Irish national team without the Englishman at the helm: 'It's a bit like how I felt at Forest under Brian Clough. Right up to the day before he announced his resignation, I was thinking, "No, he can't go." I still think he has a lot to give this team. I think he can help mature the new lads over the next couple of years. If he can give them, and me, the benefit of his experience, then if he goes in two years, he will leave the team in even better shape than it is now.

'Only a few months ago, a lot of people seemed to think that the team was over the hill and that Jack would pack it in sooner rather than later. But I think the way that the new lads are coming through has given a new lease of life not only to the team but to Jack too. Overall, I think there is a new air of confidence about the team that will stand us all in good stead.' These were unusual, contrary sentiments from a man who in his autobiography went to great lengths to ridicule Charlton and his managerial skills (or lack of them) and his relationship with the Irish nation.

And many within that nation *did* love Big Jack. Booker Prize winner and celebrated Irishman Roddy Doyle was one. Writing in *My Favourite Year: A Collection of Football Writing*, he would admit as much when commenting on Charlton's Ireland and their efforts in the 1990 World Cup finals:

> I was a Charlton man. I liked him; I loved the team
> – McGrath, Houghton, Bonner – they were all
> marvellous. They'd been dreadful on Sunday against
> Egypt, but so what? They'd been great many times

before that and they'd be great again, possibly on
Thursday against Holland. If they lost on Thursday,
it would all be ruined. There was always a gang of
miserable little fuckers waiting for things to go
wrong.

None of them are really Irish, that's the problem . . .
I'd waited all my life to see Ireland in the World Cup.
As far as I was concerned, Jack Charlton had got them
there. He had style, humour; he was honest . . .

If Keane's relationship with Charlton was ultimately
mixed, there would be no such confusion when it came to
Mick McCarthy. He could not stand the Irish Yorkshireman
– and the feeling was mutual. Charlton resigned as Irish
boss just after Christmas in 1996, quickly to be replaced by
his captain. A bit of background about McCarthy to set the
scene. As an Ireland player, he had made his name as a
tough defender during the 1988 European Championships
and 1990 World Cup. As a manager, he had turned
Millwall into one of the most attractive footballing sides in
England. And, to give him his due, all was not rosy in the
garden when he took over from Charlton. The team was
ageing and new blood was needed – and quickly. In his first
campaign, Ireland failed to make the 1998 World Cup,
going out to Belgium in the play-offs.

Some argue that McCarthy was a lucky Ireland manager.
Certainly his prayers for quality young replacements were
answered, as Ireland's youth proved they could cut it at
international level. In 1997, Ireland finished third in the
World Under-20 Championships in Malaysia, and the
following year, Brian Kerr, who would take over from
McCarthy as manager, led both Under-16 and Under-18
teams to victory in their respective European competitions,
making Ireland the only country ever to win both
championships in the same year.

The pay-off would not arrive in time for Euro 2000 – as Ireland again exited in the play-offs, this time to Turkey – but the likes of Damien Duff and Robbie Keane would join Roy Keane in a brilliant qualifying campaign for the 2002 World Cup. The team were unbeaten throughout qualification and finished second in the group behind Portugal to set up a play-off date with Iran. After beating them 2–0 at Lansdowne Road, Ireland progressed 2–1 on aggregate to qualify for their first World Cup finals in eight years.

McCarthy had arrived on the big stage, but would he bow out a hero or a villain? He owed Roy Keane: the Irishman had dragged his country to the finals with a series of inspired displays. Now it was payback time, but it would not be the payback Roy had expected. An inkling that there were problems in Saipan emerged on Wednesday, 22 May 2002, when McCarthy spoke to the BBC and tried desperately to play down a bust-up in training between Keane and the goalkeepers' coach Paddy Bonner. Keane was reportedly angry because Bonner had stopped the Republic's three goalkeepers – Shay Given, Dean Kiely and Alan Kelly – from taking part in five-a-side practice matches. It led Keane to announce to McCarthy that he wanted to go home, citing personal problems and worries about his troublesome knee as the reasons.

However, the midfielder had a change of heart and was soon back in training, with McCarthy immediately embarking upon a damage-limitation exercise. McCarthy said, 'Team morale is brilliant; there are no worries about that. The lads are the best bunch you will ever meet and they will get on with it. Whatever happens, they will put the best side out at all times; they are brilliant. They came back from training today [Wednesday] and all gathered round Roy. They are all together.

'Roy trained and is absolutely fine. He has had a change

of heart and I am delighted. He should be playing in the World Cup because he is one of the best players in the world. Roy plays for one of the biggest clubs in the world week in, week out and I have no worries about him. This is one of those things and it comes with the territory. I'd like to have had a lovely restful week and not had this to deal with, but we'll get on with it.'

He went on: 'There is some suggestion this is all to do with a bust-up at training, but that is way off the mark. There were suggestions he had a scuffle in training, and I wasn't even aware of that. Packie [Bonner] has bigger arguments with his lad over his homework. We had a number of discussions, but then he spoke to other people back at home and that resolved whatever problems there were. I know he is worried about his knee; he has treatment on it all the time. That is an ongoing thing and it will be.'

Within 24 hours, McCarthy's attempts to play down Keane's rising resentments would be blown right out of the water. Keane would be on his way home – and soon be walking his golden Labrador Triggs around the block near his Cheshire mansion. Keane had given an interview to his journalist friend Tom Humphries in the *Irish Times* in which he slammed the team's poor preparations and training facilities at the Irish World Cup HQ. Keane had said:

> The hotel is fine, but we've come here to work. You wonder why players get injured? Well, playing on a surface like that. I can't imagine any other country, countries in the world who are far worse off than us, playing on something like that. I don't think it's too much to ask, just for a pitch that's even watered. It's so dangerous. It's rock hard.
>
> One or two of the lads have picked up injuries. I'm amazed there hasn't been more but give it time. But

you know, we're the Irish team, it's a laugh and a joke. We shouldn't expect too much.

McCarthy called a team meeting in which he asked if anyone had any grievances, before producing a copy of the interview. He allegedly accused Keane of previously feigning injury, and Keane responded by insulting McCarthy and questioning his abilities as a manager. Keane, inevitably, blew up when cornered. His head had gone: how could he back down? Everyone who knew him – most especially his managers Ferguson and McCarthy – surely understood this complex man's sensitivity to criticism and that his insecurity could hardly allow him to withdraw from a tight corner without a defensive blast. They knew the nature of the beast and should have been willing to take the good and the bad. They loved the Keane who would have died for them, didn't they? Well, shouldn't they also have accepted with wisdom and compassion the other side of his make-up – making an allowance for the inner monster of insecurity and unattainable perfection that Keane could not control?

That is why I wanted to ask McCarthy the truth of that day: did he really expect Keane to just sit back and say 'Sorry, sir', given the man's emotional make-up? I have my doubts. Wasn't this merely the endgame in a bitter relationship between the two that had seen years of verbal knocks being made against each other?

Instead of backing down, Keane launched his attack on McCarthy, allegedly calling him a 'fucking wanker'. Other members of the management team were so angry they had to be physically restrained. 'It was bedlam once Roy got to his feet,' said a member of the Irish back-room team. 'He began his onslaught and it got steadily worse. The other players could not believe what was going on. Mick was left with no choice but to send Roy home, such was the level of abuse aimed in his direction.

'It was vicious and it was vulgar and he dragged up things that had happened years ago. It appeared that Roy did not want to explain or even debate anything. He just let go and never stopped.'

McCarthy said, 'I couldn't tolerate that level of abuse. It was personal and unprecedented. I had no choice but to act.' When he told Keane he was sacked, other players cheered. Keane stormed out of the meeting, saying his sanity was more important than the World Cup. McCarthy would add: 'We will move on and be all right because we are collectively strong. We all know his [Keane's] ability, but when he makes a public and open show of his opinions and makes such a public criticism, everybody starts talking about it.'

Ironically, one of those players would back up Keane's moans and groans. In *Niall Quinn: The Autobiography*, the former Manchester City striker admitted that the Republic's preparations were a shambles. He told of a drinking session in a bar on Saipan that continued until daybreak, with the start of the World Cup only days away. Keane, he revealed, took no part in that drinking binge. Quinn also confirmed Keane's claim that the Republic's training pitch was bumpy and parched and that a five-a-side training match was played without goalkeepers.

Quinn then set the scene for the final shoot-out between McCarthy and Keane like this:

> Suddenly it's gunfight at the OK Corral but Mick hasn't brought his gun. Roy goes off, rat-a-tat-tat. It is the most surgical slaughtering I've ever heard. Mick McCarthy is dismantled from A to Z. His personality, his style, his tactics, his contribution. On it goes.
>
> Words used include spineless, useless, stupid, gutless. Every grievance is ordered and filed neatly

with an appropriate insult attached. Incompetent.
Ignorant. Backward. Con man.

We're all mesmerised. For ten minutes it goes on,
and we sit there in a trance with the blood draining
from our faces. This isn't going to end in a group
hug. We came out of there like people who had seen
a ghost. 'I'll **** off then,' Roy shouts as he gets to the
door. 'I'll not go to the ****ing World Cup. Now you
have your excuse. It's all Roy's fault. See you later,
lads.' And he's gone.

Ironically, training facilities and club grounds would
improve dramatically in the Republic itself after Keane's
Saipan outburst. The Football Association of Ireland – to
whom I am indebted for many background details of the
nation's successes and flops on the football field from the
time of Jack Charlton to Brian Kerr – admitted as much to
me: 'The '90s saw an improvement for the game
domestically. Facilities at grounds throughout the country
improved, and the standard of football was also excellent.'

Back to Quinn: he had no reason to fabricate what
happened that night. His quotes from Roy leave me feeling
sad: sad that it had to end that way, that McCarthy could
not have been a bigger man and put his arm around his
best player; sad that Roy and Ireland had to miss out when
the tournament began. Mostly, as I now look back on the
incident, I feel sad that Keane the man was again so badly
misunderstood. He was no hard man and, of course, he
didn't want to miss out on the World Cup. All he wanted
was his natural right to have a say, to have a say as
McCarthy's chosen skipper. The more I look back on the
affair, the more I see Keane as the honest victim of a long-
term clash of personalities. He and McCarthy had never hit
it off. Now Keane would be made to suffer the ultimate
blow. His teammates could afford to laugh it off – they even

stuck an envelope with 'RIP' on Roy's seat on the coach as they merrily made their way to the World Cup matches. Quinn called it 'a little black joke'. Some joke when a fellow footballer's World Cup dream lay in ruins.

Another of Keane's colleagues, Republic goalkeeper Alan Kelly, heartily put the boot in, saying, 'We are 110 per cent in support of Mick. Roy has let himself down with the things he has said. They shouldn't be said and I've never witnessed anything like it. Sometimes you have arguments in football, and I had one with Roy the other day, but there's a line you cannot walk over – and that line was breached by Roy, and that's why I'm showing my support for Mick.

'I was shocked by the things Roy said. I think most of the players in the room were shocked by it. I would have no qualms about telling him what he said was unacceptable, none at all.'

Predictably, Big Jack backed boss McCarthy and made it clear he felt Keane had dropped a bollock. Charlton said, 'I think when Roy sits down and thinks about what he has done, he will have a few regrets. You don't walk out on a World Cup – and he'll have to live with this for the rest of his life. He is one of the best players in the world and he should be at the finals. He's had his complaints about their preparations but that had nothing to do with the players. This is a bad thing for Ireland. Everyone will be up in arms. Roy will have to deal with the anger of the fans and he will have to have a good excuse for this.

'You have to back the manager, and Mick McCarthy will have his reasons for what has happened. You can't have players dictating what happens just days before the tournament starts. Whatever happens, I back Mick.'

He added: 'It's the last thing that Ireland needed. We'll be lucky to get through the group now – this sort of thing doesn't do a lot for morale.'

Maurice Setters, Charlton's former number two within the Irish camp, also slammed Keane, saying, 'As skipper, Roy is right to point things out that he might be unhappy with, but it should always be kept within the dressing-room. Roy is a talented, world-class player, but he's gone OTT this time. He seems to have forgotten that his job is out on the pitch.'

The Saipan incident also had the effect of jolting Setters' memory about a young Keane in the build-up to the 1994 World Cup finals. Setters said, 'Roy was a young, inexperienced lad, and he was telling me that it was too hot for the acclimatising work we were doing. He said he couldn't do it, and got a bit bolshie about it. I told him straight that if he didn't do it then he wouldn't be playing in the World Cup, simple as that.'

But Keane's former Ireland teammate John Aldridge believed the midfielder had genuine grievances and predicted that fans in Ireland would be split over whose side to take. He said, 'You can see both sides. Personally I would have done my utmost to make sure Roy stayed, but Mick had to take a stance. When you come to the World Cup, you must have the best. Preparation is everything and the FAI should have ensured that was sorted out suitably.

'It's not about the money, because the better prepared you are, the more chance you have of progressing and the more financial reward is gained for the association. Everyone is a winner.

'Under Jack Charlton – and Roy would have had a taste of that – we just got on with it. The facilities weren't always the best but you just looked forward to the 90 minutes. Now times have changed and the standards are much higher and are expected to be so.'

Keane found another ally in the form of his biographer Eamon Dunphy. The former Ireland international claimed McCarthy had made 'a monumental blunder'. Dunphy said, 'This act of folly destroys Ireland's World Cup. The captain of the Irish team and the greatest player we have ever had is being sent from the most important occasion Irish soccer has ever had to face.

'This is not a case of somebody being caught with a lap dancer. This is the case of a man who has spoken and has earned the right to speak. It is an absolute farce.'

Dunphy believed McCarthy had felt undermined by Keane. 'That has probably been a recurring feature of McCarthy's stewardship. Sir Alex Ferguson gives Roy Keane the right to speak his mind and there is no problem there.

'But McCarthy is insecure and a figure of much less stature. He owes a lot to Roy Keane and if this is the way he has chosen to repay him, then he is a fool. Roy is not difficult; he is a lovely guy. Every football manager in the world would love to have Roy in their team – except one.'

Well put, Eamon, I agree with you. Fair enough, Ireland would enjoy some success in that World Cup, climbing out of the group stages and eventually only exiting in the second round to Spain in a penalty shoot-out. But surely they would have done even better if Roy Keane had been leading them? Surely they would have gone further? Well, wouldn't they? Logically?

NINE

WALKING THE DOG

Dublin on a crisp autumnal evening, 7 September 2005: a date worth noting in our diaries – a date at that decrepit, dilapidated, disgracefully medieval yet wonderfully magical multi-sporting venue known as Lansdowne Road – a date on which we came to praise Caesar, but ended up burying him – the date which would mark Roy Keane's last-ever appearance in a Republic of Ireland shirt.

At the time, we thought there may be more but, in hindsight, it was no bad thing to go out in such exalted company, even if the boy's last gig was destined to end in defeat. There was no disgrace at all in losing to a class outfit like France, and much pleasure to be derived in keeping such exalted company on one's last night before facing the hangman.

As midfields go, the French one on 7 September would whet any appetite. It read: Claude Makelele, Patrick Vieira and Zinedine Zidane. On his last night at the Irish office, Keane would be flanked by Andy Reid and Kevin Kilbane. The winning goal would be scored by the exhilarating Thierry Henry. No, as class company goes, Roy could not have had it much better than France for his international farewell.

Apart from, of course, Ronaldinho, Ronaldo, Kaka, Robinho and Adriano. But the Brazilians were never going to be on the agenda at this time of this year. The French rolled up at Lansdowne for a match both teams needed to win if they were going to make it to the World Cup in 2006. The dice were loaded, and the stakes were as high as you can get.

What had brought him back to the Irish camp? After Saipan, it had appeared impossible for him to return given the attitude of the manager and the players. But the ice thawed among the players, and McCarthy's days were numbered. Eventually, he jumped ship to Sunderland, with the more respected, thoughtful Brian Kerr taking over the good ship Ireland. The appointment of Kerr in 2003 eventually led to the controversial return of Keane to the international arena in 2004.

In his first interview after Saipan, with Matt Dickinson of *The Times* in August 2002, Keane had hinted that he would return once McCarthy had gone – and he explained that he would have returned to Saipan but for McCarthy's insistence that he had feigned injury. Keane said, 'People go round the houses talking about my complaints over the training pitches and so on, which were valid. But I would have played in the World Cup despite all that if McCarthy hadn't accused me of faking injuries. It is as simple as that. They dangled a carrot for me and I had a good nibble.

'I saw him on *Football Focus* saying, "I don't appreciate being called an effing w and an effing c." But if you say I am faking injury and letting my teammates down, then dead right. To me, that is the worst insult you can have. Why hasn't anyone asked him why he said what he did and why he wanted me out?

'Mick has two years left on his contract and obviously I will never play for him again. In two years, if some chairman is daft enough to give him a job and someone else comes in, I will look at it again. I would not like to finish my international career on that note. Some people seem to think it doesn't bother me. Of course it bothers me to have missed the World Cup.

'The FAI are never going to be big payers. That is why they have ended up with managers like Jack Charlton and McCarthy. The FAI have a yes man and Mick has his free time to go on *They Think It's All Over* to be a comedian, which is what he is.'

Eventually, some chairman was 'daft enough to give him [McCarthy] a job', and Keane made his Ireland return on 25 May 2004 in a friendly match against Romania at Lansdowne Road. His performances in subsequent matches earned him new accolades, including praise from some of those who had lambasted him for the Saipan incident.

Under Kerr's arm-around-the-shoulder approach, Keane settled down again: he felt wanted. Kerr knew how to deal with the boy: he instinctively understood that provocation would be met with provocation given Keane's flawed emotional make-up. In good heart and under good management, Keane helped Ireland draw away with France and Switzerland in their 2006 World Cup qualifying campaign. It looked likely they would go on to make at least the play-offs. Then Keane got injured in the France match – and the dream effectively died that night of 7 September.

The night had started brightly enough – even if the ramshackle Lansdowne Road stadium hardly lived up to the glittering picture of Dublin painted in a tourist information sheet handed out at the city's airport. It gushed: 'See how the economic boom has brought all the new clubs, cafés, restaurants, art-house cinemas, galleries, designer boutiques and all that is trendy. What makes it contagious though is its Georgian grace, famous 1,000+ pubs, fine museums, lovely parks and mostly the proud, extroverted, open-armed, open-hearted, down-to-earth people.'

Roy Keane had been brought up as a Cork man to keep Dublin and its people at a cynical arm's length. He knew all the tourist office hype about the place – its 'magic' and 'warmth' – but give him Cork and the real world any day. The night of 7 September he walked into Lansdowne Road, for what would be his last appearance in the green shirt, unmoved by any mystical charm. He was here to do a job. Full stop.

In the tunnel before the match, he caught sight of his old adversary, arguably his greatest adversary, Big Pat Vieira. The Frenchman smiled; Keane looked away grimly. It had always been that way between the deadly duo; why should it be any different now?

Before the match, I had told Vieira I was doing a book on Keane's final season at United and asked him if he had anything to say. Initially, he looked me up and down as if to say, 'Who the fuck is this fat bastard?' – a bemusement for which I cannot blame him and, indeed, hold nothing against him for – then he said, 'Yes, I admire him. He's the best I've ever played against in England. I liked playing against him; he is a great competitor and a great leader.' As Big Pat eyed an exit door, I sensed this would be a quick chat and rushed out another question: 'Is he the hardest you've ever played against?' The big man smiled at me with a glint in his eye. 'Put it this way,' he said. 'I wouldn't like to come across him alone in a dark alley – or a tunnel, come to that!'

Then the great man was off – to do the business for France, and then back to Italy to carry on his fine work for new club Juventus. It made me think back to that night at Highbury in February 2005, when Keane and Vieira had snarled at each other in the tunnel before Arsenal hosted United. In essence, they were both made of the same stock:

both strong, principled men who could occasionally let themselves down with indiscipline and a short fuse.

It was also fairly appropriate that both men should quit the clubs for whom they had been the bedrock in the same year: Vieira to Italy from Arsenal in the summer and Keane from United in the November of 2005. Also interesting to note is the fact that neither man appeared in a European Cup final for Arsenal or United – that was the key reason Vieira would jump ship for Juve, while Keane's disillusion with Ferguson and United from after the 1999 final onwards would ultimately lead to his speaking out once too often and his sacking.

Before the Ireland v. France match, boss Kerr and skipper Keane had made it plain to the Irish team that they could not afford any slip-ups if they were to have a realistic chance of making Germany 2006. Right to the end of his international career, Keane was as demanding as ever. He was right to be if you looked at the statistics of World Cup qualifying Group 4. It was the tightest of the European groups, with one point dividing the unbeaten top four. France's 3–0 home win over the Faroe Islands moved them to 13 points, alongside Ireland. Switzerland completed the top trio after their 1–1 home draw with Israel, who remained very much in the hunt on twelve points from one more game than the top three but with two matches against the Faroes to come.

No wonder, as the teams walked out on 7 September, that Keane looked as tense and grim as he ever had. He was not to know this would be his last match for Ireland, so there were no nostalgic waves to the fans or bowing of heads. No, this was Keane the warrior on a mission to take his country to glory. Even the great Zinedine Zidane looked ill at ease as the teams lined up for the national anthems. Before the match, he had conceded that a heavy weight rested on the result of this match in Dublin.

Zidane had urged his side to be more clinical in front of goal against the Republic, despite France's 3–0 thrashing of the Faroe Islands in Lens the previous Saturday. Two goals from Liverpool striker Djibril Cissé and an own goal from defender Suni Olsen allowed the French team to claim maximum points and go joint top of Group 4 with Switzerland and the Republic.

Zidane conceded Les Bleus were improving but insisted they would need to be much better when they faced Keane and Co. He said, 'We hoped we could have scored more, but 3–0 was not bad. We had a lot of opportunities and that is good ahead of the Ireland clash. But we were not perfect in finishing off. We will have to be more efficient in front of our rivals' net.

'Against Ireland, we will have less space and they will be more aggressive up-front. Our chances will lie in starting the game well by scoring fast.'

Coach Raymond Domenech agreed, saying, 'Against Ireland, we will have to be more solid and aggressive while imposing our game. If we want to finish at the top, we have to beat the Irish.'

In the event, Keane's last match for Ireland would see him on the losing side as the French notched their first win in Dublin for 52 years, thanks to Thierry Henry's goal. France's last win in Dublin – also in a World Cup qualifier – was a 5–3 victory on 4 October 1953.

Keane was booked four minutes from half-time for a late challenge on Makelele – a booking that would have kept him out of the Republic's next match against Cyprus on 8 October, even if he had not suffered the broken foot at Anfield on 18 September that would sideline him at Old Trafford and herald his last match for the Red Devils.

Yellow card apart, Keane's final showing for the Emerald Isle will be remembered as a masterful one. The United veteran rolled back the years in his battle against Makelele,

Vieira and Zidane, earning himself the man of the match award in the process. The French had the better of the first half, but Keane excelled in repelling their waves of attacks. After the interval, the Irish were more confident and – with Keane probing and directing operations – were unlucky not to go ahead when Damien Duff broke through and got his shot in on target, only for it to be blocked by Lilian Thuram.

Keane's dream would end on 68 minutes when Arsenal striker Thierry Henry, who was otherwise subdued, stunned Lansdowne Road with a beautiful curling shot beyond Shay Given into the right corner of the net. It was a heartbreaker for the Irish – but it will not take away my memories of Roy Keane that night, battling for the shirt, giving his all and ending up on an equal footing with the great Zidane and Vieira. My favourite Roy moment came when he took the ball off Big Pat in central midfield, strode past Makelele and wrong-footed Zidane before laying off the ball for namesake Robbie Keane – a wondrous moment from a world-class genius in world-class company.

Keane trudged off the pitch a beaten man, but, if he had known his final showing for the Republic would have been this good, he would have been comforted. It was boss Kerr's first competitive defeat at Lansdowne Road, and the beginning of the end of his reign. The French now shared the lead in Group 4 with Switzerland, both having gained sixteen points from eight matches. Ireland slumped to fourth on thirteen points, two behind Israel. Ireland's defeat was the first for any of the top four teams in the closely fought group.

Kerr was gutted with the result, saying, 'It was a committed, honest and organised performance. We didn't deserve to get beaten.' He knew he was staring down the barrel of a gun – he now had to beat Cyprus without key banned trio Roy Keane, Andy Reid and Kenny Cunningham. It proved too much of a challenge, with

Ireland ultimately finishing fourth in their group. Kerr's contract was not renewed.

Keane had watched in frustration as Ireland fluffed their chances of making the play-offs with a goalless draw at Lansdowne Road in their final qualifier against the Swiss. Then, on 14 October 2005, following Ireland's failure to qualify for Germany 2006, Keane announced his retirement from international football for the second time – only this time it would be final, no going back. He also showed that he can be a gentleman if managed correctly, doffing his cap in respect to Brian Kerr, offering him backing he would never have given to Big Jack and Big Mick.

Keane said, 'Like all football supporters in the country, I am disappointed that the Republic of Ireland failed to qualify for the World Cup finals. Much as I would like to continue playing for my country, I feel the time has come when I should retire from international football and concentrate on domestic football for whatever remains of my football career.

'I am aware of the efforts that Brian Kerr and his staff made in an endeavour to qualify for the World Cup finals . . . I believe the recent criticism of Brian in the media is both unjust and unfair.'

He added: 'I would like to thank everyone for the support which they have given me during my international career.'

And, with that, he was gone into that dark night, with his sixty-six caps and nine goals. He returned home to his family and his dogs. Of these latter, the loyal Labrador retriever Triggs seemed to be the most favoured by Keane. It was Triggs with whom he was always spotted walking after a crisis in his footballing career – such as after the Saipan incident, when he marched around the lanes in defiance with Triggs, and after he got the sack at United, when the media cameras would again zoom in on Roy and Triggs on another expedition.

I once thought of writing a book about Triggs and the stories she could tell of Roy and his rantings on their regular walks. It would make some book, rivalled probably only by the anecdotes of former Home Secretary David Blunkett's black Labradors, Lucy and Sadie. Lucy made her name in 1999 by throwing up in the House of Commons as Blunkett listened to the speech of a Tory opponent. After nearly a decade at Blunkett's side, she would be replaced by her half-sister, Sadie, a black Labrador–curly-coated retriever cross, in 2003. But neither of Blunkett's dogs were as famous as Triggs. Bear with me on this section of the book. It's fun for us, but it's also for Roy's benefit, to bring a bit of a smile to his face as he thinks of his beloved Triggs back home. And Triggs has certainly brought smiles and comfort to Mr Keane during his fraught final years with Ireland and United.

In a pre-Saipan interview in May 2002, the *Sunday Independent*'s Paul Kimmage managed to coax some information from Keane about the effect his mutt had on his life:

> KIMMAGE: I bumped into Eamon Dunphy recently and we spoke about your book (Dunphy is ghosting the Keane autobiography) and one of the things he mentioned was that you don't have any friends in the game?
>
> KEANE: No, that would be right.
>
> KIMMAGE: And that won't hurt you when your career has ended?
>
> KEANE: No.
>
> KIMMAGE: But you like dogs?
>
> KEANE: Yeah, I've got my dog.
>
> KIMMAGE: What is it?
>
> KEANE: A Labrador retriever.
>
> KIMMAGE: What's his name?

KEANE: It's a she. Triggs.

KIMMAGE: Why dogs?

KEANE: Loyal.

KIMMAGE: They don't let you down?

KEANE: Yeah.

KIMMAGE: They don't turn you over?

KEANE: No.

In August of the same year, Keane would reveal that Triggs had helped stop him from walking away from the sport. The previous September, he had been sent off after a run-in with Alan Shearer as United went down 4–3. Keane explained:

> I went to bed but never slept a wink. Some time during the night, I decided, 'Give it up, Roy. You've turned 30 – get out, get away, do something else. You've got to stop hurting yourself, hurting those you love.' I talked to my wife. She argued I would miss it. I said I wouldn't. Anything would be better than this madness, getting angry and frustrated, lashing out.
>
> I felt I'd lost the argument that some players were in the comfort zone. Too many people were content with what they had. It wasn't for me. I should go. Next morning, I was waiting for Sir Alex Ferguson at the training ground at 8 a.m. I told him I wanted to pack it in. He said it was a knee-jerk reaction.

Keane told Ferguson he would not play in the next game – the Champions League clash with Lille – but a walk with his beloved dog changed his mind. He said:

> On Sunday I walked Triggs a long way, running the options through my head. Another club, somewhere sunny. At least I could be miserable in a warm climate. I love my football, really love it – but could

I play for another club? My heart was in Manchester United. And if I couldn't play with my heart, I couldn't play. My mind was settled. I felt calm – a big weight off my shoulders.

I thought about it and talked it through with [my wife]. I decided to play against Lille. He [Ferguson] had stood by me – quitting would be a slap in the face for him – the last thing he needed when the club was struggling. I carried on for him. I've got another four years in me – I'm sure of that now.

So that is the great truth of it all: Ferguson owed a debt to Triggs for those extra four years-plus he would get out of Keane from September 2001 to November 2005.

Triggs would earn many notable mentions elsewhere over the years. Keane's journalist pal Tom Humphries mentioned the pet while talking about Keane in the *Irish Times*: 'Whatever reasoning was used [for Keane's departure], it worked as sweetly as a gun held to the head of Triggs, Keane's pet dog. The player won't be back and his departure has been messy.'

The possibility of Keane joining Celtic also earned Triggs an honourable name-check in the *Daily Record*. Stuart Cosgrove said:

Keane has never tried to endear himself to other players. He once said he trusts his dog Triggs much more than any of his teammates. This unusual candidness sets him far apart from the fake camaraderie that prevails in the dressing-rooms of senior football.

In November 2005, Triggs got a mention from the Press Association, who were contemplating the difficulties United would face in the Champions League now their inspirational skipper had gone. The piece began:

> Sir Alex Ferguson has admitted Manchester United's lack of experience is a major handicap to their dreams of Champions League glory. While Roy Keane has temporarily been reduced to walking his dog Triggs round the Cheshire countryside, without him, Ferguson's youngsters must negotiate their way along a hazardous path to take their customary place in the knock-out phase of Europe's most prestigious club competition.

And here's one that Roy himself will particularly like, which confirms Triggs's position at the top of the fame chart. Triggs was voted the fifth most famous animal on the planet by Warwick University's student paper *The Warwick Boar*, with the following glowing report:

> Roy Keane's dog . . . Having been sent home from the World Cup in disgrace and, more recently, involved in a fracas with a teenager, Keane has at both times sought solace in his sandy blonde dog, Triggs. Arguably the most photographed pet in football, if the adage that a dog's character reflects their owner is true, postmen in the Cheshire suburbs will be running scared.

Keane could count himself lucky to have a friend like Triggs in his darkest days. After he quit the Irish scene, there were rumours that his next return to Lansdowne Road would be as the national team's manager. Those rumours caught fire when Keane left Manchester United. Surely this was the ideal stepping stone for him into management?

Looking back at that interview between Keane and *The Times*' Matt Dickinson in August 2002, there were signs that Keane was bored with the national team – and could do with a good few years away from it. Dickinson reported that Keane hardly watched his country in the World Cup after his exit. Dickinson said:

> Some of his compatriots may be perturbed when they hear that Keane slept through Ireland's opening game of the tournament, walked his mother's dog while Robbie Keane was scoring the dramatic last-minute equaliser against Germany and cannot remember where he was when they qualified from the first round. In all, he watched only 20 minutes – including the penalty shoot-out against Spain. He can only hope that they will believe him when he says that it was not indifference but hurt that meant he could not bring himself to turn on the television.

One aspect that came through was that Keane could be tempted into the Irish job to prove that he could do it better than McCarthy. His view of Big Mick's World Cup was typical in its disdain: 'The World Cup? They did OK, but that's what they expected because the manager drums that into the team. "We've done well to qualify" – all that nonsense. That's the problem.

'That sums up the mentality. Spain had ten men for half an hour; the game was there for the taking. I think a more astute manager would have won the game. Some people have higher standards than others.'

The bookies certainly hyped up the idea that Keane would take up the post after he left Manchester United. Many of them suspended their markets as Keane's odds of becoming Ireland manager shifted from 50–1 to 3–1 in 24 hours. Betfair's Eoin Ryan said, 'This news has really livened up the betting on this market. Initially, on hearing the news, our punters piled into Keane for the Ireland job, forcing his price down to a low of 3–1. His price has drifted back out to about 8–1 now, though. Some clever punters did manage to back him with us at as high as 70–1 a few weeks ago.'

A true betting man would have guessed that 'Keane for Ireland in 2006' was a red herring. The former Man United man admitted he would one day like to manage his country, but he was wise enough to know the day had not yet arrived. You see, Roy Keane is no fool. He knows the score: that he would need his coaching badges, that he needed to learn the ropes first, maybe under another manager. And anyway, weren't the bright lights of another major club side looming as the speculation about Keane and the Ireland job mounted?

TEN

SIR ALEX SEXTON

'The test of any manager or player is how they handle adversity'
– Sir Alex Ferguson, May 2005

'We are there to provide the manager with what he needs' –
Joel Glazer, 1 July 2005

'Manchester United have sold a record number of season tickets despite the controversial arrival of new owner Malcolm Glazer and the Reds' back-to-back Premiership title and Champions League failures' – Press Association, August 2005

Let's retrace our steps a little and consider Keane's departure from his cherished club in more detail. We're back in Manchester and it's that dreadful blank period in the summer – you know, the one where cricket and athletics are all there is to watch on the box, and football's still miles away on the horizon. This particular pre-season it wasn't as bad as usual for those fans who dread the summer break: at the end of the new 2005–06 season there would be a World Cup in Germany, and so the start of the season had been brought forward to accommodate an earlier than normal conclusion to the campaign in May 2006. For Manchester United, that meant a return to training on 27 June 2005 – just five weeks after they had lost to Arsenal in the FA Cup final on 21 May.

Sir Alex Ferguson's thinking was that an earlier start would mean they would be less sluggish when the Premiership campaign kicked off in August. He claimed that the poor start they'd had to the 2004–05 season had cost them the title to Chelsea. This was a slightly discoloured way of thinking; it was actually the fact that Chelsea had the better players and team that thwarted his ambitions and led to an eventual massive 18-point gap between the clubs. Ferguson said, 'The important thing is for us to improve and learn from the early-season attack. It was a bad start for us last season and we lost the League then. Next season, the players are going to start earlier – much earlier . . . that will make sure we are ready, because it looks to me as if you're going to have to start better than normal. Normally, we start training about 10 July and make steady progress until we get to the turn, but it doesn't look as if we can afford to do that.'

He promised United's supporters that he and the players would give the next campaign a much better shot than the previous one – and he was hopeful of winning a ninth title in fourteen seasons. 'We've got a young team,' he said. 'We will improve and there is no doubt about that. I am certain of it. We have the squad; we've got the desire and the ability.'

Not everyone was pleased with the early start – and there is an argument for players being given more time to recuperate and recharge rather than less. Chelsea boss Jose Mourinho clearly disagreed with Ferguson's up-and-at-'em philosophy. Looking relaxed, he announced his club would begin pre-season training ten days later than United, on 6 July, and said with a smile, 'We'll enjoy the summer break and will come refreshed into the new season. We are the champions and it is a great feeling.'

You may not like the man – many United fans certainly do not – but you surely have to admire him. That sort of approach filters through to your team. I would argue that Ferguson's declaration of a punishing summer boot camp merely added to the tensions of a squad already wondering if they could ever compete with the Blues. Certainly, skipper Roy Keane was not that thrilled about the prospect of jogging on the spot ten days earlier than his Chelsea counterpart Claude Makelele – and told Ferguson as much.

You could sympathise with him: Ferguson's plans made still less sense when you considered United had agreed to carry out a tour to the Far East and also faced a Champions League qualifier against Debreceni VSC. Surely it would have been more sensible to bring the lads back in on 6 July? With the enormous workload pencilled in for them even before the Premiership opener at Everton, they would surely have been in shape. Ferguson's itinerary risked early burn-out, although he would have none of it, saying, 'The four games we play in the Far East will add to their stamina and sharpness before the season starts. I'm determined we're going to be more physically ready to hit the ground running at the start of next season. We must be better prepared, not simply because we'll be involved in an early Champions League qualifier, but because we don't want to be playing catch-up again in the Premiership.'

Keane and Ferguson had been growing apart little by little since the club's glory year of 1999. Keane's primary interest was the welfare of Manchester United, and I am told he felt two incidents in particular involving the United boss had reflected badly on the club. The first came in 2002–03 when Ferguson announced he would retire, only to change his mind; the second concerned the racehorse Rock Of Gibraltar. In the first instance, Keane allegedly felt that Ferguson's indecision cost the club greatly, that it led to players slacking off and not taking their work as seriously. In the second, it appears Keane felt Ferguson should not have been wrapped up in a dispute over the horse – especially when it involved the club and two directors.

Keane had allegedly also become disillusioned with some of Ferguson's transfer dealings since 1999 – some of his signings appeared unfit to wear the treasured red shirt – and also disagreed with the more defensively minded tactics that would earn Ferguson the nickname of Sir Alex Sexton among the fans: a reference to the ultra-cautious United manager of the late '70s, Dave Sexton.

Not that Keane was unhappy with Ferguson's two 'name' signings in the summer of 2005. Edwin van der Sar was the goalkeeper that United had needed for years, and Ji-Sung Park, a speedy Korean forward, would add variety to United's attack and offer much-needed breathers for the ageing Ryan Giggs.

Van der Sar, a £2-million signing from Fulham, was no spring chicken at 34, but he would bring the stability and consistency United had lacked since the retirement of the great Peter Schmeichel in 1999. Fair enough, he was no young giant like Juve's Gianluigi Buffon or Real Madrid's Iker Casillas, but he was top-notch and, just as importantly, had his own motivational carrot to strive for – he wanted to prove he was the man who at last could be relied upon to replace Schmeichel. After signing a two-year deal, he said, 'I am delighted to have signed for Manchester United, one of the most famous clubs in the world. I'm looking forward to joining my new teammates to start preparations for the new season, which promises to be one of the most exciting of my career.'

Ferguson was sure he was indeed the missing link: 'Edwin brings a wealth of experience to the team. He is an international goalkeeper with proven class.' Previously, the United manager had signed Mark Bosnich, Massimo Taibi,

Raimond van der Gouw, Fabien Barthez, Roy Carroll, Ricardo and Tim Howard – all of whom had tried and failed to command the United defence in the same manner as Schmeichel.

Park was also an encouraging purchase at £4 million. A few days before he signed on at Old Trafford, the South Korea and former PSV Eindhoven midfielder helped his country to qualify for the 2006 World Cup finals with a goal in their 4–0 victory over Saudi Arabia. Like van der Sar, he had his own ambition at Old Trafford. He explained, 'What is important for me is to develop myself faster and consistently.'

South Korea coach Jo Bonfrere was confident the move would be a good one for Park, adding, 'Moving from PSV to Manchester United is a big step, so it is good for him that he can take the step, and if he makes the step, he can prove that he is a good player capable of a high level of football.'

One aspect of the summer signings campaign that Keane was rumoured not to like was the lack of funds made available at United. In this respect, it is important that we establish the financial and other factors determining stability, or lack of it, at Old Trafford in June and July 2005, as Keane embarked upon what would be his last season as a player at the club. Of course, Manchester United had been taken off the Stock Exchange and into private hands after a protracted and hostile takeover the previous May. The Glazer family had bought the club amid much controversy and rancour, and rumours abounded that Ferguson would be handed a £20 million transfer pot each summer. Some critics argued that was not enough, but if that summer of 2005 was anything to go by, that would have been like manna from Heaven. Ferguson's total cash fund was actually zero: the readies for the purchase of Park and van der Sar were raised by the eventual exits of Roy Carroll, Phil Neville and Kleberson. Far from being a cash cow, the Glazers would slowly and quietly begin the process of reducing costs by loaning out players like David Bellion and Jonathan Spector to save on wages and implement a gradual programme of redundancies for non-playing staff at Old Trafford. The latter was a particular disgrace when you consider Joel Glazer's words to staff at Old Trafford on 1 July 2005: 'What we are looking to do is to work with you to push the club forward to greater heights. A great part of why we're here is because of what everybody in this room has done for this club, and to change that would be foolish.'

As if to emphasise the harsh nature of the new ball game being played out between the two footballing citadels of the north and the south, on the day Chelsea signed Michael Essien from Lyon for £28 million and snapped up Manchester City's Shaun Wright-Phillips for a knockdown £21 million, United splashed out the princely sum of £1 million for Ben Foster . . . Stoke City's reserve goalkeeper. At the same time, the Blues also forked out £2 million in compensation to Tottenham Hotspur for their Director of Football Frank Arnesen, whom they wanted to take control of their youth academy.

No wonder Keane was said to be worried about United's new era under the Micawbers – sorry, the Glazers. He was not the only one. A document leaked to *The Times* suggested Keane had good reason to be anxious. It claimed that Ferguson could be forced to sell before he could buy, as was the case with the purchases of van der Sar, Park and Foster. The report pointed to the existence of a £25 million budget cap on transfers, but supporters' trust Shareholders United noted with apprehension the word 'cap'. 'The transfer budget has been very subtly expressed as a cap. It could be £25 million; it could be a pound,' SU chairman Nick Towle said. 'We're doing the numbers right now. If and when he refinances these preferred securities and puts that debt into the club, and if he doesn't do a sale and leaseback on the ground, the [budget] in years two, three and four is £7.7 million, minus £12.1 million and minus £24.8 million. That's factoring in 10 per cent yearly ticket price rises, naming rights and so on. You're talking about player sales unless he puts more money of his own in there. There is no player transfer budget in years three and four.'

A few days later, the Glazers finally emerged into the public eye – entering and leaving Old Trafford in the rather ridiculous confines of the back of a police van – and claimed that United had nothing to fear from them. Brothers Joel, Bryan and Avi claimed they would not put up season-ticket prices above the normal rates of the last five years, and that Ferguson's hands would not be tied in the transfer market. But football finance expert Professor Tom Cannon, of the Kingston Business School, poured scorn on their optimism. He said, 'It's very difficult to see how they can keep these promises. They've acquired a lot of debt and there will be a lot of expectations upon them from their preferential investors.

'At the end of the day, if they put up ticket prices and tell Sir Alex Ferguson he must buy a player for £1.5 million rather than £20 million, what are people going to do? Take the club off them? This is their club now, so they will just turn round and say, "Sorry, we thought we could do this and that, but it's not worked and we're going to have to put up prices after all."'

Some fans were openly questioning whether the very heart of the club had been lost with the Glazer takeover – and whether, indeed, things would ever be the same again. According to an insider, Roy Keane would express similar sentiments to friends in private. One fan, who preferred to stay anonymous, said:

> Let's face it, the club are in decline. Third in the League three times in four years is not good enough

for a club with the reputation Man United have. Next season could be worse, with Liverpool looking strong and Arsenal and Chelsea continuing to dominate. The heart of the club that was great (Cantona, Schmeichel, Beckham, Butt, Giggs, Scholes and Keane) are all gone or nearing retirement and they have not been replaced. Rooney has bags of potential but Ronaldo lacks the killer ball Beckham had and the rest would struggle to get into many Premiership teams. Ferdinand doesn't even look like the best defender in Manchester, never mind the world. Finally, the fans fear a rise in ticket prices. Well, it currently stands at £17–£23 for members per match ticket, £19–£25 for non-members and £304–£418 per season ticket. This to watch a bunch of pretenders playing off the reputation of 1999?

Other supporters did not see the Glazers' takeover as a problem, arguing that nothing had truly changed and that there was a terrible whiff of hypocrisy around the Theatre of Dreams. One such man was Geoff Hughes, of Irlam, Manchester, who said:

Record sales of season tickets? Now there's a surprise. What happened to all those anti-Glazer nuts burning their season-ticket renewal forms outside Old Trafford? I'll tell you what happened: as soon as they got home, they phoned the ticket desk and told them they had lost the form and can you please send me another one. How these people can hold their heads up, I don't know. When the Yank tells everyone his plans for the club in the next day or two, everyone will be saying, 'Hey, this could work,' and when my team, Manchester United, start to return to the pinnacle of the game next season, all this takeover crap will be forgotten about. Think about this: Glazer never had the power and muscle the fans had and never will. All you had to do was stick together and not go to matches and this guy would have been gone after six months. You had all the power but never knew what to do with it.

Even the most powerful man in the Western world was encouraged to get in on the act with a few words about the new American presence at United. When *The Times* asked American President George Bush at the G8 summit what he thought of the takeover of United by Glazer, he replied, 'Yes, I read about that on ESPN.com.'

There were those at Old Trafford willing to comment rather more vociferously about Ferguson's obvious negligence in not identifying and buying a suitable world-class replacement for Keane. The fans felt the boss had been focusing on other transfer targets when the search for Keane's successor should have been the number one priority. Another fan's comments in June 2005 summed up their fears:

Surely, Man United have noticed that we need a replacement for Keane. They are interested in everybody, but then Chelsea follow. United should approach someone privately to replace Keane; don't let Chelsea know they are interested. We seriously have to do something about it before it is too late.

According to press sources, it was a moan even Keane himself would voice to Ferguson when Chelsea beat United to the signature of the combative Ghanian international Michael Essien, the man Keane had hoped would end up at Old Trafford. Keane's eagerness to search out a replacement for himself also highlighted how he viewed his own situation at the time at the Theatre of Dreams: he saw his Manchester United future as long-term, maybe involving a coaching role, otherwise why would he be so keen to bring in a suitable newcomer to take on his own central-midfield role? It did not make sense unless he visualised a long-term future for himself at Old Trafford.

Roy Keane turned up for pre-season training with Manchester United on 27 June 2005. It would be his last at the club. He and Ferguson had managed to keep their regular rows under wraps since 1999, but now began a period of disagreements that would lead to the two men falling out in public and, even more surprisingly, with no way back.

It was as if the full load of problems and aggro at the club weighed too heavily on United's skipper that summer's day: the Glazers' takeover, the failings of Ferguson in the transfer markets, the obvious declining of the manager's abilities and incisiveness, the emergence of the all-powerful Chelsea under Mourinho and finally, the final straw, the personal humiliation as Ferguson chose Queiroz as his confidant and second-in-command.

If anyone had contributed to Ferguson gaining his moniker of 'Sir Alex Sexton', it was Queiroz, the Portuguese who had returned to United after a failed one-year spell at Real Madrid. If Carlos could not succeed with the world-class talent at his disposal at the Bernabeu, what chance was there of him making inroads with the likes of Darren Fletcher and Liam Miller? If you claimed that Sir Alex's number two was not up to it, he would have none of it, arguing with a purple face that he had the best man from the whole of Portugal at his side (putting down Mr Mourinho in doing so).

Most thought that this man Queiroz was not fit to lace his fellow countryman's boots. As for him taking over at

United when Ferguson eventually left, it was the nightmare scenario as far as United fans were concerned. Keane had admitted to friends that he did not believe Carlos was the man to take the reins at Old Trafford. He confided that he did not rate his training techniques and was unhappy with the cautious nature of his tactics. Inevitably, if we are being honest here, there may also have been an element of envy and jealousy towards the man Keane had come to regard as his biggest rival at Old Trafford. Until Queiroz's arrival, Keane had been Ferguson's biggest ally and confidant. That all changed when the Portuguese returned in 2004 after his barren one-year tenure in Madrid.

Suddenly, Keane was on the outside looking in. It was Queiroz Ferguson turned to for quiet chats, and it was Queiroz Ferguson would anoint as his successor, although initially he had suggested Keane could take that honoured role. The Portuguese took an increasing hold over the team, often selecting the men who would play and sorting out the tactics for each match. Keane meanwhile was sidelined by the new alliance at the top.

It was not a situation Keane enjoyed – certainly not one he had anticipated. The master plan was for him to become number two to Ferguson and then take over if or when the old man moved upstairs. Now, though, if the Scot stayed in an advisory capacity, all the signs were that it would be to Queiroz's benefit. Keane put up with the new order as long as he could, but it was inevitable that he would ultimately blow his top.

That bust-up would come in the pre-season of 2005, as United headed for a bonding break in Portugal before their warm-up games in the Far East. Keane did not see eye to eye with Ferguson over the trip, and the two men fell out, leading later to press speculation that this was the reason for Keane's subsequent omission from the tour to the Far East. It was only when Keane failed to turn up for the Far

East tour that the idea began to circulate among the public and the press that there had been a difference of opinion. Ferguson would admit that he and Keane had argued, but he tried to brush it all under the carpet, claiming it was not dissimilar to many such incidents throughout their 12-year relationship. He also claimed that Keane's non-appearance on the tour was nothing to do with the fallout, that he was staying in Manchester to recover from a hamstring problem.

This was not what insiders close to Keane told me. As we have already established, Keane was not his normal self as pre-season dawned. He was unhappy about many things at United – now the steam would blow the lid off the kettle. Apparently he took exception to Ferguson and Queiroz's decision to invite families along to the Portuguese training camp. In his eyes, it was either a training camp or it wasn't. If it wasn't, and it was just an excuse for a holiday with the family, why not let the players continue their breaks a few days longer? I am told that what annoyed him in particular was that he had had to cut short his family holiday to turn up for the early training sessions. And where in particular was he taking that holiday? You guessed it – Portugal!

Another element of the Portugal saga, I am reliably told, involved Queiroz. Apparently, it was his idea to hold the training camp in the Algarve and his idea to restrict training to mornings only. The latter decision would then apparently convince Ferguson that the relaxed atmosphere and lighter-than-expected workload could allow the players to invite their families along for fun in the afternoons. No prizes for guessing who disagreed with Queiroz and who took his sentiments up with Ferguson. I am also told by a reliable top source that the first time Keane and Queiroz clashed in the Algarve that week was over the swimming pool at the United complex – with

Keane complaining that it was too cold for his children to play in!

For the record, here are the official denials of any bust-up as United arrived for their first tour match in Beijing. Keane's agent and lawyer Michael Kennedy said the claims were 'without foundation'. And Ferguson added his weight to the argument in typically blunt terms when he addressed the media prior to the encounter with the football team Beijing Hyundai. 'Roy Keane is injured; it is as simple as that,' said Ferguson. 'You can't travel if you are injured. There is nothing else to say.' But Ferguson had publicly admitted there *was* an incident, and whichever way you try to camouflage the actual details, the writing was now on the wall for the previously unbreakable – at least in public – Ferguson–Keane alliance. Writing in *The Sun*, the evergreen John Sadler summed up the point-of-no-return effect the banning of Keane from the Far East could have on the duo's relationship. Sadler said:

> Sir Alex clearly feels the need to demonstrate his authority with the player he describes as 'my mirror on the field'. On the other hand, he has never been in greater need of Keane's confidence and cooperation. Should the new season turn into one of fragmentation and frustration, it would inscribe a sad epitaph for the manager who did it all, won it all, but whose biggest mistake was his failure to choose the ideal time for his departure.

Prophetic words, indeed.

The Far East tour was a success of sorts. For the all-smiling Glazers, it sent the cash tills ringing, with replica shirt sales in the Far East, and it gave Bryan Glazer and the fans over there a glimpse of their heroes. But they were really the only plus points. From Keane's point of view, it was bad news. He had been left out of the tour, and Ferguson, in one of those false-dawn moments that had typified the man for the previous couple of years, was now starting to believe that his team could cope without the skipper. He had started the experiment of playing centre-forward Alan Smith in Keane's role and was convinced the aggressive Yorkshireman could be the answer to his prayers. He also convinced himself that his team would be able to overhaul Chelsea, saying, 'I do not believe there is a great deal between ourselves and Chelsea. They are a very good team, but so are we. They did have a fantastic season last year, but it was an unusual one which you think they might find difficult to replicate. I know they have added a couple of players to help them cope with the number of tournaments they are in, but I still do not believe there is much between the two teams.

'Our club has always had high expectations from ourselves, the fans and people outside the club. Each season, whether you have won something or not, there is always pressure. The nature of the competition has improved over the last three seasons because Chelsea only lost one match last season and Arsenal didn't lose at all the year before. The bar has been raised but the challenge it presents is perfect for Manchester United.'

One thing you can't deny about the United manager: he talks a damned good game. In another lifetime, he could have been working for the government, spinning bad news as well as anyone. At this point, in July 2005, United were simply not in the same league as their rivals from Stamford Bridge – full stop, no argument – and Alan Smith was no more a natural replacement for Roy Keane than Queiroz was for Ferguson.

The tour also confirmed Rio Ferdinand as the number one target for the United boo-boys. At the time, he had still not signed his new deal, despite the fact that United had stood by him when he had received an eight-month ban in January 2005 for failing to attend his drugs test. Ferdinand was booed by the fans at United's friendly against Kashima Antlers in Tokyo. He also had an on-field argument with Ruud van Nistelrooy. Everything was clearly not as beautiful in the garden as Ferguson was trying so hard to portray. United were in a downward spiral. Keane knew the truth of it all, but his reward for pointing out the reality was to be ostracised. Now, is that any way to treat your best player and one of your most loyal servants ever?

It seemed to me that Ferguson had started to get his priorities wrong. He was castigating Keane, whose loyalty to the club could never be questioned, over giving his negative opinions of the Portuguese training camp, yet was standing by, and at the same time having a go at United fans for booing, a player who was, in my opinion, showing disloyalty by making extravagant wage demands at a time when he should have been displaying gratitude.

While Ferdinand toured the Far East with United, Keane was turning out for a United XI at Rossendale and Walsall. His appearances made a mockery of Ferguson's claims that he was unfit. Keane played the first 45 minutes at Walsall and put in a committed performance that had Steve Hobson, a Rossendale United director, purring, 'It was a fabulous night. Roy Keane was a fantastic role model. His commitment was wonderful and he played like it was a cup final. After the game, people were swarming round him for autographs, and he must have gone home with writer's cramp.' Hardly sounds like a man who was too injured to climb aboard a plane, does it? News reached Ferguson in the Far East that people were questioning why Keane was absent. If he was unfit, why was he turning out for United back home?

With that turn of spin we have come to admire him for, Ferguson tried to defuse the speculation that Keane had indeed been banned from the Far East tour. He said, 'There is no point bringing Roy out at this stage because he could only play in one game. We play at Walsall on Saturday, so he will play in that if he came through last night's match without a problem.' Good try, boss. So, while the master was appearing in England's green and pleasant land, the old man and his boys were getting sunburnt in Hong Kong, China and Japan. By the time Ferguson was on the jet home, he was convinced that United were back in business, that he really could catch Chelsea this season and that he had a squad as good as theirs. He was wrong on all counts, but the truly sad thing was that that belief would lead him to jettison two of the midfield players he could actually count on to deliver in that problematic holding midfield role. The first to go – as we will see in the next chapter – was Phil Neville. The second man out would be the cause of the biggest bombshell to hit Old Trafford in Ferguson's years at the club, because the second man kicked out was a man who never deserved such an ignominious exit: the legendary Roy Keane.

ELEVEN

THE FEUD WITH QUEIROZ

Roy Keane's final season at United got off to a hectic, baffling start. Sir Alex Sexton was in his usual, typical start-of-the-season mood: the inscrutable one where no one really knows what his game plan is, or if he has one. He had these optimistic words to say about how he saw the season panning out for his skipper Keane: 'Roy is a player here. We admire him greatly and there is every chance he will be here again next season. We do have to start considering the age of our players. I've said to Roy, if you can give me 30 games this season, I'll be happy. To get the best out of him, we need to spare him for certain games.'

For the record, Roy Keane managed just *six* games in the 2005–06 campaign, and then he was out on his backside. Yet, until the two seismic interviews he conducted with MUTV, you would not have guessed that he was heading for the sack. OK, he and Alex Ferguson had seemingly fallen out over the pre-season training camp in Portugal, but at the time it was by no means crystal clear that the writing was already on the wall. In fact, it was: Ferguson was allegedly hurt by the criticism that Keane was said to have levelled at Queiroz when they had all argued in

Portugal, and the manager was a man with a long memory of resentments. It appeared that the bond between Keane and Ferguson had been broken in Portugal; now it seemed likely the manager would snap if Keane tried to question his authority again.

On the surface of things, though, no one could have guessed what was to come. Keane was busy taking his coaching badges, and there was lots of talk about him staying on at United in such a capacity under Ferguson. Looking more closely, we could have spotted the clues. Just how could Keane stay on when, if the hints in the press were true, he no longer saw eye to eye with Queiroz? How could he work with the man whom he allegedly considered his biggest rival?

Yet, on 9 August – the day of the first-leg European Champions League qualifier against Debreceni VSC – Rio Ferdinand agreed a new £100,000-a-week deal to stay at United for the next four years. The same day, the *Daily Mail* ran a story about Keane under the headline: 'United want Roy for the long run'. The piece said:

> Keane's future at Old Trafford appeared to be in doubt after a bust-up with manager Sir Alex Ferguson during training camp in Portugal. But not only do United see Keane playing next season, they also want to ensure the Ireland midfielder stays with the club as a coach until he is ready to become a candidate for the manager's job. As such, he will be offered a new contract in the New Year that will allow him to begin coaching as soon as he wants.

Six weeks later, on 21 September, the papers were still in the dark about Keane's situation. Again, in the *Daily Mail*, the headline was 'Keane is lined up as coach', followed by the rather excited revelation that:

OFF IN SHAME: The immediate aftermath of the incident that will forever besmirch Roy Keane's reputation – the disgraceful revenge tackle on City midfielder Alfie Haaland in the Manchester derby of April 2001.

TRIPLES ALL ROUND: The United skipper joins in the celebrations after his team won the European Cup in Barcelona in 1999 to complete their Treble. Keane had watched from the sidelines after picking up a suspension in the semi-final in Turin and would later admit he did not feel he deserved his medal, as he played no part in the final.

THE GOLDEN BOYS: Keane with goalscorer David Beckham after United beat Everton 2–1 and lifted the Premiership title at Goodison Park in May 2003. To many critics, this match would represent the end of the Ferguson glory era – with Beckham soon to be sold off to Real Madrid and United entering a period of Premiership decline.

WORLDS APART: Roy Keane and Mick McCarthy in Saipan just hours before their World Cup bust-up. Keane would be sent home alone after giving 'Big Mick' a verbal going over in front of the entire Irish squad.

MEETING OF THE LEGENDS: Roy Keane battles with Zinedine Zidane in Keane's final match for Ireland in September 2005. The Frenchman had the last laugh as his country finished 1–0 winners at Lansdowne Road – a result that would contribute to Ireland's failure to qualify for the World Cup finals of 2006 and bring about Keane's second retirement from the international scene.

DOWN AND (ALMOST) OUT: Keane hits the deck at Anfield on 18 September 2005 after a tackle by Liverpool's Spanish midfielder Luis Garcia. He would not play again for Manchester United after sustaining a broken toe in the clash.

THE SURVIVORS: Sir Alex Ferguson and his assistant manager Carlos Queiroz at Charlton, the first United League match after Keane's exit.

SWEET SIXTEEN: Hoops boss Gordon Strachan welcomes Keane to Celtic Park with a No. 16 shirt – the same number the Irishman wore for years at Manchester United. Some critics openly questioned whether Parkhead would be big enough to accommodate both the combustible Keane and the Scotsman with the legendary short fuse.

ONE OF THE BHOYS: Roy Keane goes walkabout to meet his adoring fans after completing his move from United to Celtic. Keane had always had a soft spot for the Glasgow giants and had mixed with the fans when he travelled to Seville to support Celtic in the UEFA Cup final of 2003.

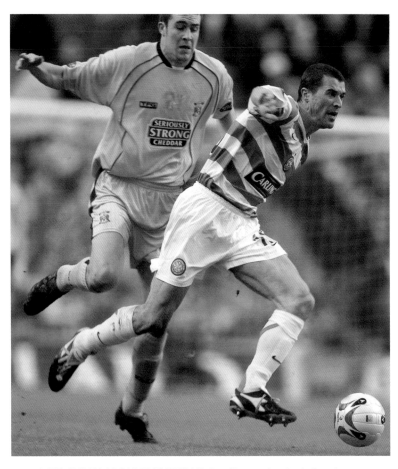

A BIT CHILLY AROUND THE KILLIE: Roy Keane wins the ball and sets Celtic on the attack in his home debut for the Hoops on a bitterly cold January afternoon in Glasgow. Keane played in the back four – a role he had previously admitted he did not enjoy – and gave a fine showing as Celtic went on to win 4–2 over Kilmarnock.

> Manchester United have told captain Roy Keane that they are ready to begin talks over a player–coach contract which they hope will one day lead to him becoming manager at Old Trafford. United believe Keane has all the qualities needed to become a top manager and will effectively tell the 34 year old to name his own job title when chief executive David Gill sits down with his representatives in the coming weeks.

The only problem with the story was this: Gill never sat down with Keane's men. What we are trying to establish here is that Keane's exit was *not* down to a sudden blow-up with Ferguson and Queiroz. Clearly it wasn't – the storm had been brewing since the Portuguese's return from his failed season in Madrid. There had been numerous behind-the-scenes rows, then the public row over the training camp and hints in the press that Keane was dissatisfied that United had not sat down with him at the start of the 2005–06 season and entered into talks over a new deal.

If Keane was being lined up for this and that at Old Trafford, why did he use MUTV to have a go at United for not offering him anything? The first MUTV explosion came on 29 September. Keane had been in a grumpy mood since picking up his injury at Liverpool 11 days earlier. One thing you quickly learn about Keane is that he is not good company when he is sidelined – whether it be through injury or suspension, but especially through injury. He sulks and broods and could offer you a fair mimicry of Chancellor Gordon Brown when the black mood really gets to him. So it was, he entered the MUTV studios on the 29th in a rebellious, contrary, slightly cynical mood.

These were the phone-in interviews the station did with the players to 'give the fans a better chance of getting to know them'. At six quid a month (£1.50 a week), you get what you pay for with MUTV: a cosseted, often unrecognisable United world as spun by the powers that be at Old Trafford. Criticism – by former players such as Paul Parker, Alex Stepney and Mickey Thomas – is gentle, the sort of easy banter you might get at a port and Stilton evening at the local Rotary club. But the club dropped an almighty bollock when they let Keane on because the show went out live (and consequently uncensored).

I looked at Keane's eyes on the night of the show and saw a mixture of anger, fear and retaliation – and that was before the questions began. Keane was clearly boiling up inside and my feeling was that he used the programme to try to manipulate United. He wanted to bring them to the negotiating table so they would offer him that new deal. The plan, it seemed to me, was that his words would leave the fan base outraged and force the board into action. Keane said, 'I would like to play another year or two, but I do not think it will be at Manchester United. There comes a time for everybody when they have to move on, and I am prepared to play elsewhere.

'I think it will be good to experience a different dressing-room. It wouldn't be an English team, though. Coming back to Old Trafford and going into the away dressing-room would be too hard for me to stomach.

'I am not putting a gun to anybody's head. But my gut reaction last season was this would be my last year, and I still feel that way. You have to learn and be prepared to move on. Life will not stop when I leave Manchester United. It might be an opportunity to go into management or coaching somewhere else, and it is best to make a clean break, because coaching at Manchester United doesn't really appeal.

'I would be surprised if I was offered a new contract, and even if I was, I would not expect it to be until the end of the season, but by then I will have already made a decision about what I am going to do.

'I'll be 35 in the summer and we've got a lot of decent young players coming through. There's a danger of staying on too long, and maybe one or two people think I've stayed here a year or two too long anyway. If you follow your heart, you want to stay as long as you can. But you've got to listen to your brain as well – and the body.'

It was Queiroz who broke the deafening silence after the interview. He suggested all was not lost in the fight to keep Keane at the club. He said, 'When the manager feels the time is right, he will address the Roy Keane situation. Of course he will address it. At the moment, we don't want to discuss these things in public. But I saw the interview and I'm not worried. At the moment, this subject is not the most important to us . . .'. However, Queiroz did give Keane a rather fine tribute and admitted it would be almost impossible for United to replace him. He said, 'You don't replace great players like Pele, Maradona, Eusebio or Roy Keane. You just create new players in new teams. That is why the game moves forward.'

Phil Neville, who had been surprisingly transferred from United to Everton just before the start of the season, also felt he needed to weigh in with the tributes. It was as if Keane had already gone. Neville P, who spent 12 years alongside Keane at Old Trafford, said, 'If he goes, it will be a huge loss for the Premiership. If you look at all the greatest games in the Premiership over the last ten years, more often than not Roy Keane has been in the middle of it all. Roy is one of the best players I have ever played with. You have got to respect his decision, whatever decision he makes. I'm privileged and proud to have played with such a great captain and someone I regard as a good friend as well. He's been the most successful captain Manchester United has probably ever had, and he will be missed by the club on and off the pitch.'

United legend Bryan Robson also had something to say

about Keane – and offered up a sensible idea about the captaincy issue at Old Trafford. Robson, the manager at West Brom, said, 'Roy has had a hip operation and a cruciate knee-ligament injury. So he is the only one who knows how it affects him, and he will make up his own mind about what to do. But when you watch him play at the moment, it doesn't look as though anything has affected him. He is a fitness fanatic. As long as he is playing to a high standard, he should go on as long as he can, because there is nothing better than playing.'

Robson argued that Rio Ferdinand should be the next United skipper – and made a case for Keane to help him make the grade. Robbo added, 'Keane is really demanding in what he expects from his teammates. When he arrived at United, there were people around like Paul Ince and Steve Bruce. The three of them are all people who would shout a lot. Keane gets them organised on the pitch. When people are getting slack, he will have a real go at them. That's what his strength is.

'When he is not there, you don't really have people who can get a grip of the team. Rio Ferdinand has the ability to do that. He has got to take it on board and learn from Keane. Then if Keane does decide to retire or move on, you will have a player in the squad who will do it.'

Even the normally urbane and reserved manager of Arsenal wanted to give his opinion on Keane's future. Arsene Wenger said, 'It is significant for Manchester United as he's been a big player for them and is coming towards the end of his career. But everyone knew at the start that he could not last forever. Of course, it will be hard to replace him. The difficulty for clubs like Manchester United is that you know Roy Keane today is not the player he once was at 28 or 29, but he's still a good player. What is difficult to evaluate is how long he can go on.

'But he has played his whole career at Manchester

United and I'm not yet convinced that he will leave. He could also be saying, "Come on, Manchester United. If you want to keep me for another year, then it's time to wake up, as I have some other offers on the table." He could still end up staying at Manchester United.'

Finally, it was the turn of United's living conscience and epitome of dignity, Sir Bobby Charlton, to add what sounded like a farewell speech and an epitaph: 'Roy is at an age where he's thinking about his future. If he wants to go into coaching or management or continue playing for a while, then he will make up his mind himself, because he's a sensible lad. He will also have talked to a lot of people.

'At Manchester United, we can't say enough good things about him. He's a wonderful player and has been a great servant to the club. We hope he will be with us for a little while longer, but we must leave it to him. I would not insult him by not letting him make up his own mind.'

All this talk, speculation, advice and platitudes, and Keane had not even left the club – he'd only suggested that he might do. It showed that he truly was one of the biggest names ever to grace the Old Trafford stage.

The tension between Keane and the club increased in the days after the MUTV chat and it would explode within seven weeks. Keane, still sidelined with his broken foot, could regularly be seen moping around Carrington and Old Trafford. He was hardly in the best of moods. Yet the feeling generally was that he would still be at Old Trafford when the dust settled – Ferguson had done a grand job in covering the tracks of their tears. Indeed, in *The People on Sunday*, 16 October, the claim was being made that he and his boss were getting on so famously that steps had already been taken to cement their relationship for the next decade or so.

Under the headline 'Keane's secret new job', we were told that 'Roy Keane has secretly started COACHING at Manchester United, giving the clearest hint that he is being groomed as Sir Alex Ferguson's long-term successor.' In breathless terms, the exclusive went on to say:

> Last month, Keane stunned the football world by suggesting he would quit Old Trafford at the end of the season. But now it seems that not only is he staying . . . but he is also shaping up as a major contender to take Fergie's mantle.

Apparently, Keane was spending several nights a week at Carrington with the club's Under-10s and Under-14s sides – which he was, but it was not part of an agreed pact between himself and Ferguson. He just wanted to get involved and turned up voluntarily while out injured. At least it helped to break his dark moods.

The real truth of Keane's situation was emerging in quiet whispers from the corridors of power at Old Trafford. It was rumoured there were no efforts being made by Gill or Ferguson to convince him he had a future at Man United. One man with a close ear to the club is the journalist Mihir Bose. At the time of *The People*'s 'exclusive' about Keane's 'secret new job', he revealed in his weekly column in the *Daily Telegraph* that:

> A new contract for Manchester United captain Roy Keane is no nearer being agreed. There has been no contact between United chief executive David Gill and the player's advisers and, on several occasions in the past few months, Keane has expressed his unhappiness in characteristically blunt terms to Sir Alex Ferguson about the club's inability to sign a midfield replacement.

That all tallied with my sources close to Keane and the club, although Bose's claims further on within his piece that Keane had 'told Ferguson that, while he wants to play, he would prefer to do so in defence as he eases himself out of the game' do not add up. I was told that Keane did *not* want to play in defence: he had made a point of telling Ferguson that he had not enjoyed the role when forced into it on previous occasions and that he felt his rather more restricted playing future would still involve him in the holding midfield role, but with less starts. That is why he had wanted Essien to sign: he knew he could play in the same midfield with the Ghanian doing the work and the running and that United would again be able to compete for honours. Put it this way, who would you count on to bring you more success: Essien or Keane's final accomplice in central midfield, Darren Fletcher?

At least the results of the latest footballing poll put a smile on Keane's face as the new season began. He was voted the hardest footballer ever in a survey of around 2,500 people conducted by the alcopop brand WKD on the eve of the new campaign. Roy beat Chelsea's legendary defender Ron 'Chopper' Harris – famed for his brutal tackles – into second place and Vinnie Jones into third. A source told me that Keane loved the accolade. It propagated the macho image he loved to portray, the image which I came to understand was just that: a tough front designed to camouflage the real man behind the mask.

Keane's treatment of Manchester City's Alfie Haaland was surely a major reckoning in this. He had harboured a long-time grudge against his rival and eventually 'got even' with him by hacking him down in a Manchester derby match – after Haaland had moved from Leeds to Manchester City. Haaland struggled to recover from a knee injury sustained in the tackle and played his last game in 2002 before being forced into retirement. A WKD spokesman said, 'Keane was the clear winner, but the rest were all pretty tough. Anyone with the nickname Chopper has to be a contender.'

If the team's early season form was your yardstick, meanwhile, you certainly would not have guessed there was any major resentment between Ferguson and Keane beneath the surface. United started like a train on fire, demolishing everything put in front of them. Inevitably, it would be Keane who bagged the first record of the season: he became the first United player to be booked, for a premeditated foul after 31 minutes of the stroll-in-the-park first-leg European Champions League qualifier against Debreceni VSC. United won 3–0 on 9 August 2005 – an early present for Keane on the eve of his 34th birthday. In my notes on the match at the time, I wrote:

> By 40 minutes, Keane had committed four fouls –
> he's becoming too slow to calculate the tackle. Would
> Ferguson's Achilles heel this season turn out to be his
> over-use of a slowing Keane and the fact that he had
> not replaced van Nistelrooy with Michael Owen?

In the event, Ferguson's Achilles heel would arguably be his loyalty to his assistant Queiroz at the expense of Keane, while Ruud would have a good goal-scoring season. In a taste of things to come, Ferguson would take off Keane after 67 minutes of the Debreceni game and send on the willing legs of Alan Smith.

For the record, these were Keane's final six matches for United: Debreceni (home, Champions League), Everton (away, Premiership), Aston Villa (home, Premiership), Newcastle (away, Premiership), Manchester City (home, Premiership), Liverpool (away, Premiership). The Liverpool match was on 18 September. Six days later, United, who were still unbeaten with Keane in the side, played Blackburn at home. Without the now injured Keane, United lost 2–1.

United's Premiership season had got under way with the visit to Goodison Park, and the occasion had thrown up yet another query about the often puzzling sides of boss Ferguson's character. He could be a pleasant, civilised man one moment: the next he would be purple-faced and ranting like a madman. He was football's answer to Jekyll and Hyde: one minute he was ushering Phil Neville out the door to Goodison, the next he was acclaiming him as a class act.

The decision to sell the loyal Bury-born utility player was a strange one. With Kleberson and Djemba-Djemba run out of town, Ferguson had just Neville P and Keane as experienced players for the holding midfield role. He was gambling with Alan Smith, but the jury was still out and, as we have seen, Keane was on borrowed time at United. So why flog the only other man who could reliably do the job? The transfer bore similarities to the cut-price sale of Nicky Butt to Newcastle almost a year previously. Butt could have done a job but was exiled in favour of Eric 2DJ and the Brazilian Kleberson.

Now Neville P – one of the most loyal servants United had ever had, a fine pro and a mighty underrated defensive midfielder (ask Big Pat Vieira and the Arsenal lads who had felt his edge in United's 2–0 win at Old Trafford the previous October) – was shunted off to Everton. Neville responded by turning in a man-of-the-match performance in his first big match for the Toffeemen: their 2–1 Champions League defeat to Villarreal.

Then, a couple of days before the Everton v. United Premiership opener, Ferguson opined that Neville P was good enough to make the following season's World Cup finals. Doesn't that beg the obvious question, Sir Alex: why get rid of him, then, if he is that good – especially given United's scarcity of resources in the role Neville P could have filled if Keane got injured? Ferguson opined, 'I am glad he has chosen Everton. It gives him an opportunity to be at the World Cup next year and I am sure he will be. He is a fantastic human being; one of the best professionals you could ever meet, and the loyalty he has given this club is amazing. It was hurting me a lot to leave him out, but I am sure he will be just as good a servant to Everton as he was for us.' Neville P handed out his own thank-you present to United on 69 minutes of the match – when he scythed down Ji-Sung Park and earned a booking for his efforts.

In the first of the six matches that would complete Keane's United portfolio, the Reds skipper had what you would describe as a quietly influential outing, directing operations from his defensive midfield role and inspiring United to a welcome 2–0 win at a ground where they had been beaten in the corresponding fixture the previous season. Fletcher did Keane's running, and goals from van Nistelrooy and Rooney completed a job well done.

Ten minutes from time, United fans provided the players with a glimpse of what to expect from them over the season after Alan Smith clambered into Tim Cahill, leaving the hapless Aussie with a dead leg. It was the kind of act Keane had often performed in his 12-year career at Old Trafford – and the crowd had loved him for his commitment. Now the mantle appeared to be passed on to the young Yorkshireman, as the Reds fans sang in unison: 'If you all love Smiffy, clap yer hands . . .'. Smith walked away smiling like a Rottweiler that had stumbled into the path of a poodle.

Ferguson was also wearing a wide smile after United's 11th victory in 14 Premiership visits to Goodison. The grin disappeared a little when he was asked what he thought of Chelsea chief executive Peter Kenyon's claim that the Premiership title would be decided from 'a select group of one'. The United manager summarily dismissed the opinions of Kenyon, his former boss at Old Trafford, as worthless. Ferguson riposted, 'Fortunately it is not the manager saying it, because it is not someone speaking with any knowledge of the game. You don't talk that way, really. Because it is not the manager, you can take it with a pinch of salt. You have to dismiss all other sources.'

Sir Alex's mood then changed as rapidly again as he extolled the virtues of Paul Scholes, who had agreed to sign a four-year extension to his contract through to 2009. Ferguson added, 'Paul has given us 16 great years of service. He's deserved our loyalty because he's given plenty back. We hope his next four years are as good as his last four.' These comments would contrast sharply with how Keane's loyal service would be rewarded three and a half months down the line. Then again, Paul toed the line and maintained a dignified silence for the most part. Roy told the truth about a crumbling empire and that was a sacking offence in the latter days of Sir Alex Ferguson.

A week later, United welcomed Aston Villa to Old Trafford for the first Premiership match of the campaign at the Theatre of Dreams. This time, Keane did not look as good and was not as effective. He was on the fringes of play, finding it hard to get involved, and some of the match passed him by. Sad to see, he seemed to be playing on memories – and Ferguson should really have taken him off on 77 minutes when Alan Smith was brought on to replace the unlucky-to-be-subbed Wayne Rooney.

A touching, sobering thought here: Villa had last beaten United almost precisely ten years previously, in a 3–1 opening-day win in the Midlands that saw David Beckham score his first goal and led Alan Hansen to condemn himself with those immortal words: 'You don't win anything with kids.' If Roy had remembered, he would probably have had a lump in his throat. Those were the days, hey, when you were truly on top of the world, old friend? This particular afternoon in August 2005, United ground out a functional, unattractive 1–0 win, courtesy of Ruud van Nistelrooy's sturdy, steady boot.

Fourth out of Roy's final six was away to the Toon. It was another relatively straightforward win, this time by 2–0. One Keane highlight was in the tunnel before the match. Roy stood side-by-side with that other veteran warlord, Alan Shearer – both lining up to lead out their sides for what would turn out to be the final time in the Premiership at St James'. Shearer was about to appear in the 700th game of his career but was set to retire at the end of the season. The Newcastle skipper tried to attract Keane's attention in the tunnel, playing and laughing with the mascots and constantly eyeing the man who had been arguably his greatest – and most bitter – rival over the years. Keane would have none of it, steadfastly refusing to have his dead-ahead glare broken or his attention distracted from the task in hand. It was classic Keane – no ground given to a rival he did not like.

After the relative disappointment of his showing against Villa, this was Keane back at his impressive best – bossing the midfield, marshalling his men and putting in tackles that were spot on. Keane would again last the 90 minutes, as United rolled over Newcastle for the fourth consecutive time at St James'. As fate decreed, Roy's last three matches would be big ones: first the Geordies, then Man City and finally the old enemy from down the East Lancs Road, Liverpool. Appropriate, really: a big finale for a big player, although we were not to know it was the end of the road at the time.

Keane's final Manchester derby would see him playing just 12 minutes of the 90, plus 3 of injury time. He came on in the 78th minute for Darren Fletcher, lining up next to Alan Smith in central midfield and showing the young novice how it should be done. In my notes at the time, I wrote:

Keane sprayed passes that reached teammates and tackled without fouling. Simple really, ain't it, but they do say simplicity is genius, and Keane at the height of his career kept it simple like no one else I know. The match ended a 1–1 draw, with goals from Ruud van Nistelrooy and Joey Barton. And no, Keane was not cautioned.

Writing in *The Guardian*, Daniel Taylor provided a perceptive eulogy for Keane that would frankly be hard to better. Talking about Roy's role in the match, he said:

> Then there was the absence of Roy Keane, a habitual excuse when things go wrong and one that now has United's fans rolling their eyes. How many more times must they witness the tradition of a vapid display when their captain has been rested?

So, Manchester City's 31-year wait for a derby-day victory at Old Trafford would continue for another year, and Roy Keane would never play in another Manchester derby. The days were counting down; time was slipping away. We're now ready for the final chapter, of Keane's final season at Old Trafford – not the final chapter full stop, but the one to wrap up the story of his last game for the club, the tapes that would bring about his demise and the final rollercoaster events that would lead to his surprise sacking. Fasten your seat belts. Tight.

TWELVE

THE TAPES OF WRATH

Ferguson: 'You shouldn't be saying things like that'
Keane: 'No. *You* should' – front page of *Red Issue* fanzine,
November 2005, accompanying a photograph of Ferguson and
Keane

'The trouble is that when Keane says some people are not
good enough for United, he is now included in that list' – a Man
United fan on the BBC 606 website, 6 November 2005

Liverpool away, 18 September 2005: Roy Keane's last
match for Manchester United. Not a bad way to go out, in
the final analysis: against the team he and Ferguson most
despised and wanted to beat. In the end, it was all square
– a 0–0 draw – but it was by no means dull. Meetings
between the five-times European champions and the two-
times European winners never are: there's always a
brooding undercurrent that more often than not develops
into an abrasive, bruising war.

This one was no different. It was bruising enough for
Keane to end his United career on 88 minutes with an
injury that – along with the bruised egos of Sir Alex Sexton
and Queiroz – would prevent him ever donning the red
shirt again. Two minutes from time, in front of a baying

Kop, Keane would walk off for the last time, with a broken foot, to be replaced by another key component of the Reds' golden generation, Ryan Giggs. Roy would be joined on the journey to the touchline by Wayne Rooney, who was brought off at the same time, with Darren Fletcher his replacement. Somehow, the sight of Rooney walking off with Keane was symbolic: old and new, past and future. Rooney, to me, was the only character within the club capable of reaching the heights achieved by Keane, the only character within the club possessing that same warrior's streak, the only man in the club in the same league class-wise and temperament-wise.

Another irony: the captain had broken a metatarsal bone in his left foot at Anfield. The same injury that had sidelined David Beckham and Gary Neville and had previously put United's championship credentials in doubt would haunt them again. Keane's broken toe – sustained in a challenge with Liverpool forward Luis Garcia – would rule him out of Ferguson's plans for two months, at a time when Chelsea were already away in the distance in the battle for the Premiership.

It was a particular blow for Keane. He had just returned from a hamstring problem, and the lay-off – like all the injury setbacks in his career – would not sit easily with this gladiatorial character. Away from the action, he would brood, sulk and easily flare up. The scene was inadvertently being set for the final act of the drama. A depressed Keane combined with a Ferguson and a Queiroz under intense pressure was an inevitable blow-up waiting to happen. Now let's look more closely at the build-up to what would be an explosive climax between them.

In public at least, Ferguson would refuse to accept that Keane's injury was a shattering blow for the club's and his own ambitions. Asked if the 0–0 draw – the first between the clubs at Anfield since 1991 – had killed off his championship hopes for another season, he bristled, 'It's far too early to say that.' He added hopefully, 'I don't think that games like this will be easy for Chelsea. I still think we had enough of the ball to win it and we showed good professionalism and composure. We just lacked a cutting edge.' They were words he would trot out on several occasions before the middle of December, as United fell further behind in the League and exited the Champions League by disgracefully finishing bottom of an easy group.

In fairness to Ferguson, I think we should say that he did have terribly bad luck with injuries in the early part of the 2005–06 campaign. The wonderful, hard-tackling Gabriel Heinze was ruled out for the season after damaging cruciate ligaments in his left knee during the Champions League group-stage game against Villarreal – a cruel blow, as he had only just returned from another injury lay-off. And England full-back Gary Neville suffered a groin injury in United's Champions League qualifying second leg against Debreceni. When he resumed training, he seemed to be making a full recovery, only for him to break down again at Carrington. He needed surgery and was sidelined for another six weeks. Then came the Keane injury to add to Ferguson's problems, or maybe that should read highlight his problems . . . the main one being that his squad was too lightweight and lacking in class when the big-hitters were forced to sit it out.

Ferguson appeared in denial over the strength of the squad, particularly over the glaring deficiencies in central midfield, given the injury to Keane and the fact that both he and Scholes were ageing. By September 2005, the United boss really *did* seem convinced that Alan Smith was the answer to his prayers. When told that Smith had revealed to the press corps that Keane had taken an interest in him, offering advice and trying to encourage him, Ferguson purred, 'I am not surprised at that. Winning is as important to Roy as it is to me. He is one of the long-serving members of the club who wants us to do well all the time. He sees certain characteristics in Alan that he saw in himself as a young person. Those characteristics could help Alan develop into a very good player in that position.'

In typical fashion, Ferguson then switched tack and used the injury situation to have a pop at Chelsea. He had earned our sympathy over the nightmare situation, and then scored a spectacular own goal by letting the monster within him free – the one that always had to have that cynical last word. He said, 'We are going through a spell of injuries at the moment, but over the years we have handled this type of thing quite well. If that was to happen to Chelsea, and they lost people like John Terry and Frank Lampard, it could make a difference to them because, up to now, they have not really had any injuries.' It didn't need to be said, Alex – as much as anything because it is patently incorrect. Chelsea's squad was good enough and deep enough to cope with injury in any department – what about Robert Huth for Terry and Gudjohnsen for Lampard?

Back to Smith and his suitability to step into Keane's shoes. I was worried about what his personal feelings were about the switch from up-front to middle of the park. Basically, I wondered if he was going along with Ferguson to ensure he had a regular spot in the first eleven, when earlier in his career he had repeatedly spoken out about playing midfield, making it clear he did not like the role and that he would only perform there in an emergency. At Leeds, in the 2001–02 season, David O'Leary deployed him there to accommodate the signing of centre-forward Robbie Fowler from Liverpool. Smith did not enjoy it, and when he signed for Manchester both he and Ferguson were at pains to say he had been purchased for his abilities as a striker.

Now, in the 2005–06 season, on the surface at least, he had become a convert. But would he ever in his deepest heart be able to honestly say he would rather play in the middle than up-front if he had the choice? I doubted it – and saw it as a cause for concern. Was his heart truly in the job? And was he ever going to be good enough? His attitude and determination were beyond reproach, but his mistimed tackles and tendency to naturally wander up-field rather than maintain a holding position would be tricky problems to overcome.

Keane's injury at Liverpool would be the making or breaking of Smith. Ferguson would now give him the extended run in central midfield he had pleaded for. In some games, he would do well, while in others he would look like a duck out of water. Analysing Smith's progress from 18 September to Keane's departure in November, he predominantly excelled against the lesser lights in the Premiership – with an honourable exception being the home win over Chelsea – but struggled when up against class opponents like Edgar Davids of Spurs and against tricky rivals in Europe.

The weeks after Keane's injury would be tough ones for Ferguson and Queiroz. In the first match without him, against Blackburn, they lost at home 2–1, but followed up with wins against Benfica, Fulham and Sunderland. The warning bells were ringing four days before the Blackburn defeat. Writing in *The Sun* on Tuesday, 20 September, Neil Custis reported that the players were growing impatient with the style and quality of play being offered up by United's management duo. Custis wrote:

> Alex Ferguson is facing a Manchester United player revolt over tactics. United have had only five shots on target in their last three games and failed to score in 225 minutes of football. Many players are growing sick of what they see as a negative style of play, with a supposed 4–3–3 formation often turning

into 4–5–1, with Ruud van Nistelrooy alone up front.

Wayne Rooney is also growing frustrated at having to play a deeper role – sometimes out on the wing. He wants to play in attack and van Nistelrooy wants him as a strike partner. But the tactics appear to be decided by Ferguson's number two, Carlos Queiroz. And he is determined not to budge from what he sees as the right way to win back the Premiership . . .

It wasn't just the players who were unhappy. The fans also made their feelings known after the loss to Blackburn. They booed the team and Ferguson, and two nutters even tried to charge a barrier and get to the United boss when he was in the dugout. Ferguson was immediately allocated extra security guards, but was confronted by more fans shouting abuse as he walked off at full-time. The incidents followed on from a bust-up at Budapest airport a month earlier when fans told Ferguson he had 'sold out' by working for the Glazers.

It was easy to see why the supporters were down. Ferguson had left his best player, Rooney, on the bench against Rovers as United adopted a cautious approach. Rooney eventually emerged and guess what? Yes, he played a major role in United's leveller midway through the second half. Blackburn goalkeeper Brad Friedel was unable to hold Rooney's 25-yard shot and Ruud van Nistelrooy hit home the rebound. United should have gone on to take all three points, but Paul Scholes gifted Michael Gray possession ten minutes from time, and from his pass Morten Pedersen rammed home his second goal of the game and the winner.

The defeat left United ten points behind Chelsea, but Rovers boss Mark Hughes claimed the crisis at Old Trafford was not as bad as it had been depicted. The former United striker said, 'There are huge expectations at this club, and those expectations will always be there. They work with that on a day-to-day basis, but this defeat will make them stronger. Once they are backed into a corner, they come back stronger and stronger. I am sure that is the reaction they will get with this defeat.

'It is still very early days as far as the title is concerned. United were hoping to win today, but they have not managed to do it. What makes it more difficult is the fact Chelsea are playing so well. If they give them too much of a lead, it will be very difficult to peg them back, so they will have to start doing it very soon.'

By now, Ferguson had raised the drawbridges, as he retreated into the role he most enjoyed: the victim railing against those who would have a go at him. A few days earlier, he had stormed out of a Sky TV interview after being asked about Wayne Rooney's temperament and had even refused to talk to MUTV after one programme on the sanitised station had had the temerity to criticise his tactics.

A couple of days after the Blackburn debacle, it was Queiroz's turn to drop a bollock. The Portuguese gave an interview to a publication in his native land in which he accused supporters of stupidity: 'Against Blackburn, we played 4–4–2 for the first time and the people in the stands were screaming: "4–4–2!" That's why football is a game in which imagination and, many times, stupidity have no limits. It was the first time we'd used this system – that the public ask for so much – and . . . we lose. Football is a sport full of opinions. But we do not play either with one or two forwards, but with three!' It was a foolish time to speak his mind, given the resentment United fans already felt towards him and the blame they attached to him for United's lack of stylish penetration in attack.

An unlikely figure stepped forward to defend Ferguson and Queiroz: Arsene Wenger. The Arsenal boss also attacked United's fans for booing his United counterpart, saying, 'You know I'm not his best friend, but I found that really appalling. Of course we, like the players, are only as good as our last game, but considering what this guy has done for the club, I find it horrendous, nearly unbelievable.'

Maybe Queiroz would have benefited from saying nothing as the crisis intensified: playing the silent role, the hard-working, loyal assistant who was grafting all hours to put things right. Instead, he came over as intransigent and out of touch with Manchester United and the stylish football their name had been built upon. He did not seem to realise that winning in itself was only part of the Old Trafford success story: you also had to win while playing well.

At around the same time, Ferguson paid tribute to the late, great Jock Stein, who had died 20 years earlier. Fergie's words would have been worth reading by Queiroz if he really wanted to know the type of man Ferguson would chew the fat with – and what his real feelings were on whether you should boast about your own abilities (or imagined abilities). The Old Trafford boss was in the Scotland dugout as assistant to the former Celtic manager for the World Cup qualifying draw against Wales on 10 September 1985. Stein collapsed before the end of the match, which the Scots drew 1–1 to earn a play-off place against Australia. But the first man to lead a British team to European Cup glory – with the Hoops in 1967 – passed away in the dressing-room at Ninian Park. Ferguson told *The Scotsman*:

> To this day, I still miss those night sessions we would have in the team's hotel when he was manager of Scotland and I was his assistant. He hardly slept, of course, and would sit up all night talking if you let

him. At about 3 a.m., I'd say, 'Jock, it's all right for you, but I'm taking training in the morning and I'll have to get to my bed.' He would say, 'Ach, you can have a nap in the afternoon.' Then he'd turn to Jimmy Steel, the masseur and a wonderful character, and say, 'Steely, order another pot of tea.'

But it was inspiring listening to him talk. With some men who get a bit of success, there is a bit of me, me, me in their conversation, telling you what they did and how they did it. Whenever I asked Jock about his great Celtic teams and how they did what they did, especially in specific matches like, say, the European Cup final, he never once mentioned his own part.

Results would hurry Keane's departure. First came the poor 0–0 home draw with Lille in the Champions League, followed by a 1–1 Premiership draw with Spurs, then the result that would break the camel's back, the 4–1 League loss at Middlesbrough. Before the Lille match, Ferguson had been praising the Champions League, hailing it as the finest club tournament and claiming it was now even more important than the World Cup in terms of prestige. He said, 'When the Champions League began, nobody could have envisaged the levels it would reach. It is a fantastically high standard, and when you think the last great World Cup was probably 20 years ago in 1986, I do think the Champions League is better than the World Cup.'

It sounded like Ferguson was trying to deflect attention away from his team's Premiership failings. Well, if that was the plan, it had a rebound effect. It focused the spotlight onto his team's Champions League failings! United really should have fared better in such a moderate group. The goalless draw with the French side was merely indicative of the lack of cutting edge that would bedevil the club's lofty ambitions.

After the match, Sir Alex again tried to take the spotlight off his team's showings by denouncing the opposition's approach and, quite correctly, lambasting them for taking Ryan Giggs out of the game. The winger had to undergo surgery after fracturing his cheekbone in three places in an aerial clash with former Arsenal defender Stathis Tavlaridis and faced six weeks on the sidelines. Ferguson's anger was compounded by the fact that the referee refused to allow Giggs to receive treatment immediately – and it was only when he was replaced by Ji-Sung Park seven minutes from time that the full extent of the damage became clear. Ferguson said, 'The referee is supposed to stop the game when a player has a bad injury. When you see the incident, I am amazed the referee didn't allow the physio on. Our doctor is not happy about it and it is something we are looking at. Ryan has suffered three separate fractures and his cheek will have to be plated. If we had been able to get on the pitch, we would have taken him off immediately, because you can see the indentation in his cheek from the TV pictures.

'Ryan stayed on due to his own courage; the miracle is he didn't get any more knocks, because something really serious could have happened. When he came off and we saw the damage, we realised Ryan had been very lucky. Lille are a very aggressive side who were committed to getting a result any way they could.

'I looked at the video, and I have never seen as many elbows and aerial challenges in all my time in England. You have to give Lille credit in terms of how far they have come as a club since we last played them four years ago, but they certainly weren't prepared to gamble and try to win. They just wanted to make sure they didn't lose.'

I certainly had sympathy for United and Ferguson after the bruising they received at the hands of Lille, but maybe the United manager could have held back from a full, verbal, public put-down of the French team. With the Premiership already looking out of reach, the last thing that was needed was to provide Lille with motivational ammunition for the return match in France a fortnight later – a match that United would need to draw or win to keep their Champions League hopes firmly on track.

More of the same dour fare was served up by United with the arrival of Tottenham at Old Trafford four days after the home game against the French outfit. The visitors deserved their point after coming back from behind. Silvestre had put the Reds ahead on seven minutes, only for Jermaine Jenas to equalise with a superb free-kick on 72 minutes. Ferguson had made Scholes skipper for the day: an unusual move given his loss of form. Even more mystifyingly, he had asked him to play the anchor role, with Smith awarded the marauding midfielder job. On such whims, reputations are smashed and empires fall.

Out of the blue, the issue of Keane's future re-appeared. The *News of the World* asked Ferguson what the current situation was towards the end of October and he replied, 'Roy is 34 years of age and it's the same for everyone else: we will assess it at the right time. Roy knows that and his agent knows that. We were never going to negotiate with Roy at this moment in time. That was decided long ago between his agent and United chief executive David Gill. His contract is up at the end of the season, but we knew that three years ago, we knew it two years ago and we knew it last year.'

The next Premiership match was against Middlesbrough, and the issue of Keane and what to do with him would very soon be Ferguson and Co.'s principal concern. In a dreadful performance on 29 October 2005, lacking confidence, drive or motivation, United were whipped 4–1 down by the Riverside, falling 13 points behind the unforgiving Blues of Chelsea. Edwin van der Sar gifted Middlesbrough the lead when he let Gaizka Mendieta's shot slip through his fingers. A mistake by Rio Ferdinand let in Jimmy-Floyd Hasselbaink for the second, and Yakubu Ayegbeni made it 3–0 from the spot after Stuart Parnaby was fouled. Yakubu set up Mendieta to make it 4–0, with United's consolation goal coming from a Cristiano Ronaldo header.

Two days later, Keane arrived at MUTV for his spot on *Play the Pundit*, in which a player gives an assessment of the team's performance the previous weekend. Keane played it rather too close to the bone for United's liking; his assessment was far too withering for their ears.

The staff at MUTV knew the show would cause more than ripples and advised their superiors of its content. It was alleged that on the orders of Sir Alex Ferguson it was shelved, and the tape was escorted out of the building by security as if it were the reincarnation of Elvis Presley. The programme was to be screened at 6.30 p.m. but disappeared from the schedule list an hour beforehand, to be replaced by Gary Neville on *Play the Pundit*. In the end, that also did not materialise, United instead putting out a half-hour feature on their youth academy. Sources told me that it had not actually been Keane's turn to play the pundit that particular Monday, but that he had contacted MUTV off his own bat following United's 4–1 drubbing and asked to do the programme. That would give credence to the idea of him becoming more and more discontented with life at United as he sat on the sidelines brooding – and even more resentful at their failure to come forward with a new deal. Was he calling Alex Ferguson's bluff and expecting the manager to back him? If so, he called it wrong.

The tapes were later burned, but not, so my sources at United suggest, before one wide boy at MUTV did a quick copy. If that is the case, he has a nice little pension to cash in on one day. The cover-up would prove damaging to the station. Several friends told me they would now cancel their subscription, and many more people rang MUTV to complain about their censorship.

So what was in the tapes? Well, according to club sources, Keane spent an hour picking to pieces his teammates' performances against Boro. He was quoted as saying, 'Just because you're paid £120,000 a week and do well for 20 minutes against Spurs, you think you're a superstar.' And, 'There's talk of putting this right in January and bringing players in. We should be doing the opposite.' His criticisms were allegedly so wide-ranging, so personal and so *honest* that Ferguson vowed they would never be shown in public. They are said to have included particular blasts at Alan Smith, Darren Fletcher, Kieran Richardson and John O'Shea. Rio Ferdinand was also allegedly in the firing line over his wages, although he would later claim Keane did not have a go at him over whether he was worth his weekly pay cheque or not. To be fair, the criticism did put Ferguson in a spot: he could hardly go into the dressing-room and say to players he had bought and nurtured that he in fact agreed with Keane's assessments, could he?

But Ferguson had lit the fuse that triggered Keane's explosion, cold-shouldering his former lieutenant in the previous months, making it clear Queiroz was now his blue-eyed boy and, all the while, refusing to confront Gill and the Glazers over Keane's contract. A week before the MUTV tapes, Ferguson may have inadvertently pushed Keane to the brink with a robust, emphatic public defence of Queiroz. He said, 'I rely on Carlos a lot. He is a very capable man and brings his experience to bear in order to widen our horizons. If I was a young player starting out with United and found myself under a coach who works as hard and puts as much thought into helping me develop as Carlos does, then I would count myself very fortunate indeed. The training is all meticulously prepared, and I know that his aim is to improve every player with each session.

'As for me allowing him too much influence, he has no more authority than any of our previous coaches – like say, Steve McClaren – but he is allowed to get on with his own job. We work closely together. He knows the theme and gets on with it without constant interference. I have every confidence in our set-up.'

After the tapes were binned, a source close to Keane said, 'Roy is surprised and angry that the club overreacted so much to his words. It is extraordinary. In his view, he just told it how he saw it – he did nothing wrong.'

That old rascal Tommy Docherty, manager of United in the '70s, was one of those who felt Keane had been right to speak out. He said, 'Roy is 101 per cent right. He said things that needed to be said. It should have been said by either Ferguson or Carlos Queiroz. Some of the United players are not good enough – and it should have been said two or three times already.

'Some are too well-off, and if you look at some of the signings, they are disgraceful. Take the goalkeepers as an example. They signed five or six before they found Edwin van der Sar, who was right under their noses all along. I know what it is to make bad signings. I bought keeper Paddy Roche and I am not afraid to say he was useless. The nicest bloke you could hope to meet but a terrible buy.'

And of MUTV, the Doc added, 'They are only interested in good publicity. If someone comes on with something negative – even if it needs to be said – then they don't want to know.'

The United fans seemed largely behind Keane and his withering assault. On the 606 website, United fan IC said:

> Keane knows what it takes to be successful, and he
> clearly doesn't see it in the next generation of

players. He's 100 per cent right about Ferdinand and the younger players – they are on a lot more money than they should be. Some of them would struggle to get into other teams.

And M added: 'If he had said this in private, would the players care? The publicity of this will make a bigger impact on them.'

While R said:

Keane has only come out and said what every United fan has been thinking. Sure, players like Alan Smith and Darren Fletcher can do a reasonable job in their respective positions, but that's not good enough when you play for a team like Manchester United – you must excel in your position week in, week out.

Z echoed these thoughts, saying:

Too often, the fans are treated like idiots who know nothing about football and will believe any rubbish coming out of the club. ('We were unlucky', 'It's just a blip', 'He works hard for the team', etc.) At least Keane is prepared to acknowledge what we can all see, that things need to improve.

However, TDE was prophetic in feeling that the incident could spell the end for Keane at Old Trafford:

The biggest fallout from Keanogate will be that he quits very soon. He quit the Republic of Ireland when he had a bust-up with Mick McCarthy, and he will do the same now. He has the respect of the fans as he cares so much, though he may not always go about it in the right way.

A was one of a minority who believed that it *was* finally time for Keane to step aside:

> The trouble is that when Keane says some people are not good enough for United, he is now included in that list. You can't criticise his commitment and desire, but he is just not the player he once was and is no longer able to control the game as consistently as he used to. If he wanted the best for the club, he should have left a year or two ago – his staying is not the cause of United's decline, but it is a factor.

There was talk in the press of a second MUTV tape – from the 2002–03 season – in which Keane allegedly had a go at Ole Gunnar Solskjaer. The Norwegian – a darling of the Old Trafford faithful – had scored just two goals in his opening twenty League appearances that season as United battled with Arsenal for supremacy, and Keane is alleged to have moaned about the number of chances he had missed. It is further claimed that Ferguson ordered that the tape be shredded and that Keane 'went mad' when he learned about it.

Yet Keane's analysis of the current United side's shortcomings seemed spot on when, two days after his banned outburst, they meekly surrendered to a 1–0 defeat against Lille away in the Champions League. Inevitably, the chant from the United fans from all corners of the ground were as one at full-time: 'Keano, Keano, Keano.' All of a sudden, their season looked at risk; they were trailing Chelsea in the Premiership and now only a win in Lisbon against Benfica would definitely take them into the knockout stage of the Champions League.

Before the Lille game, Ferguson had taken an indirect pop at Keane by intimating that he should have thrown a protective arm around the United youngsters – as former captains such as Steve Bruce and Bryan Robson had apparently done – rather than castigating them. He said, 'A big defeat like Saturday's [Middlesbrough] is a big step for them mentally. In the past, we've relied on experienced players like Steve Bruce and Bryan Robson to help the young players. We have got to pick up the resilience and substance of Manchester United teams of the past, but some of our young players have only been here one year.'

It was 2 November, and four days later, with Keane watching from the stands, United would take on Chelsea at Old Trafford in a crunch Premiership match. Keane sat alone, away from Gary Neville and Ryan Giggs, who were also out injured. Their separation highlighted the growing chasm between the skipper and his teammates: Neville G and Giggs had always been considered his closest acquaintances at the Theatre of Dreams.

Ferguson must have been rankled by Keane's outburst, because in a statement before the match he seemed to be referring to him when he said he would not tolerate public criticism of his players from those inside the club. He said, 'Of course there is criticism. The criticism has come from all directions. What you have to do as manager of our club is to make sure the criticism remains inside your doors. I am unremitting in that respect. Totally unequivocal. My stance is there and it doesn't change. You don't criticise any Manchester United player outside the doors. I have never done and I won't.'

This was as clear a sign as you could get that the bond between him and his injured skipper was broken for good. By the time of the Chelsea match, Keane was for the axe – the only questions to be determined being how and when.

Again fostering the siege-mentality environment he loved to work within, the United manager continued, 'Criticism is not a problem for me; you expect it at a club like this. What I have to look at is how the players have been affected by it. It is natural, particularly in young players, that you have a dip in confidence when you lose games. They are no different to anyone else in that respect.'

Niall Quinn, seemingly Keane's eternal adversary after the incidents in Saipan in 2002, also used the occasion to kick Keane when he was down, claiming the United skipper was selfish and that he had messed up the club's preparations for the Chelsea match by his MUTV outburst. Quinn, writing in *The Guardian*, said:

> [T]hey did not have the benefit of the best preparation due not least to the farcical and self-serving intervention by Roy Keane. As far as I am aware, humiliating your colleagues in public is not the best way to foster team spirit. From his teammates' point of view, do they really see that as a genuine attempt to get a positive reaction or was it a rant from someone supposedly so committed to United that he has let everybody know how much he loves the idea of a move to Celtic?
>
> That is one aspect of Keane's make-up. Another is his participation on the pitch, and I suppose a footballer of his stature will always be missed. Paul Scholes was also missing on Wednesday (against Lille) and, if Keane and Scholes were on form and in tandem on Sunday against Chelsea, would we be having this debate? Personally I don't think we would, and that is a part of the reason why I just don't see that what is happening at Old Trafford constitutes the end of an era.

Yet the omens for the upcoming visit from Chelsea were not good: they were on a 40-game unbeaten run and were 13 points clear of United. That is not to say that the Reds did not have a chance – they always seemed to rally when their backs were against the wall. You only had to think back just over 12 months earlier, when they had wrecked Arsenal's hopes of making it to 50 games in their unbeaten run. Ferguson said, 'There are some similarities between the two games, but this Chelsea side are made of much sterner stuff. They are a very powerful team and very committed to defending. It is certainly not going to be easy to beat them, but maybe what we need just now is the opportunity to play against a very good team. The start of the game will be so important and we need the crowd behind us. The question is can we usurp Chelsea and make them think for a bit? I know we have the ability to do it – and I think everyone else does too.'

The answer to his question was yes. United did usurp the Blues, and in some style too, although the win would ultimately prove to be yet another false dawn for this team in transition. To complete the 'Roy of the Rovers' scenario on the day, it was Darren Fletcher, one of the youngsters apparently on the receiving end of Keane's blast at MUTV, who grabbed the only goal of the game. Inevitably the TV cameras focused on the lonely figure sitting in the main stand as United celebrated their precious goal. Unshaven, dark, determined, defensive and unsmiling, you half-expected the desperado to stand up and shout, 'Come on, punk, make my day!'

Twelve days later, his bluff would be called when Ferguson told him the party was over and he was out. That picture of the desperado in the stands would be the last of Keane at Old Trafford as a United player. In many ways, it was how he would have liked to be remembered: a sharp-shooter, defiant and moody, his own man, right to the bloody, bitter end.

THIRTEEN

THAT JFK MOMENT

The end, when it came, was predictable only in its unpredictability. After all, this was Roy Maurice Keane we are talking about: the man whose career had dipped and soared on a wave of the unexpected. The news of his departure from Manchester United Football Club initially filtered through slowly, but the trickle eventually burst like water breaking a dam as the shocking truth emerged: Roy Keane, the leader of the Red cause for the previous twelve and a half years, the man who sweated blood for it, had been sacked by his mentor, Sir Alex Ferguson.

OK, maybe I'm being a wee bit dramatic here, but United fans will understand where I am coming from. The scenario seemed almost akin to a 'Where were you on the day JFK/Lennon died?' situation on that bleak November morning, the 18th of the month, 2005. In fact, one supporter rang into MUTV later in the day to say he had been in tears: he had been under the impression that Keane *had* died when he had initially tuned in to the coverage, such was the sombre, dirge-like tone.

I was in London that day, working for the *Mail on Sunday*, when a bemused-looking Andy Bucklow walked up to me with these immortal words: 'Have you heard the news?'

'No,' I replied, expecting him to tell me Ferguson had signed another Djemba-Djemba or something. Andy, let me tell you, is a United nut and a relic from the Doc's Red Army era: the K Stand boys who watched every match home and away during the seasons from around 1974–1976.

'Keane's gone,' he proclaimed, his eyes close to tears. 'He's gone . . .'.

This well-travelled, normally articulate man in his 40s then walked away from me, his words trailing into thin air, as if no more could be found, as if no more were necessary.

My first thought was to check the *United We Stand* and *Red Issue* websites – forget the mutterings of MUTV or manutd.com at this stage; they would be toeing the party line and probably would not even mention it until the lawyers had firmed all the words up. That was a correct assumption. It was 11 a.m.; they didn't lead on the news until 12.30 p.m., when a form of words satisfactory to both the club and Keane had been settled upon.

Andy Mitten's boys at *United We Stand* were already on the ball. This was their opener, under the headline 'Keane Sacked':

> We are hearing that Roy Keane has left, or is about to leave, Manchester United. We can't confirm the story as yet, but our sources are as good as you can get. Roy is currently with Michael Kennedy discussing his future. We understand he had a row this morning centred around his captaincy, a disagreement of opinions with the manager and his next contract. That led to a bust-up. More when we get it.

Full credit where it's due. Those words were the first explanatory ones on the subject. Thousands more would follow over the next two days as the Saturday and Sunday newspapers tried their best to prove they knew more inside information than the others, and yet, as a United insider would tell me on the Monday, those words at the very start of it all were as accurate as they come. Fair enough, the role of Carlos Queiroz in Keane's exit was not specifically mentioned, but it was certainly covered in the phrase 'a disagreement of opinions'.

By 12.30 p.m., many United fans were finding it difficult to digest their lunches; many I know had taken the rather more comforting option of a liquid lunch. The simple fact is this: everyone knew Keane was finished as a world-class player, but he deserved better than to be treated like 'a piece of meat' – as he once described the manner of Jaap Stam's hurried push out of the United side-door when Ferguson fell out with him.

Sure, Keane's legs had gone and United had been forced to adapt to an unfamiliar, unsuccessful tactical plan to accommodate him, one in which the likes of Fletcher would be used to do his running, giving United a 4–5–1 outlook. I am not saying that United should have continued like that – indeed, I believe it was suffocating them and that Keane should have been used sparingly when he returned to fitness – but this was no Jaap Stam: Keane should have been retained within the club, with a new contract as a player–coach or, preferably, as player–assistant manager. This, after all, was the man who had shaped the dream from which Ferguson bathed in the glory. He and Keane had always worked from the premise that loyalty was the key to continued success and harmony; now loyalty, along with self-protection, would see Keane evicted as if he were a petty thief.

The loyalty that ended the affair was Ferguson's – and, in the minds of many, it was misplaced. He chose to be loyal to Queiroz; he chose the Portuguese over the man who had laid his body on the line for him for all those years. Don't get me wrong: Queiroz is a lovely guy, a gentleman, and much more refined than Keane. But his impact on United had been disastrous since his return from Real Madrid, as he implemented a much more cautious, defensive approach upon the team. Senior players told me they did not enjoy his training methods as much as those of previous coach Steve McClaren. They were much more of the slowly-slowly, steady-as-you-go type rather than the high-impact, let's-get-at-'em ones employed by McClaren.

My feeling was that Ferguson was wary of being seen as a soft touch by the Glazers, and that perhaps he needed to stress he was still the man in charge by allowing Keane to leave. Ferguson had been living on former glories since the last Premiership title win in 2003, and probably the last thing he would have wanted was to get the boot himself. He was a proud man who wanted to go out a winner; plus there was the small matter of money. I imagine he did not want to lose his £4 million-a-year salary – who would? He would battle to stay in charge and keep his income, just as he had done in the dispute over the Rock Of Gibraltar racehorse and his row with John Magnier, which nearly tore the club apart. (Quite rightly, Sir Alex had wanted to make sure he got his fair cut of the readies when it went to stud.) When he now saw Keane making waves and noted the reported worry lines on the faces of the Glazers, I believe Sir Alex would have felt himself in a similar situation.

Yet the departure of Keane was still a calculated risk by Ferguson. If United continued to struggle under his and Queiroz's reign, he would surely be next out of the door with the Portuguese. But at least it bought time for him to hopefully turn the club around. In one way, it could be argued that Ferguson had done Keane a favour. By not making him his assistant, and by allowing him to go before things got worse, he indirectly ensured Keane would not be tarred with the same brush of ultimate failure that he and Queiroz would fall foul of if success eluded them and they were frogmarched out of the building.

By the afternoon of 18 November, the statements were coming in thick and fast from Old Trafford. The first was from the club itself. It said:

> Manchester United has today reached agreement with Roy Keane for Roy to leave the club with immediate effect. The agreement allows Roy to sign a long-term deal with another club to enable him to secure his playing career beyond what would have been the end of his contract at United in the summer.
>
> The club has offered Roy a testimonial in recognition of his 12 years at Old Trafford. The club thanks Roy for his major contribution to the club during his years of service.

Then Ferguson had his say:

> Roy Keane has been a fantastic servant for Manchester United. The best midfield player in the world of his generation, he is already one of the great figures in our club's illustrious history. Roy has been central to the success of the club in the last 12 years and everyone at Old Trafford wishes him well in the rest of his career and beyond.

Chief executive David Gill did not want to be left out. He said:

> Roy has been a towering figure at the club for over a decade. His dedication, talent and leadership have been qualities that have marked him out as one of

the true greats. On behalf of everyone at the club, we
wish him every success in his future career.

Finally, it was Keane's turn:

> It has been a great honour and privilege for me to
> play for Manchester United for over 12 years. During
> my time at the club, I have been fortunate to play
> alongside some of the best players in the game and
> in front of the best supporters in the world. At all
> times, I have endeavoured to do my best for the
> management and the team.
>
> Whilst it is a sad day for me to leave such a great
> club and manager, I believe that the time has now
> come for me to move on. After so many years, I will
> miss everyone at the club.
>
> I send my best wishes for the future to the
> management, players, staff and supporters of the
> club.

Each statement was akin to the sort of formal letters that
exchange hands when a Cabinet Minister is forced to leave
his position. They had the air of false sentiments used to
cover up the truth. Let's cut the crap here: they were written
by solicitors and they did not cover anything up; they
merely reflected badly on each player in the drama. Come
on, Roy, we all know you weren't responsible on the day of
18 November for your sudden exit, but on that day you
were complicit in the corporate hypocrisy and disdain for
the supporters who had backed you to the hilt.

This was the man who had called some United fans 'the
prawn-sandwich brigade'. OK, I know he would say he was
talking about those in the corporate seats, but they were
also the ones who, in a large part, helped finance his £4.5
million-a-year wages. Now they were part of 'the best

supporters in the world'. Similarly, Dazza Fletcher, Rio Ferdinand and Alan Smith, whom he had allegedly knocked a couple of weeks earlier in that infamous MUTV *Play the Pundit* interview and whom he had hinted should be sold in January, were now people he 'will miss'.

Also, he had described it as 'a sad day for me to leave such a great club and manager . . .'. Yet, for some time, he had had his doubts about Ferguson, privately confiding to his allies that he felt the old man had lost it, publicly questioning his buys, lambasting him for not finding a quality replacement for himself in midfield, and complaining about the boss's reliance on Queiroz.

The word from behind the scenes was that Keane had been given a £5 million pay-off for his silence. Knowing the Scrooge-like nature of the Glazers, that was unlikely, but some deal had certainly been cut.

The subterfuge was extraordinary. While the news of Keane's departure was finally released by United at 12.30 p.m. on the Friday, Keane had trained with the other players earlier that morning and Ferguson had given his usual Friday morning press session without mention of the Irishman's exit, even claiming that he was recovering well from his injury and would soon be available for selection.

I am told that the deal that would see Keane go had been worked out at the start of the week. The only reason he, his lawyer Michael Kennedy, Ferguson and United's lawyer met at 9.00 a.m. on the Friday was to sign the contract that would see his wages for the season paid up in advance and, presumably, to sign the deal that bought his silence. That meeting in itself was foolish if the idea was to maintain a conspiracy of silence about Keane's future until 12.30 p.m. – it alerted the vigilant *United We Stand* and led to a breaking of the news before the planned hour.

The whole handling of the skipper's exit had been a shambles – from his own silence on the matter, to

Ferguson's refusal initially to even acknowledge it, to the very fact that a man of Keane's stature deserved to be treated better. This was the man who had always fought like a madman for something he believed in; now he slipped away meekly and red-faced into that quiet night.

Why did Keane go? He had got to the stage where he had to know: him or Queiroz? It was reported that he had shouted at the Portuguese, in front of Ferguson, letting him know exactly what he thought of his abilities, and Ferguson made his choice. I was told Keane had become resentful at the outsider's closeness to the boss; he had become jealous. He lashed out on MUTV at the deficiencies within the team Queiroz was shaping as Ferguson handed him more and more responsibilities, and then, two weeks later, finally, had a go at the new holder of the boss's affections in front of Ferguson.

Queiroz had seized the role that Keane himself had hoped to be occupying at this stage of his life and career: that of Ferguson's assistant, the man who would be moulded for the role of king should the Scot be able to engineer the situation so that, upon his retirement, he would move upstairs and nominate his own man for the accession. To Queiroz, at least for the moment, the victory; to Keane, the unusual, unpalatable taste of defeat.

The eerie sense that we were watching history being made that November day grew as tributes began to pour in for the departed Irishman. That person ringing MUTV to say it was as if Keane had died made more and more sense as day turned to night on 18 November. I cannot remember any other occasion when so much has been made of a player merely leaving a club – not retiring or dying. The first accolade came from the Professional Footballers' Association, which lauded the 34 year old's contribution to the Old Trafford club. Deputy chief executive Mick McGuire declared Keane would be a hard act to follow, saying, 'He's been a magnificent player for the club and has been as instrumental as any player in ensuring that United have been a leading club in the Premiership and have achieved so much in the last decade. He is unique, and he's going to be very, very difficult to replace.' It was to be only the first of many accolades.

Arsenal boss Arsene Wenger may have been holding back a laugh that his old enemy Ferguson had lost his greatest ally when he said, 'He was certainly their most influential player in the last ten years. It's a complete surprise that he's gone in the middle of the season. It looked like he was a bit upset recently. Why, I don't know.

'I must say that, for many years, you didn't hear anything from Roy Keane. But this season you have heard from him in the newspapers, and I feel that is a dangerous game. I've had disagreements with many players, including Sylvain Wiltord, but he didn't leave in the middle of the season. Sometimes you have disagreements with people, but it doesn't mean you don't respect them.'

As to whether Keane might go to another Premiership club, Wenger replied, 'I wouldn't be surprised.' However, the Frenchman dismissed suggestions that Keane might be Highbury-bound. 'We have put our confidence in our players and will keep doing that,' he said.

Former Manchester United and England midfielder Ray Wilkins admitted he was 'flabbergasted' when news of Keane's departure broke. He said, 'This will be a total shock to everyone in football. There was a lot of talk about him leaving the club in the summer, but for him to go before the January transfer window is a major surprise. Roy was an extremely powerful figure at Manchester United and an exceptional player. I'm flabbergasted.'

Wilkins added that he would not be surprised to see Keane join Celtic, the club at which the midfielder once stated he wanted to end his career. 'Roy has publicly stated that he wouldn't want to play against United in the Premiership, so that might be the obvious choice for him,' he said. Wilkins then made a very valid point: 'It would be interesting to see Roy working with Gordon Strachan. Two Celts together might be a bit fiery, but he survived twelve and a half years with Sir Alex so I'm sure he wouldn't have a problem. One thing's for sure: this will be music to Chelsea's ears. It's another major boost towards their goal of retaining their Premiership title.'

The controversial Michael Crick, the man behind an unofficial biography on Ferguson, said he believed Keane's canned interview to MUTV was one step too far for the United boss to accept. Crick told the BBC, 'Ferguson laid down very strict rules for all his players, but then he made exceptions to the really great players like Cantona and Keane. Ferguson gave Keane a huge amount of leeway. He turned a blind eye to some of the things Keane's been up to and some of the comments he's made.

'We don't know the full story, but it may be that Ferguson just decided that this was, you know, a move too far by Keane and he had to go.'

However, Paul Parker, a former teammate of Keane's at Old Trafford, was not convinced the MUTV interview was solely to blame. 'There's more to it than that,' he said. 'That didn't help Roy, but that was Roy, and I think the club and the boss understood that. But I think a lot of it all was down to what he wanted to do, and it wasn't that one isolated situation.'

Fanzine king Andy Mitten accepted that Keane would be almost impossible to replace: 'I feel he had something to contribute. He was such a big influence on the club, and the fact he is driven by success would only have been a good thing for the club. He's the best player I've ever seen in a Manchester United shirt, the driving force behind much of the club's success since he joined in 1993 and a legend in the eyes of most United fans.'

Shareholders United vice-chairman Sean Bones admitted he was surprised by the sudden departure of Keane, and felt the exit would put pressure on the Glazer family to prove they truly did have the interests of the club at heart by providing the readies for a top-notch replacement. 'As supporters, we have to thank Roy Keane for the wonderful service he gave to Manchester United,' he said. 'He was without doubt the best midfield player of his generation. Sir Alex even rated him above Bryan Robson, and that just shows the calibre of player he was. We as supporters particularly loved him because he sweated blood for us on the field; he gave everything.

'He is part of the fabric of the club. It's always a surprise when something like this happens. I think what it does is put added pressure on the Glazer family because not only do they have to replace Roy, who is irreplaceable, they also have to acquire another player to keep their promise to supporters. The trophy haul has been unbelievable in the time he has been here.'

Former United and Republic of Ireland striker Frank Stapleton argued that the MUTV interview was at the centre of the decision to axe Keane. 'In some ways, I'm surprised, and in other ways I'm not,' Stapleton told *Sky Sports News*. 'It is a reaction to what happened a few weeks ago, when he criticised his teammates publicly, plus a combination of the fact that maybe they weren't ready to renew his contract at the end of the season. He probably said, "I'll go now rather than wait."

'The programme is at the centre of this. Just before, he had said he didn't think he'd be at the club after this season, maybe to force them into giving him a contract. At this stage of his career, Roy knows it is very straightforward. He wouldn't have thought twice about saying "Right, let's call it a day now, let's move on," and the club have obviously made the decision not to renew his contract.

'In the period that he has been there, he has had unbelievable success. But in my mind, no player has ever been bigger than Manchester United. The club will go on and look to get stronger.'

Another former United player, Lou Macari, was shocked by the news. He was also the first man to say he thought Keane would be devastated that United no longer wanted him. 'It's a real bolt out of the blue. I've always thought of Roy Keane as a major part of Manchester United,' he said. 'There is always a place for Roy Keane in the team, and it is only when the likes of Keane, Paul Scholes and the Nevilles have all gone that people will realise their value. Trying to replace Roy Keane is almost impossible, and no matter what Roy will say over the next few weeks and months ahead, Roy will be gutted that he is no longer a Manchester United player.'

Nicky Butt, Keane's former midfield partner who was now at Birmingham, paid tribute to Keane's leadership – but did not accept he was irreplaceable. He said, 'He was one of the best players the club has ever had. And he was a leader – that's how he will be remembered. But he is not irreplaceable – ten years ago, you could have said that about Bryan Robson.'

Never one far away from the media spotlight, David Beckham got in on the tributes act, taking time out from training in Madrid to describe Keane as 'one of the most inspirational captains I have ever played with'. He told the Press Association, 'He is a player who will lead from the front and get a team going. He is also a player who will tell you when you have done something wrong and something right. You know where you stand with him; he'll tell you in his own special way.'

Beckham was eager to stress the importance of Keane's role at Old Trafford, adding, 'I think he had one of the biggest impacts on a club anyone could have. The players responded to him in every game. I am shocked he has left, because I thought he would be there for a few more years, but he has made his decision and everyone will respect that. People now have to look at what he has done with Manchester United, because in the last 12 years he has won everything there is to win in club football. He has done it gaining respect from so many players that he has played with and against.'

Beckham conceded he had no idea what the future would hold for Keane: 'I don't know what his plans are. I hope he'll play for a few more years. Whether he finishes playing or carries on, I don't know. I said last week he could become a manager, not right away, because it is difficult when you are as young as he is, but I believe his potential in going into anything and succeeding is high. Maybe he'll just spend time with his family. He's a family man and has a lovely wife and kids.'

Middlesbrough boss Steve McClaren – who had worked previously with Keane as Ferguson's number two at United and who had earned the Keane thumbs-up for his innovations in training and overall approach to the game – made it clear he would love to sign the midfielder and help him develop into a coaching role. McClaren also admitted he was 'shocked' by the news of his exit. He said, 'Only Manchester United and Roy and their representatives know what's gone on behind the scenes, and obviously that will come out in the next days, weeks, the speculation about that. But all I can say is I was shocked. It's the end of an era. What a player – one of the greatest players ever to pull on a Manchester United shirt. I'm delighted that I had the pleasure of working with him for the three years in that period when he was, for me, the best midfield player in the world.'

Asked what might have prompted the shock parting of the ways, he said, 'I honestly don't know and it's difficult to speculate. I just know that Roy is very much his own man, makes up his own mind, and once he makes that up, there's no changing it. Obviously, that's what he's done. He's proved that in the past – that's why he's the player that he is, and that's why he will be the player again that he wants to be.

'It's the end of that kind of generation. He's still going to be playing and still going to be an influence wherever, but you won't get many players like Roy Keane ever again in football – a leader on and off the field, a combative midfield player, but who can also play and influence a game. He'll be sadly missed by Manchester United. That kind of player is very difficult to replace.'

Keane had not indicated where his future lay amid speculation linking him with Celtic, but McClaren believed there would be no shortage of takers for a player who himself contended he still had plenty of good football left in his legs. McClaren said, 'For that calibre of player, there will be a queue, I'm sure. He's still a very, very good player. You never lose your leadership; you never lose the aura he would bring to any football club. I know Roy, and whatever he does, he gives 110 per cent, so there's no question of motivation. He's always motivated, so there's quite an asset there.'

The Boro boss also predicted a bright future for Keane in coaching: 'I think he's looking to go into that – he was always interested when I was there. He's certainly got a coach's and manager's head on him, and if he wants to branch into that, then it's the perfect opportunity now.'

If it was a ploy to attract Keane to join him at Boro, it was a clever one. The Irishman would give Boro much thought as he plotted his return to football in January 2006. His obvious move was to his boyhood heroes, Glasgow Celtic, but could he stand the midweek trips to outposts like Inverness and Livingston? For his love of the

Parkhead club, yes, probably. But Boro was also worth considering, for two reasons: one, he would enjoy working with McClaren again, and two, the link-up could even see him returning one day to Old Trafford as assistant manager to McClaren at United.

By the Monday, it was clear what his options were, and what they weren't. It had been suggested in a 'World Exclusive' in *The Sun* (which also appeared in the *Daily Mail*!) that Keane was on his way to Juventus. It was suggested that the move would appeal to him because it was the only option out of the clubs eyeing him that would allow him one more realistic crack at winning the European Cup. For worldwide 'dream team' fanatics, it also offered the mouthwatering possibility of him teaming up with his former arch rival Patrick Vieira, who had joined Juve for £13 million from Arsenal in the summer.

By Monday night, the dream appeared to be over. Juve, who would have had to drop the brilliant Brazilian Emerson to accommodate Keane in the team, said, 'Juventus is very strong right now and we do not need any more players.'

Their spokesman refused to confirm reports that Keane's lawyer Michael Kennedy had made contact with Juventus to see if they were interested. But it was pretty obvious why they felt they did not need Keane: at the time, they were top of their Champions League group and within sight of the next stage, while also leading Serie A by five points.

Celtic, who were favourites for his signature, did not sound too keen on Roy in public, but that was just a ploy. Their chairman Brian Quinn said, 'Would he fit into Gordon Strachan's plans? The team is playing very well at the moment and they look settled. You wonder whether you would want to interrupt things, but that's up to Gordon. The other question to consider is the business side.

'We would have to wait and see what Roy Keane is

proposing, if indeed he's looking for anything at all from Celtic. When he first talked about leaving United, as far as I can see, the word Celtic didn't pass his lips.'

Apart from Boro and Celtic, the only other ports of call for the ex-United skipper appeared to be West Bromwich Albion and Everton. Baggies boss Bryan Robson, in that typically determined style of his, had telephoned Keano the very night he left Manchester, trying to persuade him to sign. In public, Robson said, 'Everyone in the Premiership will have an interest in Roy Keane. We're no different, but it is about what Roy has got in his mind and what he wants to do. I have tried to phone Roy, but all I kept getting was his answer machine. If he wants to come to West Brom, I will try to make it happen with the chairman.' However, I couldn't for the life of me give you a second reason – the first being his friendship with Robbo – why Roy Keane would move to the Hawthorns. Could you?

In the case of joining David Moyes at Everton, again it was hard to see why. The talented Scottish manager had sounded out Michael Kennedy about the Irishman's plans, and whether he would be interested in a player–coach role. But if that was the choice, surely Boro, and McClaren, would be a better bet?

The conjecture about whom Keane would join brought a breath of fresh air to the whole affair of his leaving United – taking it on from the rather funereal smog that continued to hang over Old Trafford. One thing was for sure: it would be some time before the vast majority of United fans would come out of mourning . . .

FOURTEEN

WE THOUGHT HE HAD DIED (REPRISE)

'Back in 1997, '98, '99 – or whenever my prime was – when people said "You're the top player", well … I never believed that for a second. In the same way, over the last couple of years when there's been criticism or whatever, you try not to believe that either. People have said I'm finished. Yeah, well, that's OK. I think that's part of life and part, I suppose, of a journalist's job, of trying to sell papers. I try not to take too much notice' – Roy Keane, 25 July 2004

The fans at Old Trafford were far from happy at their leader's departure. The chap who rang into MUTV was not the only one who thought Keane had passed away. Many others had come to the same conclusion for a minute or two as they cottoned on to the fact that something big had happened at Old Trafford that day.

For many United fans, it would be as if he had died. It sounds ridiculous, but some of them could have used some therapy to overcome the feelings of loss they experienced for weeks afterwards. You would probably need to have been a United fan for the years encompassed by Keane's reign to understand.

Plus, someone very special to Manchester United

actually was fighting for his life the night Keane was forced out, highlighting how rather dramatic and ridiculous some of the highly strung emotions greeting the news had become. By coincidence, I was staying in London on 18 November, in a budget hotel I use in Earls Court. My route from working at the *Mail on Sunday* to the hotel took me down past the Cromwell Hospital. That night I felt a bit choked as I walked past the hospital and looked up at its blue windows, each the focal point of a patient's room. In one of them, the greatest player ever to don the red shirt of Manchester United lay fighting for his life. I said a little prayer for Georgie boy and felt the tears welling up as I looked up at his bedroom window, where he was fighting what had become his toughest battle as his life slowly ebbed away. For all your faults with booze, women and life itself, George, you truly were the Best. God bless you, mate.

For days, the websites, radio phone-ins, TV football shows and the sports pages of newspapers were preoccupied with the Keane exit story. Here's a selection from manutd.com/talkingreds, a typical example of how the fans, for the most part, found it tough to come to terms with what had happened:

> It is up to Keane to decide what his future ends up as. I wish Roy all the best for the future and hope he makes it a success whatever the matter. Good luck, Keano! A Red Devil through thick and thin – Gav

> I'm absolutely gutted! Roy, you will be sorely missed, and I hope you find your way back someday! – MJ

> Can't believe this . . . absolutely gobsmacked! Thank you, Roy, for many great years . . . you will be missed – April Chamberlain

> Gutted! Keano has been my hero for so long now. I'm
> in total shock. Oh my God. I want to wish Roy all the
> best and thank him for being a true United legend
> – EK UTD

> Roy has, quite rightly, been awarded a testimonial in
> recognition of the service and loyalty he has given to
> the club for over 12 years – so this will be our chance
> to give Roy the send-off he so richly deserves. God
> bless you, Roy, and our heartfelt and warmest thanks
> for giving your all for us and the club – Carol Steele

Oh, yes, the testimonial . . . offered by the club as a thank-you to Keane for his 12 years of service. If it happened, it would go some way to making up for the sense of injustice the fans felt at the way their leader had been forced out by the back door.

One man who refused to be taken in by the United PR machine on the day was Mark Longden, the chairman of the Independent Manchester United Supporters Association. He was fuming mad and did not mince his words as he hit out at the so-called 'mutual parting of ways' as 'absolutely crazy'. Longden also expressed the fear that United's stuttering season could now take an even more dangerous turn for the worse. 'I'm absolutely staggered,' said Longden. 'We've been trying for years to find a Roy Keane replacement and then we get rid of the one we've got in the middle of the season. It seems absolutely crazy to me. We've sold Nicky Butt, Eric Djemba-Djemba and other players who can fill the Roy Keane role. Phil Neville could play that role, but he's now at Everton.

'Now we get rid of Roy Keane without any sign of a replacement. How does that work? The season seems to be going from moderate to worse.'

Longden cited Keane's sterling show away to Juventus in

the European Cup semi-final in 1999 as the highlight of his glittering career at Old Trafford. He said, 'That will be the one overriding memory. He virtually got us through to the Champions League final single-handedly, even though he knew he was going to miss the final. That was the measure of the man. He's up there. He's a legend, up there with Best, Robson, Cantona, Whiteside and that company.'

Praise indeed, from a fan who knows what he is talking about. Other supporters voiced their anxiety about a future without Keane, wondering if, how and when the Glazers would finally free up some cash to find a quality man to step into Keane's shoes. One fan, on the BBC's 606 message board, summed up those fears, saying:

> Top class midfielder? With what money? Do you realise the mire United are in? They are now even struggling not only to sell out 'chumps league' games, but they are struggling to sell Premier League games. Wigan tickets are still on sale to members four weeks after going on sale! These tickets are usually gone the weekend that they go on sale! We might see United's true position after the Tuesday game with Villarreal – one *huge* game for the club in its ambitions both on and off the pitch.
>
> United are no longer the solvent club they were when they could sponge up the loss of a great player and then afford to replace him, or even someone from inside the club taking over the mantle. Where from within United is the leadership and inspiration going to come?

Another United fan expressed the view that the club was foundering after the Glazer takeover seven months previously, that the Keane departure proved the very structure of the club was now at risk:

Glazer ripped the soul out of United, now the heart [Keane] has gone. What direction are United going in? Yes, Fergie has survived players going before – Hughes, Ince and Kanchelskis ('95) and Cantona ('97) – but I am afraid people will recall the end of the great empire of United falling on Friday, 18 November 2005. Who is next: Fergie? Ruud van Nistelrooy to Madrid with Ronaldo? Rio to Chelski? Glazer has poisoned United to the core and the cancer he has brought will spread.

United have no money to replace Keane, and the fact that they couldn't afford to keep him happy (wages) and also insure him against further injuries shows the financial mire the club are in. It will cost United at least five times more to find a suitable replacement for Keano.

At least some fans were happy at Keane's departure – but they were the hopeful variety at Celtic Park, the ones praying they would be the beneficiaries of the situation. Peter Rafferty, the secretary of the Affiliation of Celtic Supporters' Associations, is an intelligent, thoughtful man whose comments on the beautiful game are always worth listening to. His opinions on Keane proved no exception to the rule, his words providing a welcome reality check. Yes, admitted Rafferty, Keane would receive a warm welcome at Parkhead, but no, it would not be the end of the world if he didn't arrive. Rafferty confirmed, 'It would be a good acquisition for Celtic – but it all depends on Gordon Strachan's terms and whether he would fit into his wage structure. If Roy Keane isn't prepared to take a considerable drop in wages, that would be difficult for Celtic to manage.

'There has been a lot of discussion about this, even before today's news. I know most supporters would like him, but some think he is now on the old side and he isn't the first-class player he was. He has obviously had his injury problems and those still appear to be plaguing him. The big question is whether Gordon Strachan wants him, and so far there have been no answers to that.'

Rafferty also asked whether Keane's arrival would hold up some of the younger talent coming through at Celtic. After a shaky start at the club, Strachan's brave decision to turn to youth – with the likes of Shaun Maloney, Craig Beattie and Aiden McGeady – had paid dividends. Rafferty added, 'We have a lot of young Scottish players coming through now from the youth academy. Gordon Strachan sees the future being in the hands of these players and he has been willing to play them. They have been playing particularly well this season, so it all depends on whether Gordon Strachan wants him. Whatever he decides, the supporters will back him.'

Others associated with Celtic were not as keen on Keane. Lisbon Lion Jim Craig was worried that Keane would use the club as a retirement home if he arrived. Obviously, he did not know Keane that well. Craig said, 'What you have got to look at is would Roy Keane bring something to Celtic? He has more experience than all the players, he is a Champions League winner, but you have got to ask is he the same Roy Keane at the height of his powers? The answer to that is no.

'Is he able to play even a third of the season through injury? He has not been able to do that with United. Will things get any better next season and thereafter? Will he also be a disruptive influence behind the scenes? He occasionally was at Manchester United.

'Somebody has to answer those questions. Will he also take a considerable drop in wages from what he has been on? Why should Celtic be the graveyard or retirement home for players who are not at the height of their powers?'

Craig was seriously out of touch if he thought Keane would

be a passenger at Celtic Park, or anywhere else for that matter. OK, the Irishman had not come out of his leaving day with much integrity, but no one could deny that his career with United was typified by his indefatigable spirit and that unwillingness to give up or give in, however bad it all looked.

We've now examined why Keane was ousted on the day of 18 November and come to the conclusion that his back-door exit was a shabby way to treat a legend. We've also focused on the dramatic reaction of former players and the fans. Now let's take a closer look at the actual merits of whether he *deserved* a new deal. The press had a lot to say on the matter, with most pundits agreeing that he at least deserved to have been allowed to make a dignified departure.

On the subject of whether the exit itself was correct, there was, naturally enough, a mixed reaction. One writer, whose name is perhaps not widely known to the public, summed it all up the best for me. Frank Malley, chief sports writer at the Press Association, had this rather perceptive take on events:

> The end came, like so many incidents in Roy Keane's tempestuous career, with a devastating suddenness. One minute, he appeared destined at least to see out the season at Old Trafford, the next his Manchester United career was over, wrapped in the diplomatic envelope of 'mutual consent'. The tributes flowed, of course, as they always do when a respected warrior is carried out on his shield for the final time. A 'towering figure'. A 'true great'. The 'best midfielder in the world of his generation'. And there's no doubt Keane was all those things.
>
> But the indecent haste and careful wording surrounding his departure also suggests Keane had become the man United could no longer afford to indulge, the captain whose searing honesty and

growing disaffection was in danger of fraying the fabric of the world's most famous club. Having an injured and ageing Keane on the sidelines in recent times was tantamount to a deranged sniper with a hair-trigger on the rooftop. Anyone in range was in danger of becoming a target – even Sir Alex Ferguson it seemed . . .

That's a fine piece of journalism. Malley went on to say that 'friends of' Ferguson had indicated that one of the big reasons Keane had to go was that he had spoken out of line on MUTV. But Fergie had never directly discouraged his captain from having a go in public. The boss had always made a lot of 'keeping criticism in-house', but it certainly appeared that he had at times also been only too happy for Keane to speak his mind for him.

Also, Ferguson never held back once a player had moved on. I'll never forget his comment about Paul Ince on 5 May 1999. The former United midfielder was now in the red shirt of the Koppites and throwing himself about and getting stuck in against Keane. United were winning 2–1, with goals from Dwight Yorke and Denis Irwin with a minute left, when Ince leapt in to equalise. Fergie, already in a bad mood from Irwin's sending off, could not stop himself when asked what he felt about his ex-midfield king stripping him of two points. 'He's a fuckin' big-time Charlie,' Fergie growled. In fairness, the man had called himself 'The Guvnor' at Old Trafford and driven around with the number plate 'GUV1'. Ince would learn there was only one governor at the Theatre of Dreams.

Back to Malley's piece: I loved the line about Keane being like a 'deranged sniper with a hair-trigger on the rooftop', but would argue that that situation could have been avoided if mentor Ferguson had taken care of his biggest student. As my psychoanalyst friend says, 'He felt left out as Ferguson opted for Queiroz to be his right-hand man. That frustration and resentment would have to boil over sometime, and it did – with the MUTV show and Keane's attack on Queiroz in front of Ferguson.

'You'd think a hard man like Roy Keane would not need a protective arm around the shoulder or a bit of love now and again, but you'd be wrong. The public persona of the man is much different to the real man. He is a shy, insecure boy at heart – and it looks as if he felt he was being pushed away by Ferguson, the one man in football he truly admired, apart from the deceased Clough.'

I accept that Keane's time as a top-class player at the Theatre of Dreams was almost up, but again would argue that he should have been made to feel wanted. Then, I am sure, he would have taken what Ferguson said about talking out of line on board. I am equally sure that if Ferguson had sat him down and told him he was going to make him a player–coach who would have a say along with Queiroz, he would have jumped at the job. Manchester United Football Club ran through the boy's soul and blood.

There was talk that Keane had stormed out of the meeting at Carrington on 18 November because he had been stripped of the captaincy. I am told by a reliable senior United source that this is not true. It was never mentioned and Keane did not storm away – he was devastated to be leaving and apparently had to be helped away, grief-stricken, by his solicitor Michael Kennedy. He knew the separation was inevitable days beforehand; the Carrington get-together was purely to sign the divorce papers.

Another interesting, provocatively opposing angle came via Paul Wilson, writing in *The Observer*, two days after the sacking. He made a claim that Ferguson had actually been *over-sympathetic* towards Keane, by allowing him to stay on when his powers had been on the wane for some time. I'm not sure Wilson got it right in arguing that Ferguson overindulged his skipper – for me, Ferguson is not a man prone to nostalgia – but Wilson's contention puts forward an interesting alternative side to the whole issue. He said:

> The divorce may be directly traceable to heated rows between captain and manager following the former's ill-advised punditry at the start of this month, but the real question is why Ferguson has clung so tenaciously to Keane for so long. By his own admission, Ferguson has been searching for a replacement these past few years, since it became clear how compromised Keane's contribution would be by surgery, yet strangely no business resulted.

Other columnists and writers tended to back up the theory that Keane had got a raw deal at the end of his illustrious United career. Daniel Taylor of *The Guardian* was one such:

> Perhaps the saddest part of Roy Keane's fall from grace at Manchester United is that he will be remembered in future years for the callous nature of his departure rather than what he did on the field. Ushered out of the door by the most ruthless manager in the business, Keane's exit could hardly have been less dignified for a man who has graced the Old Trafford pitch for the last 12 years. Even by Sir Alex Ferguson's standards there was something remarkably brutal about Keane's final few hours as a United player.

Continuing to balance the picture, the celebrated Paul Hayward, arguably one of the triumvirate of sporting columnists who made up Fleet Street's finest in 2005 (along with Patrick Barclay and Patrick Collins), set out a case for Ferguson to be applauded – that, rather than sidestepping the Keane issue, he had actually put the 'Irish rebel' in his rightful place. Hayward said:

> When the blood is wiped from the dagger, this will be remembered as the week when Manchester United restored the power of the badge over the private agendas of superstar individuals.
>
> When the wailing of Keane-obsessed fans has ceased, the vast Old Trafford congregation may even give thanks that Sir Alex Ferguson's authority has been restored . . . when the shock wears off, there may be a welcome sense that a ghost in the machine has been exorcised . . . His [Keane's] mistake was an old one. He assumed he was bigger than the club. The drop of blood on the tip of the dagger tells him he was wrong.

Brilliant writing, articulately put, but I'm not sure I agree with it all. For me, Keane never thought he was bigger than the club; he just wanted a fair deal after the loyal service he had put in, not to be treated like a wicked old has-been by the man for whom he had shed blood.

To round off this section, one more critical analysis, this time one I am in full agreement with. It comes from the aforementioned, excellent Patrick Barclay, writing in the *Sunday Telegraph*. He contended that Keane had every right to talk 'out of line', and that he was peerless in that central midfield spot. Barclay said:

> As for his recurrent, and increasingly frequent, criticisms of fellow United players, they were always interesting for us to hear. Players of high class have a special right to express themselves . . .
>
> Under Ferguson's aegis, Keane perfected the role of the holding midfield player . . . Even today, only

Claude Makelele could be said to perform the same art to anything like the same standard. But Keane in his prime was peerless: the very model of the modern midfield general.

Beautifully stated: Ferguson had thrown his masterpiece in the bin, instead promoting and showcasing more moderate pieces of work in his football team and his back-room team. Just how much of an extraordinary gamble the United boss had taken, we will expose in the next chapter.

FIFTEEN

AND THE SKIPPER WORE GLOVES

'I am only interested in playing for a team that could win the Champions League, so there is no possibility of that at Manchester United' – Juventus goalkeeper Gigi Buffon, 2005

'Roy Keane would not have been fazed by the night ...' – Andy Gray at Benfica as United lost 2–1 and exited the Champions League in the group stages

One hundred and fifty-one words. That, when Ferguson finally got around to giving his personal views on Keane's sacking, was the verbal legacy the United boss decided his skipper's 12-year tenure deserved. And he didn't even stand up in public and say it; he didn't tell it straight through the press – presumably in case they asked him about something away from the agreed script, something not to his liking. He treats the Fourth Estate so badly. Most of the poor hounds who have to deal with him week in, week out are too frightened to throw him a bouncer anyway.

It's just the nature of the man – a man who, like Keane, can be so contrary and so infuriating. But surely it is part of the package that he should carry out his duties with the press? Isn't he actually denying information to United's fans by hiding behind his self-imposed partition? Gary

Lineker in particular has a case against Ferguson. He is made to suffer, along with the millions who watch *Match of the Day*, because the big, bad United boss refuses to speak to the programme – because he feels one of his sons was badly depicted in a BBC documentary. What did that programme have to do with *Match of the Day*? Why should United's fans – and, indeed, football fans throughout the UK who are keen to hear his wisdom – be made to pay the price? Maybe the Glazers can show a bit of muscle and put Sir Cry Baby in his place – get him off his pedestal and in front of those cameras and press hacks; stop him from cancelling press conferences just because he has a quibble with someone who has written something he doesn't like. Talking to the press *is* part of his job, part of his commitment to the fans who cannot afford Sky or MUTV.

Ferguson even stormed out of an interview with MUTV in 2005. Now that really takes the biscuit. How can you fall out with an organisation that panders to your every whim and need? That paints you as the man who is still on top of his game when the days of wine and roses are long gone? It was within the United media empire that Ferguson finally spoke those 151 words of homage to Keane. They would appear in the *United Review* match programme on the night of the European Champions League group encounter with Villarreal. Even within that brief 'tribute', Ferguson couldn't help trying to manipulate the fans onto his side. He said:

> As you are well aware, Manchester United and Roy Keane have parted company, a decision we consider to be in the best interests of club and player. As I said at the time of the announcement, Roy has been a fantastic servant for Manchester United. The best midfield player in the world of his generation, he is already one of the great figures of our club's illustrious history.

>Roy has been central to the success of the club in the last 12 years, and everyone at Old Trafford wishes him well in the rest of his career and beyond. It's always sad when a great player departs the scene of his triumphs, but football doesn't stand still, and I know Roy would be the first to agree we must all focus on tonight's match as a crucial moment in our bid to reach the knockout stage of the UEFA Champions League.

Typical Fergie, that: 'and I know Roy would be the first to agree'. He probably would, but surely the manager could have left out the spin on this one occasion?

The clash with the Spanish outfit was United's first home match in the post-Keane era, and it gave a few pointers to how things would shape up without the great man. Ruud van Nistelrooy was captain for the night, in the absence of Gary Neville and Ryan Giggs. He came out clapping the fans in a pair of black gloves. Can you imagine Roy Maurice Keane *ever* wearing a pair of gloves? Even in the depths of Antarctica? Don't get me wrong here: I think Ruud did a fair job in his mini-run as skipper after Keane's exit, but surely he was sending out the wrong message with his hand-warmers. United needed strong leadership after Keane, not a softly-softly, gently-gently approach.

Ferguson was a little more forthcoming on the subject of who would be his next skipper. He admitted he had drawn up a short list of three to take over from Keane: van Nistelrooy, Giggs and Neville. Before the Villarreal match, he said, 'I have been very lucky to have had a lot of good captains during my time at the club, and Ruud has the right attributes. Every time I have listened to Ruud after games, he has always spoken well. He is clear, precise and speaks with intelligence.

'Ryan has worn the armband many times, purely on seniority, and that is quite right. A player who has served this football club the length of time Ryan has deserves to be recognised. Then you have Neville, who, like Ryan, has served his time. He is a loyal man, a great servant. He is a very emotional and enthusiastic person and has great qualities. There are others in the squad, like Alan Smith and Wayne Rooney, who would love to be captain – Wayne is always telling me – while Rio is another possibility, but I will choose from those three.'

My choice would have been Rooney. Yes, I know he is only 20, he has a history of being a hothead and he would have had to learn quickly, but he was also the closest United had to a Keane-clone in his temperament. He had that unforgiving, brooding dynamism and determination to win, that fierce streak you sometimes need to set you apart from others in the dressing-room. And, from a manipulative point of view, making Rooney captain would have probably secured him to the club for life. Without the armband, he would arguably not feel as tied to United, and, if the domestic domination of Chelsea continued and United did not improve in Europe, he could conceivably be tempted by pastures new. Rooney had left Everton – his home-town club, the love of his footballing life, the club his family supported through the generations – to join United for one reason. It wasn't the money; he could have earned the same £50,000-a-week wages if he had stayed at Goodison. No, it was to better himself, to win medals and to compete in Europe. If he could be that tunnel-visioned with his boyhood idols, why should he feel any more loyalty to a club he had no natural love or allegiance to?

Rooney would have been a fine choice of captain, a brave choice. If Ferguson truly wanted to break for good from the Keane era (of which Neville G was an integral part), Rooney would have helped to draw that line. I'm not denying that Neville G is the best of the rest of the bunch. He is United through and through and a deep, determined, strong character. But where was he when Big Pat Vieira had a go at him in the tunnel at Highbury on 1 February 2005? Hiding in the shadows of his skipper Roy Keane, leaving it up to Keane to fight his corner for him, that's where. For me, that highlighted the difference between the two men: Keane didn't have to think about whether to stand up for his seemingly cowering teammate – he just did it.

Ferguson eventually plumped for Neville, and had no doubt he had made the correct choice with the right-back who had been at the club for 12 years and made close on 500 first-team appearances. He said, 'Given the service Gary has given this club, it is the right decision. Ryan was under consideration, but you cannot expect someone of his age to be running up and down the touchline every game. He will still play a lot of matches for us, but we want to try and keep the freshness in his legs, so he will not play every week.'

Ferguson certainly took a gamble with own future by jettisoning Keane before the Villarreal game. United had huffed and puffed in their Champions League group matches and defeats by the Spaniards, and Benfica a fortnight later, would see them out of the competition. Given the Glazers needed every penny they could lay their hands on to service those massive debts, an early elimination from Europe could conceivably have resulted in a similarly prompt exit for the United boss.

Ferguson admitted he was throwing the dice and hoping for good fortune. He could certainly have done with Keane's steadying hand on the tiller as the Spaniards arrived at Old Trafford to face a relatively youthful United. With Keane gone and seasoned performers such as Giggs injured and Gary Neville only just back from a three-month groin-injury absence, the United manager conceded that his young team were lacking crucial top-level experience for a game they could not afford to lose. Ferguson said, 'We have not got enough experience in the team at this time, and that is a handicap for us. If you look at the graph of teams that have success in Europe, they are mainly very experienced teams with an average age of between 28 and 30. You can't say that about our team at the moment. We do have young players with incredible ability, but consistency is the key to going on a run in European football, and young players do have dips in form from time to time. Our job is to get as much experience into them as quickly as possible.

'Over the last couple of years, we have tried to build a new team. The 1999 team couldn't last forever, and the horrible part of this job is that you see great players getting older. The demands are so great at this club that you have to change things quicker than at other clubs, but the only reason for doing that is to make United better.'

United keeper Edwin van der Sar also admitted that a positive result against Villarreal was vital if the club were to ease the pressure brought about by Keane's departure. He said, 'We are not concerned about the result going badly, but we are out of the qualifying positions at the moment and we have a duty to perform well and win. It's important that we ease the pressure on the players, the manager and the club by getting a result. I think that we turned the page by beating Chelsea two weeks ago, and the confidence we gained from that allowed us to win at Charlton, but we have to play that way against Villarreal.'

In the event, United would draw 0–0 against the Spaniards – a result that meant they would have to win in their final group match in Benfica to guarantee qualification for the knockout phase, having drawn a blank for the fourth time in their five Champions League encounters.

It was a stuttering show from United, the gloom lifted only by the man-of-the-match display provided inevitably by Rooney. The Scouse youngster appeared keen to take up Roy's mantle as United's spiritual leader. He was everywhere, trying to inspire the troops, and, with a bit more luck, could have had a goal or two. The fans did not try to hide where their allegiances lay in the great Ferguson–Keane debate. One banner hung from the Stretford End bore the simple but poignant words: '12 YEARS – THANKS FOR EVERYTHING ROY' and chants of 'Keano, Keano' echoed around the stadium from start to finish.

One man in particular seemed to miss Keane more than most. He was Paul Scholes. Without his central-midfield partner for most of the season, Scholes had looked a pale imitation of the player who, since the departure of Cantona, had become the team's creative fulcrum. Alan Smith was still learning the Keane role, and it was debatable whether he would ever be able to fill Keane's shoes. For now, the closest he had got to emulating the master was having a skinhead crop to make himself look more fearsome. His tackling outside the box, with consequent free-kicks awarded against United, was still a cause of major concern but, to give Smith his due, he was a tryer and a battler and he deserved a chance.

It's just that he didn't seem to have bedded in with Scholes. The ginger-head played like a little boy lost. No, in the immediate aftermath of Keane's departure, United found it tough, both physically and emotionally, as the full extent of Ferguson's act sunk in. One major criticism I have of Ferguson is that he does not appear to be able to spot a gift horse when it is presented before his very nose. Why didn't he shake off the gloom by throwing in the brilliant Giuseppe Rossi? He could have allowed Scholes a much-needed break and let the American-born Italian youth international blow away the cobwebs of the Roy saga.

After the Villarreal game, Ferguson was asked about Rossi, and his eyes lit up with excitement. He accepted the link between Scholes and Rossi and, indeed, was happy enough to hail the boy as the best natural finisher to come through the United ranks since Scholes. So why not give him an extended run-out in the first team, then – at a time when a breath of fresh air was most definitely needed? Sometimes, Ferguson's decisions must have baffled even Queiroz. Rossi had already netted two senior goals for the Red Devils, including one on his Premiership debut at Sunderland in October. The 18 year old had also found the net 14 times in 13 matches for United's reserves.

No wonder Ferguson admitted, 'Without question, Giuseppe is the most natural goalscorer we have had come through the club since Paul Scholes. He is a wonderful finisher and not dissimilar to Paul in a way. When Paul first came to the club, he was a centre-forward. Then he started to learn the game and how to drop in behind the striker. Probably Giuseppe can play straight through the middle more than Paul would have done, but there is a great similarity in the cool head he has in the box. You can't really teach finishing to that level. We do coaching sessions every day, but the natural ones are there for everyone to see. Giuseppe is a terrific finisher, and that gives him a real chance.'

Lady Luck had not deserted Ferguson in his moment of need. After the poor show against Villarreal, United suddenly came together as a unit. Smith started to make more of an impact in the Keane role, and Rooney and Ruud did what they are paid to do: they scored goals. It may have had something to do with Ferguson's decision to take more control at training and on match days. Previously, he had left much of the day-to-day organisation to Queiroz, but now he would be seen regularly pacing the touchline with coach Mickey Phelan, encouraging his post-Keane boys on. The Portuguese stayed motionless in his seat. Maybe Keane's departure had one unexpected bonus for United fans if Queiroz's wings had been clipped. Ironic if that was the case, given Keane had blown up over the ever-expanding role allocated to his rival, ultimately forcing Ferguson to choose between the two. The Reds won their next match 2–1 at West

Ham: a fine result as the Hammers were settling well back into the top flight. They also beat West Brom 3–1 in the Carling Cup and Portsmouth 3–0 in the Premiership. Scholes would finally look like the player of old in the latter encounter, scoring his first goal of the season and creating chances for Ruud and Rooney.

Were United now emerging from the haunting shadow of the departed Keane? Sir Bobby Robson certainly thought so. He told the *Mail on Sunday* that Keane's exit was already paying dividends, as highlighted by United's form in their last three matches. He said:

> Keane is still a great player, but there comes a time when an individual can get too big and start doing things beyond his remit. He tried to criticise his teammates, and I've noticed how well those teammates have played since Keane left. It's like a big weight has been lifted from their shoulders.
>
> Darren Fletcher scored against Chelsea, and you only have to look at John O'Shea's form as well. He can't be intimidated by Keane now and has found a new lease of life in the last couple of weeks. I don't think it's coincidence he has scored goals against West Ham and West Brom recently. His confidence has improved – it helps when the captain isn't always carping at you.

There were rumours that Ferguson would not be long joining Keane out of the door, and the United boss did nothing to discourage the speculation exactly a week after Roy was sacked. It was clear United were a club in transition, what with the continuing uncertainty of the Glazer takeover, the departure of Keane and the possible end of the road for the Scot who had built the empire and brought unprecedented glory to Manchester United. It was a shame that his latter days were likely to be branded as days of failure after all he had given to the club. On 25 November 2005, he confirmed the United job would be his last in football, saying, 'I don't have a long time left, but I still have some time left, I hope! When I complete my service, I will retire and I will deserve it. I'm finished once I leave United. I've said that many times.'

The key game of the season for Ferguson would be the Champions League final group match at Benfica. Victory and his decision to axe Keane would not be brought up for discussion. Plus, more importantly, from his point of view, a win would shoo away the wolves from the door, those who wanted time called on his stewardship. If he didn't get the result, all hell would break loose.

Given those outcomes, the match was arguably Ferguson's most important since Mark Robins saved his job in 1990. Many believe that a defeat back then to Nottingham Forest in the third round of the FA Cup would have ended Ferguson's reign. But he survived and prospered after Robins's goal knocked out Forest. As for the Benfica clash, Ferguson would claim he did not feel under any extra pressure before the match – even though the Glazer family's business plan was dependent upon United reaching the latter rounds of the Champions League. Ferguson said, 'The finance does not come into it for me. I feel responsible for picking the right team, the right tactics, the right motivation and the right atmosphere in the dressing-room. That's my job.' Fair enough, but his job was also to produce a winning, successful side at the world's biggest football club – a new side, and one that would have to do it without the inspirational Keane in either a playing or coaching role.

Against Benfica, all Ferguson's chickens came home to roost. If you believe in karma and that Keane's sacking was unfair, the night of 7 December 2005 was the one when Ferguson's treatment of him rebounded like an unforgiving boomerang in his stunned face. His United team were outshone by a second-rate European force, one incidentally missing their top three players. United went down 2–1, but it could have been worse. Balls were punted from the back to the front like a poor-man's Wimbledon, and the midfield was a joke. I watched the match on Sky Sports and, at the end of a rank 90 minutes, the incisive Andy Gray would put the ultimate boot in on Ferguson, probably without realising how much the one particular weak spot he had identified would hurt. 'They missed the big man,' he began, his words slow, then working up to a hammer-blow crescendo. 'They missed his leadership; he wouldn't have allowed half of what happened out there tonight to have come about. Roy Keane would not have been fazed by the night – he would have got stuck in and sorted United out.'

They sounded like words that could eventually form Ferguson's footballing obituary. The result confirmed the current state of Ferguson's management and the team he had built: this was the first time that United had failed to get past the group stages in the Champions League since the 1994–95 season. And by finishing bottom of Group D, United did not even have the consolation of a place in the UEFA Cup.

Ferguson is not a pretty sight in defeat. He bristles in his defensiveness and can come across as arrogant. He refused to answer questions about his future after the game and claimed the critics were wrong to knock him – after all, he had the basis of a new all-conquering side. He must have been watching a different match from the rest of us. When asked if he was worried about his future, he growled, 'I am not going to answer that. I've got a job to do, it's a great job and I've confidence in my players. We have a job to do, and the rebuilding will carry on. We are disappointed, there's no doubt about that. It's a blow, and you have to regroup. This club has always risen from difficult situations, and we will again.'

To give him his due, Sir Alex did admit that a lack of experience in the team had made it extra tough for United. He said, 'We probably lacked that experience and ability, and when we needed top players, they weren't there. The confidence is coming back into the team, and in the last few games there's been a growing sense of confidence in the club and they've played well.' One expression there says it all: 'when we needed top players, they weren't there'. No, Roy Keane was probably watching the game on the box at home in Cheshire, and also probably shouting at Ferdinand to get back into his correct position and telling Ronaldo to cut out the thrills that were leading to a dead end.

New club captain Gary Neville had not seemed an imposing enough figure in the Stade de Luz. It was his job to sort the mess out, but he did not appear to get among his players and have a word, as Keane would have done. Afterwards, he said, 'Qualifying for the knockout stages has been par for the course – but we have not been good enough in this group. We know over the next few days people will criticise us, and rightly so, because our performances haven't been up to our standards. But we have to stick together and perform in the League because we have to close on Chelsea.'

Close on Chelsea? Surely the next thing was to bring some realism to the club? Forget Mourinho's men – and keep your eyes peeled for Liverpool, Arsenal and maybe even Spurs. The fact was this: United had consolidated their position as one of the top dogs in the second tier of the Premiership immediately after Keane's departure – you know, the one that contains the three aforementioned teams, the one that could not hope to compete with Chelsea, unless the London club suffered an illogical, unlikely collapse. Once upon a time, United were the Chelsea of the day – now the Reds even resorted to giving away a souvenir poster in their match programme to commemorate having beaten the Blues 1–0 at Old Trafford. How times and perceptions had changed in the latter days of the Ferguson era.

Ferguson outlined his vision post-Keane in this manner: 'The whole logic of the past couple of years has been building a new team. Fletcher is 21; Rooney and Ronaldo are 20. They will get better for sure. And Pique and Rossi will come through in the next wave.' But who would be the new Keane? The obvious man was Rino Gattuso, the bearded warrior at the heart of Italy's midfield. He was a proven winner with Milan, with one European Cup and two Italian titles. And the good news for Ferguson was that a year beforehand he had made it clear he would love a move to Old Trafford with his Scottish wife, Monica. Another plus for Sir Alex was that Gattuso had developed his play under former United number two Walter Smith, when Smith was the manager of Glasgow Rangers. He had spotted Gattuso playing in a youth tournament for Perugia and enticed him to Rangers at the age of 17. The combative midfielder won a Scottish Premier League title before Smith departed for Everton and Rino returned to Italy.

Gattuso admitted: 'Walter was like a second father to me when I went to Glasgow, because I was just a young boy. He gave me my chance to play for a big team, and he will always be in my heart because of that. I learned a lot from him. I love the British style of football. It's about running 100 per cent for 90 minutes and tackling like men. In Italy, if you tackle a player, they moan to the referee. The Scots will not do that.'

What more of an invitation did Ferguson need? The man was ready and willing – all it needed was, say, £15 million of the readies the Glazers had promised and a call from Ferguson. It was surely time for the Glazers to put up or shut up? They hadn't contributed a penny to the transfer pot since May – although Joel had been talking big figures to the press and whoever would listen.

There had been much talk that Germany's captain

Michael Ballack would be the man to replace Keane. It looked as though Ferguson was counting on it when he gave the Irishman his marching orders. The press were on high alert for an announcement: it appeared plausible, a way of consoling the Old Trafford faithful after the dismal treatment of their favourite son. United had been sounding out the Bayern Munich midfielder for months and were 99 per cent confident he would come to Old Trafford.

As a replacement for Keane in his role of captain, he would have been ideal. He possessed an arrogant air, a quality that would have stood him in good stead in the cauldron of the Premiership. He had already got up the nose of Mourinho by diving for a penalty when Bayern had visited Stamford Bridge in the Champions League a year earlier. That would help to endear him to United for starters. Plus the Glazers were happy that he would not command a fee, as his contract would expire in the summer of 2006. Sure, his wages would be around the £100,000-a-week mark, but they could probably ship out a couple more big earners to accommodate Ballack.

The real problem with Ballack was that he was not a replacement for Keane the holding player. He was more in the Paul Scholes mould: attacking was his forte, rather than defence. He was no Gattuso, although if United could have lured both of them, it would have been an excellent coup.

By the end of November, Ferguson faced a problem he had not anticipated. Ballack, the man he had staked all his bets on, decided he did not, after all, want to move to Manchester. His head had been turned by the prospect of a move to Real Madrid and by a continued campaign by Uli Hoeness at Bayern to undermine United. The German club's general manager taunted the Red Devils through the media, asking why Ballack would want to take what he saw as a definite step down. Even the legendary Franz Beckenbauer, who thrived on a whiter-than-white image, joined in the muck-slinging aimed at United. The Bayern president said, 'I know Manchester United and AC Milan are in the hunt, but Michael will only improve himself by going to Madrid. Anywhere else and it will not be a step up. Much as I want him to stay, I feel he will probably leave. If he does, the decision will only make sense if he goes to Real Madrid.'

Ferguson faced another public loss of face when Ballack finally decided United were not for him. Sir Alex and United had already looked rather foolish and negligent when they had let Arjen Robben and Ronaldinho slip through their fingers – now they were about to face a similar nightmare over Ballack. Step forward spin-master Ferguson, who would personally make sure United would not lose face again. The only problem was that everyone knew Ballack had cancelled on United, rather than the other way around. Ferguson tried to hide his blushes, saying, 'He's a great player, and we have considered it and have had discussions with his people. But he is similar to players who play in that position already, like Wayne Rooney and Paul Scholes. We want to target players in other positions. The biggest problem for us is numbers. We have been operating with a lot of young players in the team and we badly need a stronger squad. That is why we are targeting a couple of other positions.'

United were lucky enough to already have a replacement for Scholes – his name was Rossi – so the loss of Ballack was not the end of the world. However, the quest for his signature marked another unsatisfactory episode in Ferguson's 2005 dealings at Old Trafford. Other names were mentioned but they were, frankly, not fit to lace Keane's boots, let alone replace him. One was Aldo Duscher, the Argentine who played for Deportivo La Coruna and whose claim to fame was his cropping of David Beckham before the 2002 World Cup finals. Inevitably, the name of Thomas Gravesen, the former Everton journeyman and current Real Madrid reserve, was thrown in for good measure.

It was rapidly turning into a farce. Ferguson had apparently given no more thought to the timing of Keane's departure than he had to Beckham's. Ferguson confirmed he had acted without enough thought when he admitted he did not even know if the Glazers would stump up any readies in the January transfer window. He said, 'You certainly can't guarantee that January will be a buying time for us. The players we would all like are cup-tied in Europe, and any club doing well will not want to sell anyone, let alone to Manchester United. So you're immediately eliminating a large percentage of clubs.' In the event, the Glazers did loosen the purse strings to the tune of £12 million, thus allowing Ferguson to snap up two defenders, Patrice Evra and Nemanja Vidic – although, of course, that did not solve the most pressing problem, namely finding a replacement for Roy Keane.

Surely Alex Ferguson and United should have been ready for Keane's exit by having someone lined up? Well, they did have – Ballack – but there was no Plan B when the German walked away. How can you let the only two reliable holding midfielders – Keane and Phil Neville – leave the club within months of each other and have no realistic alternative in place?

Still, there was Smith, wasn't there? Maybe Ferguson had kicked Keane out knowing Smith could handle the heat? But here's Ferguson again, talking after he got a kick in the Ballacks: 'We're fairly lightweight in terms of numbers and physically, too, when it comes to midfield, certainly when compared to Chelsea. Unfortunately, it's not an easy task. We've been talking about replacing Keane for two or three years, but the difficulty is finding someone.' So why didn't Ferguson act on these thoughts? And did he really think Smith was 'lightweight . . . physically'? The sad truth is that a lot of people were left wondering what was going on at Old Trafford in the two weeks that followed the skipper's sacking.

SIXTEEN

KILLER ROY WAS HERE

'Even when I play cards, I play to win' – Ireland captain Roy Keane to journalists the day before his side were due to play the Netherlands in September 2001

'Somebody once said to me, because they are not my words, that if you are second in a big club, you are the first of the last. You cannot be second, only first. If you are in Real Madrid, Barcelona, AC Milan, Juventus, Chelsea, Manchester United or Bayern Munich, you cannot be second in the eyes of the people' – Jose Mourinho, 2005

'I'm not at Manchester United to keep everyone happy' – Roy Keane

We have spent a fair amount of time eulogising over Keane's achievements and his worth to Manchester United and Ireland, but there's another side to the boy that made me shiver a bit as I worked on this book: the mean, illogical, inhumane Keane who would deliberately crop an opponent, or stamp on him; the blustering, fighting Keane who was out of control. That's the Keane some fans adored, but for me, and many others, it was the Keane we abhorred. This side to his nature makes it hard to respect him, let alone love him, and threatens to bring his ultimate, overall footballing legacy down to a baser level.

It seems to me that in between the years 1999 and 2000 Roy Keane hit rock bottom in his battle with the demon drink. During 2000, there were suggestions that he had been treated for depression – although both he and Michael Kennedy laughed it off, while, at the same time, threatening to sue anyone who said it had happened. Well, I am not saying it happened. All I am saying is that after 2000 I cannot recall any major stories about Keane and the effects of alcohol upon him, so it seems fair to speculate that the problem ended around that time. Keane himself told *The Observer* that his binge drinking came to an end in May 1999, when he spent a night in the cells after a brawl in a Manchester club. Alex Ferguson had to make the trip to a Manchester police station in the early hours, just four days before the FA Cup final and ten days before the European Cup final. In his autobiography, Keane admitted, 'There was a pattern here, the story of me, drink and cities: Cork, Dublin, Nottingham, Manchester. It adds up to aggravation.'

The Observer asked Keane if his brief jail experience was the turning point for him and drink. He replied, 'Maybe, yeah. It was obviously getting me in trouble. I mean, without drink, that whole thing would not have gone beyond first base. I wouldn't have been there to begin with. Or, I would have walked away. It really pissed me off, the gaffer having to come and get me, and all. That was a long night. That was a hell of a long night.'

There was talk that Keane had been attending the rooms of Alcoholics Anonymous for help. Again, that was strongly denied, and we are glad to state that. But there was definitely a change in the man after 2000.

The more I got into Keane's make-up while carrying out research, the more I felt compassion, empathy and sympathy towards him – and I never thought I would say that. Far from being a mono-dimensional tough guy, the Roy behind the mask emerged as a defensive, shy, introverted character who found it difficult to mingle and mix, the natural recluse who is essentially a good, decent, loyal person. He did remarkably well given his nature, but he may have to develop even more as a person if he is to achieve his aim of one day becoming manager of Manchester United. Sometimes the big stick doesn't work; sometimes you need the arm-around-the-shoulder approach, as Ferguson would learn in Keane's final days at Manchester United.

Stories of Keane's excesses and bust-ups are legendary and could probably fill a book by themselves. That is not our remit: instead, let's look at a few and examine how, morally and professionally right or wrong, Roy allowed himself to get involved . . .

In 1992, Keane was arrested after rowdy scenes outside a Nottingham nightclub, but he was released without charge. It was part of the learning curve he found himself on after making the journey to England from Cork, but clearly the early warning signs about booze and its effect on him should have been heeded.

In 1993, he was thrown out of another nightclub after being caught up in a brawl. Again, the booze was doing him no good and he hadn't yet suffered enough pain to kick it into touch.

In 1995, he was sent off for the first time in his career for stamping on Crystal Palace's Gareth Southgate during United's 2–0 FA Cup semi-final replay win. Keane was hit with a disrepute charge by the Football Association and later fined £5,000. Keane's defence was, 'He shouldn't be lying on the floor. Defenders shouldn't be on their backsides. I felt that he got in the way.' Of course, his defence was laughable and well out of order. The stamping itself was no laughing matter: it bore the imprint of a callous, ruthless, inhumane being. It was nothing to be proud of. Glenn Moore, writing in *The Independent* on April 1995, also pointed out that Keane's action was still more deplorable after a fan had died during the first match between the clubs. Glenn said:

> There were less than 18,000 to see it, the lowest FA Cup semi-final attendance for 50 years, but it would have been better if Manchester United had reached their record 13th final behind closed doors last night. Instead, the faithful, and a television audience, watched a match which was already overshadowed by the death of a supporter become disfigured by a double sending-off and a mass brawl.
>
> It was not the way to remember Paul Nixon, who died during fighting before Sunday's drawn first match. Neither was the game much of a tribute. It was a scrappy, niggling affair, short on quality and won by United with some ease through first-half goals from Gary Pallister and Steve Bruce. United now meet Everton, at Wembley, on 20 May. Roy Keane, who was dismissed for stamping on a prone Gareth Southgate, will probably have served his suspension by then. United should make a stand and ban him themselves.

In 1996 and 1997, Keane had several run-ins with new Irish boss Mick McCarthy. In March '96, as mentioned earlier, he was sent off on his 30th appearance for the Republic in McCarthy's first match as manager. And two months later, as we know, he failed to report for McCarthy's testimonial and Republic training after going on holiday to Italy and was consequently left out for six matches by the national boss. Then, in April 1997, he missed a penalty for the Republic against Romania and escaped without punishment after being involved in an alleged butting incident.

September 1997 was a particularly bad month for Keane. In the early hours of 25 September, he was caught up in a scuffle at a Stretford hotel following the 2–2 draw with Chelsea but escaped action after witness statements were withdrawn. He was also interviewed by police over claims that he had threatened a neighbour during a row over Keane's straying dogs. The month also saw him injure his knee in the famous brush with Alfie Haaland at Elland Road.

On 17 May 1999, Keane was arrested after a woman alleged he kicked her in a bar, but he was released without charge. As we have seen earlier in this chapter, this was the moment when Keane came to his senses and realised he and booze would never be a marriage made in heaven. In the same year, he was angered by the new contract United had offered him, saying, 'I was a bit annoyed with the first offer put to me. Deep down, they must have known it wasn't something I could sign. Our dealings have to be realistic. I am not naive enough to settle for anything less than a reasonable valuation of my worth.'

In 2000, Keane branded United's decision to blame his £52,000-a-week wages for the hike in season-ticket prices as 'a stupid mistake'. As we have previously noted, the club had sent a letter to fans claiming that one of the reasons for the ticket increases was Keane's wage rise. I think Roy had a fair point here – why should the club use his name to blackmail the fans? The letter stank more than a little of resentment that the board had been forced to pay fair wages to their best, and most influential, player.

Also in 2000, after a Champions League clash against Dynamo Kiev at Old Trafford, Keane had his go at the corporate fans at United, saying, 'Sometimes you wonder, do they understand the game of football? We're 1–0 up, then there are one or two stray passes and they're getting on players' backs. It's just not on. At the end of the day, they need to get behind the team. Away from home, our fans are fantastic; I'd call them the hardcore fans. But at home, they have a few drinks and probably the prawn sandwiches, and they don't realise what's going on out on the pitch. I don't think some of the people who come to Old Trafford can spell football, never mind understand it.' I can laugh at Keane's comments, but could also accuse him of hypocrisy. Without those corporate fans, would he have been able to secure such a fat new contract at Old Trafford? Weren't they actually paying his wages? Wasn't he biting the hands that were feeding him? Plus, surely they were entitled to have an opinion and be able to voice it. Why should they simply toe the line set by Keane? No, it struck me that on this occasion Roy was highlighting himself as being one of those who loves to dish stick out, but can't take it when it is returned.

In 2001, Keane's problems with the Football Association of Ireland escalated over the players being treated in a second-class way: 'I am not pointing the finger at anybody, but if there was anything to make me say "I am going to spend the week with my wife and kids at home" that would be it. Where we trained in Clonshaugh it was abysmal, and it has been for as long as I've known it. I was fairly critical of the seating arrangements for the flight over here when the officials were at the front and the players behind.' Roy was spot on to have a go at the blazers: why should they be treated like lords? They were representatives, pure and simple. They were not the stars; the players were.

In the same year, Keane revealed that he did not think that Manchester United at the time were a great side: 'The great teams get back to finals and win it, and this just shows we are not a great team. We're just an average team in a lot of areas, but it's up to the manager and the rest of the staff to look at that. We seem to be falling further behind these teams like Real Madrid.' This was one of the great bugbears of Roy's career at Manchester United – and it can be traced back to that night in Turin in 1999 when his foul on Zidane and subsequent yellow card ruled him out of the European Cup final. He would never forgive himself for missing what would have been the biggest match of his career; he never truly believed he had earned the medal that was his when United beat Bayern Munich in Barcelona.

It was also bad news for any of his teammates who appeared to him to be slacking off. Like Ferguson, Keane needed that second appearance and victory in a European Cup final. Their attempts and subsequent failures to achieve it would evidently haunt them both: both appearing to believe they had not fulfilled their destinies.

In April 2001, Keane was sent off after again clashing with Haaland. Having suffered a serious knee injury in the foul against Haaland earlier in his career, Keane finally took his revenge in the derby against Manchester City. A crude stamp on the Norwegian's knee earned a red card and left Haaland badly injured. In his autobiography, Keane admitted, 'I waited until five minutes before the end. I hit him hard. Even in the dressing-room afterwards I had no remorse. My attitude was "What goes around comes around." He got his just rewards. My attitude is an eye for an eye.'

This is the big one – the incident for which Keane will be most remembered by many fans – and it is his own fault. The attack on Haaland was disgraceful, and Keane compounded the problem by boasting about it in his autobiography, as if it were something to be proud of. It was actually a disastrous self-inflicted stain on his own character. He would later admit that he would not want his children to be raised with the 'eye for an eye' approach – surely, in doing so, admitting that he knew he had done wrong?

When, 18 months later, Keane conceded he had deliberately set out to get Haaland, there were calls for him to face fresh punishment (he had been banned for three games for the original offence), but Alex Ferguson rushed to his defence, saying he had 'no case to answer'. In the event, he was fined £150,000 by the FA and banned for an additional five matches. The split between fans who backed and condemned Keane was roughly fifty-fifty on websites and phone-ins at the time.

These were three of the many voices backing Keane posted on the BBC's Sports Talk on Friday, 30 August 2002:

> Just because a person has the balls to admit what we all know occurs week in week out doesn't mean he should receive extra punishment on top of a suspension already served. Chopper Harris prided himself on such things and players like Gerrard, Le Saux and Vieira consistently do it but have yet to admit it. Honesty, it seems, isn't always the best policy.
>
> – Ciaran, Ireland

> He was punished enough when he received the three-game ban after his red card. If there was no revenge, aggression and, in some cases, hatred in the game, football just wouldn't be as interesting.
>
> – Alastair, N. Ireland

> Where is this ridiculous witch hunt going to end? Perhaps any boxer who throws a low punch should be charged with ABH? Or maybe high tackles in rugby could carry a mandatory jail term? Roy Keane plays a physical contact sport at the highest level,

and as such is required to demonstrate such aggression to be able to compete successfully. He should not be punished – every footballer in the country commits revenge tackles. Roy is just passionate – he is a red-blooded male and is just being honest. I have seen far worse tackles than that where the player didn't even get booked. Football has become a sissy game! All they care about is their pretty cars and their huge pay cheque.

– Tim, England

And these are three of the dozens who argued that Keane should be punished anew:

It is quite staggering that the only defence offered for Keane's premeditated attack on Haaland is that other players do the same but do not admit to it. Does it follow that criminals who confess should not be prosecuted, since there are bound to be other criminals at large who have not confessed to their crimes?

– Tim, Cardiff, UK

I thought there surely couldn't be anyone on the planet who could put forward a constructive defence for Keane. But sadly there are. Talk of a witch hunt is pathetic. So too is all this 'he's been punished already' (the same nonsense we had with Cantona). It's a simple concept. That is the law. If you assault somebody in your job, put them out of work for 18 months and stupidly admit it, you don't just get punished at work but by the law too. Football is no more a place for intentional career-ending assaults than cricket or tennis.

– Mark, England

> Keane is a disgrace to football, and should be severely punished for his actions. He is an embarrassment to both club and country.
>
> – Mary Smith, Ireland

Journalists on the sports pages were also split in their views, although the former editor of the *Today* radio programme Rod Liddle, who is also now making a name for himself on the sports pages of the *Sunday Times*, had no doubt about Keane's guilt, saying that, if he had his way, Keane 'wouldn't get the chance to sign for another club because he'd still be banged up and certainly banned from the game for life'.

If there can be any defence for Keane's crime, this would be it: Haaland played in an international game for Norway a few days after the tackle, and the injury that ended his career was to his left knee, whereas Keane had crunched the right knee. You could also argue that the additional five-match ban and £150,000 fine were punishment for his honesty. If he had kept his mouth shut in the book, he would not have brought the FA down on top of him. Then again, the comments he made about the incident were *the* key selling point of the book's serialisation, the words that ensured Keane would profit well beyond the sum of £150,000. My view remains that the Irishman was bang out of order on both counts.

Keane was in the spotlight again in August 2001, after centre-half Jaap Stam was shown the door at Old Trafford after a conflict with Ferguson. Stam signed for Lazio in a £16.5 million deal – a move that upset the fans and Keane. The Irishman said, 'His transfer illustrates how little power footballers have in the game. Contracts mean nothing. He has discovered that, to football clubs, players are just expensive pieces of meat. The harsh realities remain, and when a club decide they want to sell, there is little you can do.' I back Roy on this one. Clubs complain quickly enough if a player wants away or asks for an improved deal, but when the boot is on the other foot, they show no mercy. Stam was merely the latest to feel Sir Alex's ire – Beckham and Keane himself would follow.

In September 2001, Keane was sent off for the ninth time in his United career, after raising his hands at Newcastle's Alan Shearer. It appeared he was trying to chin Shearer as United lost 4–3. Later, he would admit the incident nearly drove him to quit football. Keane said, 'I try to maintain control, try to stay calm. But the red mist sometimes descends – and once that happens 50,000 people would not be able to stop me bursting into a fit of rage.' I had sympathy for Keane here in that the Geordie skipper had seemed to have drawn him in – but that was still no excuse for losing it.

In the same season, Keane lashed out at his teammates for taking it too easy. He questioned their commitment and prophetically warned that the Reds could end the 2001–02 season without a trophy. Keane said, 'Players should be proud to play and give 100 per cent. We're not asking for miracles. We're asking them to do what they should be doing. When players don't do that, it's bloody frustrating. We're going to find it hard to win the League, and if we end up with no trophies, there's something wrong.' Fair enough. He was the skipper and it was his job to motivate any passengers within the side.

In May 2002, he was thrown out of the World Cup after the infamous row with McCarthy over the Republic's preparations and training facilities. Keane said, 'You've seen the training pitch and I'm not being a prima donna. Training pitch, travel arrangements, getting through the bloody airport when we were leaving: it's the combination of things.' When talks to clear the air with McCarthy descended into a 'slanging match', the Republic boss promptly sent his best player home. I have already expressed my feelings about this in an earlier chapter – I backed Keane against Big Mick – but, of course, there were those who stood against Roy. The issue divided Ireland, split it down the middle. BBC TV pundit Mark Lawrenson publicly declared himself to be on McCarthy's side, saying, 'the bottom line was this: if you or I talked to our boss the way Keane spoke to Republic of Ireland manager Mick McCarthy, we would have been sacked on the spot. It was such a tirade of personal abuse that I just didn't see any way back for Keane. I mean, how on earth could McCarthy let Keane back in the squad for the World Cup? I think that McCarthy would have had to resign if Keane reappeared. Despite all this talk of an apology from the player to patch things up, I never thought it was possible. After all, the squad said they didn't want him back . . .'

In September 2002, Keane was dismissed for elbowing Jason McAteer during Manchester United's 1–1 draw at Sunderland. It was the tenth dismissal of his United career and followed his disagreements with McAteer over his sending home from the World Cup the previous May. Again, Roy was reeled in by an opponent; again, he could not control his anger. McAteer had mocked an earlier foul committed on him by Roy in the match by mimicking a writing action with his hands, as if to say, 'Will this be going into your book some time?'

On 25 February 2004, Roy was red-carded as United lost in Porto in a Champions League last-16 clash. United's captain was sent off for a stamp on goalkeeper Vitor Baia. His irresponsibility cost United big-time. He missed the second leg at Old Trafford as United were knocked out of Europe by Jose Mourinho's eventual champions.

In 2005, he had that confrontation with Patrick Vieira before the clash with Arsenal. The duo had always been at loggerheads, and Keane had commented afterwards on the fact that Vieira was born in Dakar, Senegal, and yet had opted to play for France. Underneath the nonsense, though, both men had major respect for the other.

Arsenal's other golden boy of the last decade, Thierry Henry, also had major respect for Keane, and also realised there was more to the man than met the eye. Henry said, 'People often talk about Roy Keane as if he was a hooligan, but the lad knows how to play football. Yes, he is aggressive. Yes, he is cantankerous. Yes, if the ball is between him and you in midfield, he makes you jump. But beyond that, he is a super footballer. He scores, he influences his team and the crowd. He'll be respected for ever. He is a football legend with Republic of Ireland and Manchester United.'

On 16 May 2005, Keane committed another faux pas: angering Southampton fans by mocking their relegation plight with downward thumb signs, before being ushered off the pitch after a 2–1 win at St Mary's, a result that contributed to the Saints' drop from the Premiership. His actions were childish and unnecessary. Saints had been beaten – was there really a need to rub their noses in it as well?

On 21 May 2005, Keane was denied the opportunity to pick up a record-equalling fifth FA Cup winner's medal as Arsenal won through on penalties at the Millennium Stadium. United finished the 2005 season without a trophy, and Keane said, 'Results don't lie and the table doesn't lie. Our performance levels have not been good enough. Everyone at this club needs to look at themselves and ask whether they are giving 100 per cent to the football club.' Captain Perfection was at work again, trying to motivate his troops in the only way he knew: as indeed he had done throughout his United career.

Now those days were over. Keane would never again win silverware as a player at United. Indeed, his sights would soon be set on whipping a new set of bhoys into shape at Parkhead in Glasgow. How would he go down there? Could he fit in with Gordon Strachan? And how would he cope if everything wasn't to his own impeccable standards? Exit the wild man of Old Trafford: enter Roy the Bhoy.

SEVENTEEN

ROY'S THE BHOY

'I have said I wouldn't mind finishing my career at Celtic, but as long as United want me, I am happy' – Roy Keane, 2000

'I've been fortunate to work under two of the game's great managers, in Brian Clough and Alex Ferguson, and the thought of being manager of Manchester United would be fantastic' – Roy Keane, 2003

'He has the strength of personality, communication and intelligence to go into it [management] if he wants to do it' – Brian Kerr, former Republic of Ireland manager, 2005

Right up until the eleventh hour, this chapter was provisionally entitled 'The Real T'ing' and was being structured to explain why and how Roy Keane had plumped for and finally signed for Spanish legends Real Madrid. Then, suddenly, on Wednesday, 14 December 2005, Keane typically changed tack. He got sick of waiting for the Real deal to materialise and signed for Celtic the following day.

It was back to the drawing board and a series of calls to insider sources in Spain and Scotland to ascertain exactly what had happened to a deal that appeared, on paper at least, better suited to a 34 year old in the sunset of his career. Instead of a Champions League swansong and the chance to team up with Ronaldo, Raul, Zidane and Beckham (again), Roy would be heading for the likes of Clyde and Dundee in the frozen winter and a much more – how shall we put it? – austere finale to his footballing life.

Unravelling the transfer trail that led to Celtic Park took some doing. My sources tell me the basic facts are these: Keane wanted to sign for Madrid but got sick of their dilly-dallying and indecision and, hardly being a man of patience, decided enough was enough and to put the saga to bed by joining Celtic. Of course, there was a certain misty-eyed romance in joining a club he professed was close to his heart. He was finally going home to where he 'belonged', and he certainly received a rapturous hero's welcome from the fans at Celtic Park. But Keane's allegiance to the Hoops was not as deep-seated as the legend would have it.

As a boy, his idols were actually Tottenham Hotspur, and his favourite all-time player was Glenn Hoddle. Celtic never really came powerfully into the equation until around the year 2000, when he came out with the quote at the top of this chapter. Only then did the misty-eyed links gain full credence, the slow burn reaching a crescendo when he joined the masses of Hoops fans at the Celtic v. Porto UEFA Cup final in Seville in May 2003. Keane did love Celtic, but in a more Johnny-come-lately way than he would have us believe – hence the delay over his move there. It seemed that he wanted to check out all possibilities before committing himself – hardly the decision of a diehard fan desperate to go home for good. He admitted that Seville 2003 had been a key moment in his growing affection for the club, saying, 'I met a lot of Celtic fans in Seville, and I've always enjoyed that banter . . . I think it's important you don't lose touch with reality, because again that has crept into the game a touch. I think fans have lost touch with the players, and I think players are guilty of that as well. Seville was brilliant. I think I lost two stone that night because of the heat, but I think it was a great occasion. Not the result, but it was great that Celtic were even there after beating teams like Liverpool and challenging for a European trophy.'

After finally putting pen to paper for the club, Keane explained, to an extent, what his thinking had been: 'I spoke to Madrid and told them I wasn't prepared to wait another week. Coming up the motorway last night, I was going over things. I got my head down last night after a chat with a good friend of mine, and it was the right decision this morning. There has been a lot of speculation over the past few weeks about where I was going. But I gave every club a chance and spoke to every manager. Madrid explained to me they were looking to wait another week or so, which is fair enough. Having spoken to the Celtic manager and having been offered the contract, I knew this was the club for me. I took my time and made the right decision. I feel this is where I belong.'

Putting the pieces of the transfer jigsaw together, it appears Real president Florentino Perez desperately wanted Keane to sign a £70,000-a-week deal for six months – after a glowing endorsement from Beckham – but was dissuaded at the last minute after journalists savaged the proposed move in Spain's biggest-selling dailies. They felt Keane was over the hill and that younger blood was needed to provide a more potent mix with the likes of the ageing Zidane. They also wondered why Keane would be good enough for Madrid if he was no longer good enough for Manchester United.

Perez, who had been making encouraging noises about Keane, suddenly changed tack, saying, 'Nobody has spoken about it yet [signing Keane] and we won't speak about it until these next two games are over.' Keane is no fool: he read the warning signs and settled on Celtic, rather than delay and be made to look silly by Madrid.

There had also been talk about the Irishman signing for an English club. Bolton, West Brom and Everton had all laid their cards on the table and admitted they wanted him. Keane met representatives at each and examined their offers, but this was very much a red-herring trail. Even before the great chase for his signature, he had admitted that he would not sign for another Premiership outfit as he could not even contemplate the prospect of playing against his beloved United in the English top flight.

Keane signed an 18-month deal with Celtic that would keep him at the club until the summer of 2007. Speculation was rife that Celtic's majority shareholder Dermot Desmond would be paying half of Keane's reported wages of £40,000 per week. But Celtic chief executive Peter Lawwell claimed Desmond would make 'no financial contribution' and insisted Keane was not breaking any existing pay structures at Parkhead. My information was that Keane would draw a basic £18,000 a week and that any other arrangements would remain private between him and Desmond. I don't want to get involved in any lawsuit over Keane's wages, so would simply suggest it is best to draw your own conclusions. Desmond claimed Keane could have earned much more money elsewhere, saying of the transfer, 'From the word go, it was the manager's decision and the board's decision to go after Roy Keane. In fairness to Roy Keane, he left a lot of money on lots of tables because of his love for Celtic. What swung it for Roy was his love of Celtic, and I would hope that he respects Gordon Strachan, respects the team.

'I am very comfortable with Roy, as are other members of the board, so we have no fears that he will be an unsettling influence. On the contrary, I think he will harness all the good things that are in Celtic Football Club.'

Fair enough, Dermot, all rather fine words, but I must admit I found Keane's claim that he was not bothered about the money at Celtic rather amusing. After Sir Alex Sexton, this was the man who had always fought his corner most staunchly when pay negotiations came around at Old Trafford. Keane said, 'Football has been good to me. If it was about money, I wouldn't have gone to Manchester United when I left Nottingham Forest. I could have left United many times over the years when my contract expired, and they will tell you that. But if you concentrate on your football and follow your gut feeling, then the rest will follow.

'Money comes into the package, and I leave that to my solicitor to negotiate, but as far as I'm concerned it's about what is the best for me in terms of football. There is a new mentality in terms of money being the priority for some players, but it never has been for me and, believe me, it never will be.'

After his exit at United, questions were being asked about how Keane would settle at Celtic Park. His abrasive, fiery nature would be called into question given the similar fire in the bellies of the Glasgow club's manager Gordon Strachan and skipper Neil Lennon. In his autobiography, *Managing My Life*, which Keane has surely read, Sir Alex Ferguson accused Strachan of breaking his word, and added, 'I decided this man could not be trusted an inch. I would not want to expose my back to him in a hurry.' But Keane remained his own man, with his own opinions, who would make up his own mind. He had been impressed by Strachan when the two had met in London a couple of weeks previously and, when signing for Celtic, was at pains to point out that public perceptions did not necessarily give an accurate reflection of the private man, and this was true of himself. Keane said, 'I have been misrepresented, without a doubt. I probably don't tiptoe around people at this level, but generally, as a professional for 15 or 16 years, 99 out of 100 players that I've played with either like me or have enjoyed playing with me. A few of my teammates have already called from United, so I couldn't have been that bad. I'm sure I will change my personality at Celtic – for a day!

'The two best players over the past four or five years in Scotland have been Neil Lennon and Stiliyan Petrov in midfield. The players at Celtic have done very well, so I am under no illusions that I will walk into the team. I have never taken my place in the team for granted. I aim to train hard and give the manager a problem. At my previous club, when they bought a few midfielders I saw it as a challenge, so I'm hopeful those here will do the same.'

Keane added that his move was not based on replacing Lennon as skipper. He said, 'The captaincy is a bonus. I am all about the team. The team always comes first and the captaincy doesn't bother me one bit. I have not come up here on an ego trip or to unwind. I am here to win matches. I am a team player, despite a lot of reports. I feel I can help the club move on to the next level, which is winning trophies. That is what I am in the game for. I am not necessarily in the game to be popular. I like pushing myself and the people around me hard, but there seems to be a fault with that in the modern day.'

Keane insisted he was still a Manchester United fan, despite his relationship with Ferguson coming 'to an end'. He said, 'I was contracted to Manchester United, and I was convinced up to last year I would end my career there, but things change. I had a great time at Manchester United – they are a fantastic club. If you had told me again I would spend twelve and a half years there, I would be lucky. The manager was great to me there, but our relationship came to an end.'

His new boss Strachan revealed captain Lennon was

consulted over his signing. Strachan said, 'Any major decisions I make at training and in terms of picking teams, I always speak to Neil Lennon. If I am going to change tactics, then I will ask him what he thinks. Something major like this, you have to speak to your captain. Roy knows Lenny is the captain.'

Strachan also quickly put to bed the idea that Keane's presence would intimidate the Celtic dressing-room, saying, 'If you think we've got a bunch of shrinking violets, don't tell Sutton, Lennon and Thompson, because they are aggressive as anyone in training and demanding. But to add to that is fantastic. It was too good a chance to miss out on one of the world's great competitors.'

Indeed it was: a massive coup for the Glasgow club – arguably their biggest-ever signing. There were suggestions that Strachan himself had not really wanted Keane to join the club – that he even saw him as a threat to his own job. I am reliably told this is nonsense – if Strachan had not wanted Keane, the Irishman would not have signed. Strachan is a strong man, confident in his own abilities, a clever manager and, most impressive of all, a master tactician. He knew that having a player like Keane would actually benefit his position. With the Irishman controlling operations, Celtic could finally hope to make an impact on the Champions League the following season. The two men were similarly combustible characters, but they were both honest professionals.

Strachan had jetted down to London to meet Keane a couple of weeks before the deal. It was his enthusiasm and projection of a successful partnership that had helped Keane to make his final decision. And let's not forget this key fact to the whole plot: both men shared a major something in common. They both left Manchester United aiming to prove that their talents had not evaporated for good. Strachan went to Leeds and won a Championship medal at the expense of his former employers, and Keane was kicked out of Manchester because, among other things, Ferguson considered him expendable.

Strachan no doubt mentioned that Keane could copy his example and prove he was not washed up. He was full of admiration for Keane's decision to switch to Celtic Park, seeing it as an example of the Irishman's continuing determination to achieve success on the football field: 'I told him [Keane] where I was going. He said he was up for it. He's all right financially, but I know millionaires who want to add more and more. He could have gone to other clubs that couldn't give him trophies. That's him.'

The Celtic boss admitted he would not be frightened to leave out one of his regular big-name players to accommodate Keane – or vice versa should the occasion arise. He added, 'I have to sacrifice, but I have to sacrifice eight players every week. I have sacrificed Alan Thompson, Shaun Maloney, Aiden McGeady, John Hartson and others this season, and they are big, big players. There are loads of big players who have been left out for other people. It is a hard job, but it is a great job picking from these players.'

The goodwill towards Keane upon his arrival was widespread: from the board, the manager, the fans and former heroes. Jim Divers, secretary of the Celtic Supporters' Association, summed it all up: 'We know we are getting someone exceptional in British football. Everyone here in Glasgow – and fans around the world – is excited at the prospect of seeing Roy Keane in green and white hoops. Everyone has their opinion, but the majority of fans I have listened to are excited by the fact he is coming to Celtic Park.

'The Celtic fans pay their money and they want the best in the world. We have secured one of the best players in the world for 18 months. Under Gordon Strachan, we are playing exceptionally well and have so many young players coming through. Keane is a master on the training pitch and can pass on his experience.'

Former Celtic boss Martin O'Neill was another at the head of the queue of those who welcomed Keane's arrival, saying, 'If I had been the manager, I would have taken him. He can offer Celtic an awful lot. Roy Keane has the competitive instincts that set him apart. Loads and loads of footballers across the country are competitive – generally, professional players thrive on that. But Roy Keane has something special. He is a wonderful footballer – one of the great players Manchester United have had over the last 30, 40, 50 years.'

Next up with applause was Lisbon Lion Bertie Auld, who said, 'It's a great signing. Roy Keane is a magnificent player and will give us that extra bit of professionalism. Apart from being a good player himself, the great thing is he has and will get tremendous respect from the other players and will make them play. People talk about him not being able to play alongside Neil Lennon, but good players can play together in any team.

'Gordon Strachan has done a magnificent job since he came in, but, although he has a good squad of players at the moment, he doesn't have strength in depth.

'Roy had tremendous respect in Manchester, but there comes a time in every player's life when the surroundings seem to be closing in on you, and I think that's what happened to Roy. Maybe he has been outspoken at times, but I don't think that's a bad thing – it keeps everyone on their toes.'

When Keane signed for Celtic, they were enjoying a *17-point* lead over their Old Firm rivals, Rangers, at the top of the Bank of Scotland Premier League table. Ibrox skipper Barry Ferguson was big enough to admit, 'It's a fantastic signing for Celtic. He is a player I have always admired. When you look at the career that he has had, he is an excellent player. As a young boy, he was somebody I always looked up to and admired. He's a world-class player. But we just have to focus on ourselves. Hopefully the manager will get a bit of money and bring in a few players himself.'

Kilmarnock manager Jim Jefferies even went as far as to claim that signing Keane was the equivalent of bringing in two new players for Celtic. He said, 'The one thing about Roy Keane is that he has been a top player. You can see how Sir Alex Ferguson will never say anything bad about him on the football side. The only concerns Celtic might have is that he has missed a lot of games with injury. When you get to 34, injuries happen a lot more often than when you're 24. That's a fact of life for any player. But if he is fit and he does play a lot of games, they have strengthened their team in a big way. It's as simple as that. He's probably worth a couple of players to them.'

Even Keane's disappointed suitors from England had nothing but praise for the man they had missed out on. Bolton manager Sam Allardyce said, 'Not being able to clinch Roy's signing is particularly disappointing because that is a world-class player you are talking about. From my point of view, it was a top-class player, who, on 1 January, I could put into the team and say, "This man is going to make us better." I had no doubts at all about that. Where I can go and find that now is virtually impossible.'

And West Brom boss Bryan Robson added, 'I spoke to Roy Keane last night and he told me his intentions to go to Celtic. I never spoke about money to Roy. It was about what challenge he wanted. I think it is a decent move for him. If he picked a Premiership club, it would have been awkward for him going back to United.

'Roy has always been challenging for trophies at United. So if he had selected an Everton, West Ham, West Brom or Bolton, they are not really going to be challenging for trophies, so Roy might have found that difficult. Celtic are still going for the League and they'll probably have the Champions League next year, so it is a different type of challenge for Roy – and that is what he is after. He is in a dominant team in a league where Celtic are going to dominate most games, and that will suit Roy down to the ground.'

Inevitably, there were also doubters – although they remained in the minority. Former Celtic striker Charlie Nicholas warned Keane's arrival could signal a selection dilemma for Strachan. He said, 'Stiliyan Petrov used to play wide right for Celtic, and he hated the position. So I don't see how they can play Roy Keane and Neil Lennon together without moving Petrov to the right or the left, and that is not suitable. I think there could be a few problems, and I will be very interested to see how it goes.'

And *Mail on Sunday* journalist Andy Bucklow suggested that Keane was better off in Glasgow purely because his ego would not have been able to cope with the megastar teammates he would have found in Real Madrid's dressing-room. Bucklow said:

> Keane said on signing for the Bhoys that 99 per cent of his former teammates loved playing with him. It would be more accurate to say 99 per cent knew his value as the best player in the team, and the stronger and more talented ones among them could take, and in some cases dish back, the verbals he gave out in the strive for success. But in the ego-fest that is the Real Madrid dressing-room, Roy, being Roy, would have lit the blue touch-paper. One can just imagine Zidane's reaction if he was on the wrong end of a Phil Neville-style bollocking after a misplaced pass. Or Roy having a quiet word with Ronaldo about losing half a stone to become a proper professional.

The situation would only have intensified if Cork's finest was enjoying first hand the latest galactico balls-up from the discomfort of the Real bench.

The *Daily Mail*'s Ian McGarry had his doubts about how the club's senior players would take to Keane, saying:

> The Parkhead dressing-room is a notoriously fragile environment, and suspicion and allegation of favouritism will inevitably follow because of the way Keane was recruited. Senior players, especially, who have done so much to secure success at the club . . . have seen the wage cap placed on them obliterated . . . Keane will have to win the confidence of his teammates quickly if they are to be persuaded that his presence is not merely the indulgence of a whim by the club's most powerful figure.

Former Republic boss Jack Charlton put the boot in the hardest of all. He said, 'Let's be honest: Roy is past his best. He's made the right decision, as the SPL will not be as demanding as the Premiership or a move to Real Madrid. It won't be as hectic in Scotland, and Roy will find it easier to push forward from midfield. I'm convinced Keane would never have been allowed to leave United if the manager felt he could still make a contribution to bringing back the glory days.'

Ultimately, of course, the yardsticks that would define Keane's time at Celtic Park would be his form on the pitch and the heights of glory to which he inspired his teammates. If he were to earn a place in the history books on an equal footing with the likes of legendary Hoops midfielders Bertie Auld, Bobby Murdoch and Paul McStay, Keane needed to make a major impact. Auld and Murdoch took Celtic to their greatest triumph – the European Cup final win over Inter Milan in Lisbon in 1967 – while the stylish McStay remains a fans' favourite thanks to his tremendous efforts and loyalty to the club in the modern era from 1981 to 1997.

That journey to potential Celtic Park immortality would begin within the confines of Broadwood, home to little Clyde, on Sunday, 8 January, as Keane made his debut in the Tennent's Scottish Cup third round. The arrival of Keane brought the world's sporting media to the 8,200-capacity, sold-out ground. Bully Wee boss Graham Roberts had promised the Irishman a full-blooded welcome to Scottish football, and his players were as good as his words. Roberts had said, 'Roy Keane is a world-class signing, but he will know he has been in a game against us. It will be a full house, and we are looking forward to it. But it is a big signing for Scottish football. The quality of the player is absolutely unbelievable. This is a big coup for Celtic, and we are delighted he will be making his debut against us.'

Every man and his dog had wanted to be there for the great man's debut. A Celtic Ticket Services spokesman had told the club's official website, 'The demand for tickets went through the roof when it became clear that Roy's first Celtic match could be at Broadwood.' True to form, Roy did not disappoint the crowd – or the millions tuning in on TV – as his opener provided the sort of unexpected outcome we have come to expect from the Irishman. Little Clyde emerged 2–1 winners, and the vultures started to circle – even though Keane provided a decent enough performance. It was his first competitive match since Manchester United took on Liverpool the previous September, and he stroked the ball around. Inevitably, he was a bit ring-rusty at times, but no way could the result reflect upon him – although some commentators south of the border were gleefully glad to be able to put the boot in.

Paul Hayward, writing in the *Daily Mail*, led the way:

> Too late now to accept one of those tempting offers from Italy or Spain. Roy Keane's new career descended into comedy in Cumbernauld yesterday when tiny Clyde, known as the 'Bully Wee' to their sprinkling of fans, wrecked the wee bully's Celtic debut by bouncing them out of the Scottish Cup.

A clever turn of phrase, but hardly fair. Keane was not the culprit for the Hoops' biggest upset since the defeat by Inverness Caledonian Thistle six years previously – poor defending and a lack of attacking options were. Clyde, who had started at 50–1 shots, won with goals from Craig Bryson and Eddie Malone, and it could have been worse because they also had two goals disallowed. Two facts were clear: Keane would find it difficult to form a world-class partnership with Neil Lennon, and he would eventually find it difficult to work under Lennon at all. Keane was born to be a captain – the way he cajoled the Celtic defence against Clyde told you that. Lennon might have had the skipper's armband, but how could he be the true man in charge when Roy Keane was next to him on the pitch?

It was a charade. Surely it could not last long. Also, it was hard to see how Keane and Lennon could play together in central midfield. Keane needed young legs next to him to do his bidding and his running, and Lennon hardly fitted the bill.

What we are saying here is this: from day one, it was apparent that Celtic Football Club would have to build the team around Keane if they truly wanted the best out of him in the swansong of his career. If they didn't, he would probably walk away before the 18 months of his deal were up.

On the Celtic websites, the fans were largely in

agreement, and there was little sign of Keane-bashing. Their main target after the calamitous defeat was boss Strachan. One writer said:

> How much longer have we to suffer? 5–0 against Artmedia; humiliation against Clyde; woeful against Livingston, Falkirk, Inverness (lucky to get a draw – Boruc saved a penalty), Hearts, Hibs. In fact, the only time I have seen Celtic play well this season was against Dundee United at Tannadice – and I think this was one of the rare occasions Sutton was playing.
>
> I have struggled to believe some Celtic fans this season; some of them seem to think that Strachan's building a good team. Being top of the League doesn't mean you're a good team. The only reason we're top is because Rangers have been atrocious. I have been saying this from the start of the season; the guy hasn't got a clue, and this is clear to see with his team selections. Telfer, McManus, Wallace, Camara, etc.: he has probably picked the worst players that you could possibly pick from the selection of players that he has. I still believe that you have the players there to be a decent team, but Strachan is picking the wrong players. He picks defenders that cannot defend, cannot tackle, cannot head a ball, weak, slow, etc.
>
> He has sold our best striker (Chris Sutton) and his signings have been woeful, apart from Boruc and, at a push, Nakamura. And, by the way, all you Celtic fans who wanted rid of Balde, do you see what happens when he's not playing? This is what happens when you take your only defender away.

Another replied:

No doubt some people will give you grief, and say you are overreacting, but I totally agree. We've had GS for just over half a season, and in that time we have had two of the most disgraceful results in our history. I'm sick of coming into work and being abused over our performances!

I thought Keane had a very decent game yesterday; he just didn't have much help around him. Lennon, who I am a supporter of, didn't seem to have a good game at all. Boruc, Maloney and Keane were the only three that looked decent. I think Du Wei has actually been made a bit of a scapegoat. McManus didn't have a good first half and made a few mistakes. Hartson just isn't mobile enough and makes it hard for whoever is playing up front with him. Surely with Sutton's wages cleared, we can bring in two or three young players now?

It was all crisis talk, but wasn't that the very situation in which Keane had always thrived? Of course it was: he was a battler, a warrior. Ironically, a day later, his mentor Sir Alex Ferguson was also suffering, as Manchester United struggled to a 0–0 draw in the English FA Cup away at Burton. Funny how their fortunes continued to intertwine, despite their falling out. Both men would live to fight another day; the great tragedy remained that they would not live to fight it together. Maybe one day Ferguson would realise just how bad his treatment of Keane appeared to many onlookers at the end of it all and offer Keane the hand of conciliation that Clough never got round to doing with Peter Taylor. Old Big 'Ead would admit it remained the biggest regret of his life when Taylor died early.

On Saturday, 14 January 2006, Keane finally made his home debut against Kilmarnock but suffered an annoying injury setback. The Irishman's Celtic Park bow was in the rather unusual position of centre-half, a role he had made clear at Manchester United that he did not enjoy. That Roy did a job – and did it without complaint – was a good sign for Gordon Strachan and Celtic Football Club. Nor were there any moans and groans that he had been shunted backwards so that Strachan could accommodate Stiliyan Petrov in Keane's favoured midfield spot alongside Lennon. Of course, Roy received a rapturous hero's welcome as he walked onto the hallowed Parkhead turf, and he was clearly moved by the occasion. On his home debut, it appeared to me that Roy Keane was happy at last after his nightmare exit from Old Trafford – that he truly did feel like he had come home. It was apparent just what the club and their wonderful fans meant to him as he saluted them with a clenched fist. Celtic would go on to win 4–2 to complete his joyful entrance.

Eight days later, he was back in a position he had been in for four months before his Celtic home and away debuts – on the sidelines. It was a position he did not enjoy one bit, and it meant he had to sit out the 3–1 win at Motherwell. Newspaper reports suggested Roy could face another long spell out, but boss Strachan moved quickly to allay fears, saying, 'It's a nerve thing. He will probably be able to do some light training soon.'

Yet as February 2006 dawned, reliable, respectable sources in Glasgow were telling me that things were not hunky-dory between Keane and Strachan, that the honeymoon period had been short and that the two men had argued behind closed doors over Keane's spell on the bench after his quicker-than-expected return from injury. He had missed the away win at Motherwell but had expected to be back in the team for the SPL home match with Dundee United. Instead, Strachan kept him on the bench. The official line was that Strachan was about to bring him on late in the second half to bolster up the defence – as Celtic were leading 3–1 – but that Keane had wandered off to the toilet. By the time he had returned, the visitors had made it 3–2, and Strachan decided not to put him on after all.

Just looking at the story logically, it hardly makes sense. Why would a top pro like Keane be nipping off to the loo in the middle of a match? I had never known him do it before – and why then would Strachan not still send him on to bolster a clearly leaky defence?

The word was that Keane had got peed off rather than gone for a pee – and had reportedly gone down the tunnel in a huff, only for Strachan to apparently smooth things over. If there was a bust-up at this early stage of their relationship, the last thing they needed was to have it all over the sports pages.

Strachan claimed afterwards, 'We had one plan at 3–1 and another plan at 3–2. It was going to be a shutting-up job, but we didn't have the time to get him [Keane] on, and I had to keep all my attackers. It's happened before. It's not Roy's fault. I felt a bit sorry for him, but he has taken it well.'

Yet four days later, Keane was still on the bench for the CIS Insurance Cup semi against Motherwell at Hampden. Celtic won 2–1 to take Strachan to his first cup final as Hoops boss, yet afterwards he lashed his players for giving the worst performance of his seven-month reign. Strachan said, 'That was quite comfortably the worst performance since I've been here. Tonight there was a nervousness about us which spread right through the team to our best players. I will enjoy the cup final when it comes around, but I can't enjoy it tonight. People say, "Never mind, you're in a final", but I'm not having that. I'm not enjoying it one bit at the moment, because there are standards we have to set at this club. I feel absolutely no euphoria, excitement or happiness right now.

'Tonight has crystallised what I have to do here. There are things I have to address, but it will be done in-house. Players here have to be mentally strong, or you can't play for this club. Simple as that.'

Fair enough, but didn't all those fine words beg the question – why not play a man who is definitely mentally strong, why leave him on the bench again, until the last minute? Yes, Keane had played just one minute plus stoppage time after he replaced the hapless Adam Virgo – it was certainly no way to treat a legend. Certainly not if you wanted to earn his respect, and even at the time it left me worrying about Keane's future at Celtic Park.

A Celtic fan summed it all up like this: 'This is a man who in his last game in England ran the show in the United v. Liverpool game . . . in his last international game against France he was superb and is still Ireland's best player. Is Strachan deliberately trying to bring him down a peg and trying to be cheeky with him? Did Strachan ever want Keane in the first place?

'Yes, I know he is just back from injury, but make no mistake about it – at any other club, a player of this quality would still get his place in the team. Here was I looking so forward to the Old Firm game at Ibrox, but Keane needed games . . . in the midfield to be ready for this.

'I wouldn't be surprised if Keane walks very soon, because this must be so degrading and embarrassing. I hope it doesn't come to this, because I am a huge Keane fan and this would give all the knockers something to feed on. Celtic in the last few days have become really embarrassing.'

A series of good points. Would Roy stay the full 18 months, or would he walk?

The mystery about why Keane was not in the team deepened on 8 February when Neil Lennon told the *Daily Telegraph* that Keane had never been signed as an automatic shoo-in for the first eleven, but merely as a back-up to him and Petrov.

Lennon said, 'Gordon Strachan told Stilian Petrov and me at the start of the season and again when Roy was coming in that we would be his first choices and, credit to him, having someone like Roy there keeps us on our toes.'

Yet that night, Keane did start for the first time since 14 January and scored the first goal – his first for the club – as Celtic beat Falkirk 2–1 at Celtic Park. Keane had lined up in tandem with Petrov and had an outstanding game at the expense of the 'rested' Lennon. It was getting more baffling by the day – clearly three into two did not go, and Keane was hardly the world's most patient footballer on the sidelines.

It did improve – short term, at least. He returned to the team and helped Celtic win another League title and the League Cup. It had been touch and go whether Keane would get a medal for his efforts in the League, as a hamstring injury he sustained in the 3–0 CIS final victory over Dunfermline ruled him out of action from 19 March. The Irishman was playing again by 16 April in the 1–1 home draw with Hibs and eventually managed the ten games needed to secure that medal. Hoops manager Strachan had said he would even have asked the SPL for a special dispensation to ensure Keane was awarded the honour – but, in the event, that appeal was not required.

In public, the club were making confident noises about the next season – that Keane would be there to play a big part as they planned an assault on Europe. But by the end of April 2006, my sources in Manchester and Glasgow were telling me that Roy had no plans for the next season – that he was actually planning to bow out at his testimonial at Old Trafford on 9 May, playing one half for Manchester United and one for Celtic, and that he would donate all the proceeds to charity.

Typical of Roy to leave us all swinging – keeping us all guessing about what he would do. But, in this instance, the guessing game would not last long . . .

EIGHTEEN

THE END

'Having received medical advice from my surgeon and the Celtic club doctor, I feel my only option is to retire' – Roy Keane, 12 June 2006

Straight to the point, no messing about with colourful phrases or fancy concepts: just I'm off and why – typical Roy. But was it actually all as clear-cut and transparent as those mere twenty words would suggest? Was there anything strange about the fact that six months into an eighteen-month contract Keane should suddenly announce that his hip injury had finally beaten him? Well, let me ask you this: if he was still at Manchester United and had been promised he would be captain of the team as they attempted once again to conquer Europe the next season, would he have just packed it all in? Or would he have carried on regardless – business unusual as usual, with the hip and his creaking body aching but the pain put to one side for the cause as it had so often been over the years?

My take on it was that Roy had reached a point of no return, both mentally and emotionally. Still devastated by his savage sacking from Manchester United the previous November and unable to put the pain of his abrupt departure from the club he adored behind him, he just could not go on. Of course the hip injury was real and painful, but perhaps in some ways it was also a form of camouflage behind which he could hide the hurt he still felt over his Old Trafford dismissal. As I have frequently said, underneath the macho exterior this is a man who feels and hurts like the best of us. A sensitive, decent man whose ultimate reward for his toils at Old Trafford was an end worthy of a Shakespearean tragedy, with Ferguson playing Brutus to his Caesar.

There was another element that had to be taken into consideration when trying to work out the reasons behind this momentous decision – his working relationship with Strachan at Celtic. On the surface, the two men had managed to put on a display of unity and harmony, but, according to my sources, all was not as it seemed. In the previous chapter, I touched on how they had rowed over Keane's appearances (or lack of them), and I was also told that, despite the fact he loved the fans and most adored him, Roy was not enjoying the game up in Scotland as much as he had hoped. This was not solely a reflection on the difference in quality between the Scottish and English premier leagues – let's not forget he would have had a European campaign to look forward to at Celtic in 2006–07. The heart of the problem appeared to be that Keane's heart was no longer in football.

He would never admit it while still in Glasgow, but his heart remained in Manchester. Although seven months had passed since his departure from Old Trafford, Roy Keane still felt like a boy kicked out of his home by an angry parent. He still missed being the king of the Stretford End, *the* man at United. The club was in his blood, and he would never get over it unless – maybe make that until – he returned. This was Roy Keane, the legend of Manchester United. He was never built to play a secondary role to the likes of Neil Lennon and John Hartson at Celtic Park.

It was ironic that what would officially end his career would be the hip injury. The problem dated back to September 1997 when he suffered severe knee damage in that first incident with Alfie Haaland at Elland Road. Keane underwent hip surgery in 2002 but continued to be plagued by the injury through the rest of his career – and it all began with that episode at Leeds, an incident that would become one of the most controversial in recent football history.

It was also ironic that when announcing his retirement Roy should steal the headline news in a World Cup year. His public statement on Monday, 12 June, took a little heat off England after their demoralising performance in a 1–0 opening win over Paraguay two days previously. It struck me as darkly appropriate that he should bid farewell during the World Cup – only four years earlier he had been the major talking point as the event kicked off in Japan and South Korea after his bust-up with Mick McCarthy. Now he was in the limelight again. It also made me think how gutted he must have felt back in 2002 at missing out on the biggest football show on earth and how much Roy would no doubt have given to have been leading out the Irish in the 2006 finals in Germany. If not playing in the 1999 European Cup final was Keane's biggest regret, not far behind must have been missing out for his country back in 2002.

Funnily enough, on the day Keane quit football Strachan was in Germany for the BBC as part of their pundits' panel, analysing the match between the Czech Republic and the USA. Knowing he would be on, I tuned in at 2 p.m. and awaited the inevitable questioning over Keane in between discussion about the match itself. Now, I am no mind reader, but I could see that Strachan was clearly ill at ease when asked for his comments on Big Roy. His discomfort on the TV screen in front of me and his seeming lack of any background information about the disclosure made me think that Strachan had perhaps not been the first to hear the news, as you might have expected. My feeling – purely a gut instinct – was that the wee man had probably not been told directly by Keane that he was off for good. Strachan, his manager at Celtic, had allegedly found out like the rest of us – second hand. On screen, he talked up the idea of Keane quitting solely because of that troublesome hip – how it meant 'some days he could play, others he was in too much pain' – but I also sensed pain in Strachan's own body language.

Inevitably, though, he led the public tributes to the great man, saying, 'Roy Keane is one of the greatest ever players to grace the game of football. It was fantastic we were able to bring him to Celtic, and it has been a privilege to work with him. Even in his short time with the club, Roy made a great contribution and played an important part in bringing success to the club last season. We were delighted to make Roy's dream come true when we signed him for Celtic, and we were happy when he made our dream come true by helping us to win the title. While we would have very much liked Roy to continue for the remainder of his contract, everyone at the club fully understands and respects the decision which he has made.'

I am not sure about the line 'We were delighted to make Roy's dream come true' – it sounds patronising, as if Strachan saw himself as the big benefactor who kindly took the little boy Keane into the sweet shop and treated him after seeing him looking in longingly through the window. Roy Keane made the Celtic dream come true because he was Roy Keane, not Strachan – even if Strachan had not wanted him there, the club's directors would surely have overruled him.

One of those men, Celtic chief executive Peter Lawwell, added his own words on 12 June: 'While we are disappointed, it is important Roy's health comes first, and we fully respect the decision which he has made. Despite losing Roy, our supporters can rest assured that we are working hard to strengthen the squad for next season to face the domestic and Champions League challenges which lie ahead.'

Like Sir Alex Ferguson previously, Lawwell and Strachan would find out just how difficult, nay impossible, it would be to replace Keane. As this book went to the printers in July 2006, Chelsea midfielder Jiri Jarosik was being signed by Celtic to take Keane's role. The 28 year old would no doubt be a good buy: he was reliable and efficient. But he was no Keane.

The tributes continued to pour in as 12 June progressed. Eamon Dunphy, who wrote the first book on Keane in 2002, said, 'He will be remembered as a great footballer and a very charismatic, candid and intelligent man – quite a unique figure. He has taken his coaching qualifications, and he would be a great coach and manager. He has all the qualities for the job. He was Sir Alex Ferguson's enforcer on the field at Manchester United, his leader.

'He had turbulent periods in his life. He's an extremely candid man, and that can land you in bother from time to time. But when the smoke of the controversies fade away, a great career of a great Irish footballer will be remembered.'

Former colleague Paul Parker wanted to make a point about Keane's leadership, saying, 'He was one of the best captains Manchester United have ever had, alongside, or maybe ahead of, Bryan Robson. When he came to United, he was loud and said what he thought – he didn't care what he said to anybody – but when you could play the way he could, the players put up with the other side to him.'

Gary Pallister, another former teammate at Old Trafford, was thinking along the same lines. He said, 'He is the closest thing to Bryan Robson I've ever seen: you would probably have to put them on a par. They were both terrific players for United, and if you want to go into a battle, they're the type of people you want alongside you. He made the game seem so easy, his passing, the energy levels he had and even after his cruciate injury he still inspired his team and his teammates.

'He amazed everybody. He was a fantastic player, a leader, an inspiration. When things were going tough, he was the one the players and the fans looked to to spark things into life. None more so than at Juventus in the European Cup when he scored that header that inspired them on to win the trophy. Of course, he missed out on the final itself, and that is probably one of his biggest regrets, but the fans and the players alike will remember him for the player he was on the pitch.'

Peter Rafferty, press officer of the Celtic Supporters' Club, said, 'I am surprised and disappointed by the news. Obviously he had a genuine problem with his hip, and we understood that. Over 30,000 fans went to his testimonial at Old Trafford a few weeks back, so that tells you what we thought of him.'

Sir Alex Ferguson temporarily put his differences with Keane to one side to add his own tribute:

> Roy's obsession with winning and the demands he put on others made him the most influential player in the dressing-room. He became a great captain through that and, to my mind, he is the best player I have had in all of my time here. Over the years, when they start picking the best teams of all time, he will be in there. His display in Turin in 1999 was selfless, just wonderful. It was a tragedy that he wasn't able to play in the final in Barcelona.

Even the Irish Taoiseach Bertie Ahern got in on the act:

> Today is a sad day for his legion of Irish fans, his immense footballing genius is unlikely to ever be forgotten. Roy Keane is one of the most decorated Irish players of all time. Over the past decade, he has been arguably the greatest midfield player in world football and has established a reputation as one of the true legends of world football.

Pick of the tributes from the press came from *The Guardian's* David Lacey, who added a typically eloquent overview:

> A footballer's true worth is measured in part by the difficulty with which he is replaced and for this reason alone Roy Keane will always be numbered among Manchester United's greatest players. His retirement from the game, following a brief appendix to his career at Celtic, finds United the poorer for his absence. While recurring injury problems indicated that Keane would have to give up playing sooner rather than later, Sir Alex Ferguson's failed attempts to find the Irishman's successor in midfield have underlined the immense contribution Keane made to Manchester United's growing domination of the English game through the 1990s and beyond.

United legend Paddy Crerand went as far as to say Keane would be his top choice if he was ever asked to pick the greatest United star under Ferguson. Crerand said, 'Cantona will top many polls about Fergie's best ever buy, but for me Roy Keane was the No 1. Eric was brilliant, but it was always Roy for me who was the driving force behind all that success. You need a real leader, and Keano was just that. I don't think United would have won as much as they did without Roy in the side.

'He deserves to go down in the Old Trafford history books as one of United's greatest players. He had the will and unbelievable desire to win. He was the manager in a football kit. How often does that happen when a player mirrors everything about the manager?

'All footballers want to be winners, but Roy had that extra edge that put him beyond most others in the hunger stakes, just like Fergie as a boss. Bryan Robson was exactly the same. If Sir Alex was able to go out and buy a Keane and a Robson this summer, then you might as well say next season is over. You could wrap it up, say "Thank you very much" and hand United the Premiership title, the Champions League, FA Cup and Carling Cup! That's why it has been and will be so tough and probably more or less impossible to replace Keane.'

One of Keane's most recent teammates, Stiliyan Petrov, also felt sadness that Roy had called it a day, saying, 'It is really disappointing for football, not just Celtic. It was a great honour for me to play with Roy. Every game with him was special, and I feel very lucky because not too many players have had the chance. I am really pleased that I had the opportunity, and I am sure every other Celtic player feels the same. Roy achieved so much as a footballer and a person – and I am very sad he has played his last game.'

Of course there were those who disputed the idea that Keane had given good service to Celtic in his six-month spell. Chief among them was former Hoops skipper and manager Billy McNeill, who had this to say: 'I hate to say it, but I warned Gordon Strachan against signing Roy Keane in the first place and yesterday my fears were realised. Celtic were never going to get the sort of return from the veteran midfielder that they were looking for. Just thirteen games and one goal in six months in Scotland – if

I'd still been in charge, then I would have been bitterly disappointed with that.

'But then if I had still been in charge at Parkhead, I wouldn't have signed him. Yes, he was once arguably the best midfielder in the world, but Celtic were always getting a player who was trudging towards the end of his career. Because of the punishment his body had taken in over ten years at the top in England, he was never going to set the heather on fire in Scotland. The glory days were firmly behind him. I knew it, he knew it and, more worryingly for me, Celtic knew it. For me, the whole exercise has been a gamble that hasn't paid off.'

Colourful, tough words from a legend – although you could argue that the gamble did pay off in that Celtic fans got to witness a true legend in action and those 13 games helped win the SPL and League Cup, as well as raising Celtic's already major profile still further all around the world.

Former England skipper David Platt felt that Keane's decision to quit may have resulted from his realisation that he could never again hit the peaks of performance that had once come so naturally to him. Platt said, 'Only time will tell. When I was at Arsenal, I realised in my last year I couldn't reach the standards I wanted to meet – not just at the weekend but also in training, and I think that may be a part of it. To maintain those standards, it becomes very difficult. Somebody like Roy would look at that and think it's time to move on. Yes, there are regrets, but you have to be bold enough to make that decision. It's not a case of not giving 100 per cent; it's what that 100 per cent is. He could probably have picked the money up at Celtic . . . I'm sure morally Roy would say, "I go into football to earn the money and if I can't, I'll just walk away."'

And finally Portsmouth manager Harry Redknapp made the point that most of us had in our minds – that Keane would be back in the game as a manager one day. He said, 'He's had a great career and was a magnificent player for Manchester United. He'll be a big loss for sure, and I'm sure Gordon Strachan and Celtic would have liked to have got another season out of him, but Roy feels it's time to call it a day. I'm sure we haven't seen the last of Roy; I'm sure he's got a big future in coaching and management and will be involved in football for many years if he wants to be.'

The fans' forum sites on the net were also packed with views on Keane's retirement. The majority were once again tributes, but, as with McNeill, there was one dissenter – Barry O'Loughlin, from the Republic of Ireland, who said:

> Here in Ireland, there is an element of the 'Emperor's new clothes' about Keane – people are scared of criticising him. It's almost seen as a form of treason. But to call him a legend is an insult to football and the true legends and gents that went before him.

Rob, from Fife, was typical of most of the United and Celtic fans in his gratitude for Keane's contribution to his club. Rob, a Celtic fan, said:

> I just want to thank Roy Keane for coming to Celtic. The guy's a Celtic fan and it was great fun having him play for us. All the first-team players raved about Roy Keane's attitude, and his professionalism raised our whole level for last season.

Even an Arsenal fan known as 'Dictator' on the BBC's 606 wesbite had these kind words for Roy:

> As an Arsenal supporter, Roy Keane was not always my favourite player, but, that said, he was a winner and gave everything he had when he was on the

pitch. Players like that don't come along often and most of them today are more worried about how they look and how much they can earn rather than helping their team win matches.

For the record, Roy played in a total of thirteen matches for the Hoops in his six-month stint at Parkhead, scoring that one goal. His final 'official' match was on 3 May 2006, when he turned out in the 2–0 win over Kilmarnock at Celtic Park. But that night-time fixture will not be the one his thousands of fans at Celtic and United will remember in their old age. No, his testimonial six days later at a packed Old Trafford will always burn brightest in the memory. That was a night when the full relevance of Keane's massive contribution to Manchester United Football Club, and his short but worthy impact at Celtic Park, was brought home for the final time.

More than 30,000 Hoops fans made the trip south, contributing fully to a marvellous, special night that left Roy close to tears. United had originally offered Celtic 20,000 tickets for the match, but the Celts quickly sold out their entire allocation for Old Trafford's massive North Stand – which holds 25,500 people. It was a superb turn-out and tribute from the Scots who had taken Keane to their hearts and who, along with Manchester United's fanatics, can always be relied upon to fill any ground with their magnificent support. They are arguably the only two groups of supporters who could be do that – indeed, the Celtic fans I spoke to on the night were joking that they are now used to being the 'rent-a-crowd' team when English clubs needed someone to fill their grounds for a testimonial. Not that United's fans would not have filled the Theatre of Dreams by themselves if there had been no away fans present. Of course they would have: Keane was their absent idol, their exiled leader, and would remain so until he finally returned one day.

But it felt good to see the fans of both sides joining as one to celebrate the legend of the man on his big night. United and Celtic have always been closely associated, and it was a great atmosphere to be part of. Even my little five-year-old son Jude Cantona, who was making his first visit to Old Trafford and was notorious for his short-term concentration, did not want to leave early. Knowing in advance that Keane would be hanging up his boots after this match, I had brought my whole family to see him off – it was that kind of landmark occasion you wanted to be a part of so that you will be able to remember it in your old age.

This was the third goodbye to a United player against Celtic at Old Trafford I had witnessed – and it was easily the best. As a young lad, I had watched the Bhoys come down for Bobby Charlton's testimonial match on 18 September 1972 – a match that had attracted a crowd of 60,538 – and then had also witnessed the big farewell to Lou Macari in 1984. Yet neither had possessed the sheer emotion and unity of Keane's last hurrah.

A crowd of 69,591 turned up to watch Keane play, as predicted, the first half for Celtic, the second for United. For the record, Keane played a blinder in what turned out to be a competitive match, even having a hand in the one goal scored on the night, as he combined well with Paul Scholes and Ryan Giggs to set up Cristiano Ronaldo to slot home United's winner after 55 minutes.

Keane, who had made his way on to the pitch before the match with his wife and children to chants of 'There's Only One Keano', was clearly emotional at the end. He walked around every part of the Old Trafford pitch and told the crowd, 'This is something I'll remember for the rest of my life.'

Later that night he would add, 'I'm grateful to both clubs, the players and of course the supporters. It actually surprised me how much I enjoyed it! Coming back finished things off very nicely, and it was a great occasion.'

With it being Roy, the evening did not go off without some controversy. There was a suggestion that Sir Alex Ferguson had asked to address the crowd with a few words about his former skipper but that Roy had said no. Keane's body language as he approached Ferguson during the pre-match pleasantries also seemed to indicate that the Manchester United manager had not yet been forgiven – although both men would afterwards go to great lengths to say there was no problem between them. Throughout their careers both had been known to find it difficult to let go of a grudge even after many years passed by, let alone six months.

Another factor that made it seem highly unlikely that all was actually well between the two emerged when Ruud van Nistelrooy admitted his hurt at being unable to play in Roy's big match. Earlier that day he had phoned Roy to tell him he would not be present as promised because Ferguson had apparently banned him from the ground. Roy took the news in a civilised manner, but sources told me he was 'very angry' at Ferguson yet he 'would not kick up a public fuss as he didn't want to wreck the testimonial night'.

The news of Ruud's exile would become public by the evening of 9 May after he spoke out at Holland's World Cup training camp near Eindhoven. He said he was glad to be in training because 'It's good to get my mind off it, especially as I can't be there tonight. For me it's painful. I wanted to respect Roy; I wasn't allowed to, really. It was painful, that was the most painful thing. I spoke to him [Keane] as well, and it should be fine.'

Van Nistelrooy, the scorer of 150 goals in 200 starts for United, had become the latest to feel the cold wind of Alex Ferguson's ire when he was left out of their final league match of the season – the 4–0 victory over Charlton at Old Trafford on Sunday, 7 May. Initially, it had appeared that he had made the decision himself, but sources at United told me that it had been Ferguson who had told him to stay away from Old Trafford 'because of his bad attitude' in training.

After the testimonial match, Roy was in an uncharacteristically talkative mood, even giving Celtic fans hope that he might still play on. He said, 'It's time for me to step back and reflect on the way the season has gone. I'm due to see the specialist pretty soon, the hip specialist, I'll bounce a few things off him and obviously the Celtic doctor, and I'll try and make the right decision for me and my family and for Celtic. I'll try and be fair to everybody, but again I'll enjoy the next few days now and rest the body and make a decision, hopefully, I'm sure it'll be the right one.'

Sir Alex Ferguson, when questioned, also felt Keane might still play on. He said, 'If he wants to stay on, he will do it; he'll manage that because he's got a capacity no other player's got. He'll probably take a rest and then make a decision. He's never said to me what he's going to do, and I haven't broached the subject with him, but I'm sure that when he gets a rest, he'll be able to make the right decision.'

Before the match, Keane had said he believed United would return to the top – despite the ever-looming shadow of Roman Abramovich and his fortune at Chelsea. In the match programme, Keane said: 'You get clubs who are happy to come second or third. Not United. The fans don't deserve anything less than winning, and that's what the manager and the club are about.'

Afterwards, he had a few more words to say about the immediate future for Manchester United, and from his defiant backing of the club you would have thought he was still skipper at Old Trafford. Keane said he expected to see some new arrivals at Old Trafford during the summer and that United had enough promising youngsters – like

Rooney and Ronaldo – to peak again. He said, 'It's going to be tough, but hopefully United will bounce back next season. I'm sure there will be one or two players leaving, but I also expect there to be one or two coming in.

'The club have got some good young players coming through – I watched the reserves win the league and the Treble last week – and they've got some excellent youth players as well. I'm sure Manchester United is in very, very safe hands.'

Roy even talked about his sad departure on 18 November 2005, amazingly insisting he had no regrets and claiming that he and Ferguson had smoothed things over. He said, 'It was all very amicable. The manager and I shook hands and both agreed it was the right thing to do and it was, there's no doubt in my mind about that. I've met up with the manager on a couple of occasions since then and it's been fine. I'm a grown man, I accepted it and moved on. My heart will always be with United, but things happen and you have to get on with your life.'

So what now for Roy Keane? If he had stayed at Parkhead, it was conceivable that Keane could have ended up as assistant manager to Strachan, then manager. And after that . . . maybe assistant to whoever took over from Ferguson at Manchester United and then maybe his ultimate dream of the manager's chair at Old Trafford?

Perhaps, but Keane being Keane he would do it his way. He did not want an easy run at management just because of who he was. No, I was told that he wanted to start at a lower level and work his way up. He was as old fashioned as his mentor Ferguson in that way: he believed a hard apprenticeship was the best way forward.

What we did know for sure was that this driven man would not give up easily, that the demons within him would push him to the limit, that the competitive streak and the search for perfection to cover up that divisive inner insecurity would continue to dictate that he had to be the best.

Roy Keane: the man who never accepted second best; the man who became the most successful captain in Manchester United's history, having led the club to ten major trophies; the man who played for and managed Manchester United; the man who proved Sir Alex Ferguson wrong. Yes, that would be the epitaph Roy would most want. And the odds on him achieving it?

Well, put it this way: would you ever bet against Roy Keane?

EPILOGUE

KEANE GREAT, CANTONA BETTER, GEORGE BEST

So just who was the greatest-ever at Manchester United, and just how did Keano fit into the grand order? A question and a topic beloved of any Old Trafford anorak, but one of the most difficult to get your head around and definitively answer. The question took on a certain poignancy as November rolled into December 2005 and the great Georgie Best died and was buried in his native Northern Ireland. Indeed, the title of this chapter is indebted to Georgie boy: it is a gentle rewording of a wonderful message adorning a banner near the Best family home on the Cregagh estate. The banner read: 'Maradona good; Pele better; George Best.'

Indeed, Besty did fill our lives with so much joy. Every one of the people I spoke to about United's greatest-ever agreed with that – and also agreed that was why George was head and shoulders above everyone else in United's modern era. He was a genius, a marvellous forward with speed and accuracy, nimble feet, a clever brain, and he could score goals and dribble like nobody's business. He did his job, but he did it with a smile on his face and, just as importantly, brought a smile to the faces of those on the terraces.

Inasmuch, it is a fairly futile business to try to compare him to someone like Keane: it is not a comparison that can accurately be made. However, comparing the impact of Keane on the team and their fortunes and comparing him one to one with, say, Bryan Robson is an altogether different matter.

I asked fans, journalists, players and managers within the game whom they rated the best in the modern era, and I got some interesting results. By modern, I mean from the late '60s onwards. I know there is a case in particular for Busby Babe Duncan Edwards to be in the list, if not top of it. Many believe Edwards would have been the greatest player in United's history and even better than Bobby Moore had his career not been cut tragically short when he died as a result of the Munich air disaster aged just 21. But I just felt it unfair to throw him in among the modern-day wolves, particularly as most of us had never seen him play in the flesh.

I also asked if our commentators believed that Keano would get a similar send-off to Besty when he finally joined the great XI in heaven. The general consensus appeared to be that Keane was a great – and arguably better than Robson – but that Cantona was better, and better loved, while Georgie was simply the best. In my view, you could also have made a case for Bobby Charlton and Denis Law. Sir Bobby was strong, powerful and a great leader and ambassador for the club, while the Law-man scored a phenomenal 171 goals in 305 League games. And from the more recent era, you could certainly ask if Peter Schmeichel was worthy of a mention. He was a goalkeeper without peer, a mountain of a man who even had the nerve to bully the likes of Steve Bruce and Gary Pallister.

Anyway, enough of my mutterings: here's what our panel reckoned, starting with journalist and loyal fan Martin Creasy. Back in the 1970s, Martin and his pal Robin Burnham ran coaches to Old Trafford from their home town of Crawley in Sussex. 'It was the only way we could afford to go, because we were too skint,' Martin recalled. 'I had a job at the local paper and I put a free ad in one week to see if we could fill a coach. We could have filled it twice over, such was the magic of United. It was a bargain too – £4.50 return to Manchester – a round trip of nearly 600 miles. It was great. The punters were happy at those prices and we had free seats for ourselves. We even made a few quid to pay our entrance to the Stretford End. Mind you, nobody on the coach had tickets, so we prayed that the driver got his foot down because if you got there late in those days, you didn't get in!'

Martin has been a United fan since he was a child in the 1960s, when Best, Law and Charlton were mesmerising defences up and down the country. And like many fans of a certain age, he believes there is one United player who stands head and shoulders above the rest. 'Georgie boy! Best by name and best by far,' he says. 'Sadly, I was just a bit too young to see George play in the flesh at his pre-1969 best, but I was privileged to see the great man in action for United many times in the early 1970s.

'And what a player he was. The way the team played in those days – with devil-may-care flair and excitement. That was the reason people like me loved them, even though they were hundreds of miles away. It was the way football should be played. You could keep your Leeds and Liverpools – all snarling aggression and win-at-all-costs defending. We wanted football with magic attached, and Georgie typified that. Georgie, Denis and Bobby Charlton – anything could happen at any time. Of course, by the 1970s the team wasn't always winning, but it was still United who played at stadiums where almost as many were locked out as got in!'

United's attacking philosophy meant entertainment was always on the agenda. 'There was the famous match at Crystal Palace when United were 2–0 down just a few minutes before half-time. Then Georgie and Denis Law shared five goals in twenty-five minutes either side of the break to completely turn the match on its head. Fortunately, that was one of the few times when the TV cameras were there to capture it. Football didn't enjoy the celebrity hype in those days, and only a few matches were covered by television. The sad thing is that future generations will only have glimpses of the Belfast boy's magic on grainy old black-and-white footage. Believe me, when you were there to witness it, Besty's wizardry will never be surpassed.'

Martin believes that the send-off George Best received in Belfast and the extraordinary reaction from the football world were more than just compliments on his skill. 'To be honest, I was amazed at the reaction around the country. Whole grounds rising and cheering to the rafters in honour of a famous player from the opposition. I honestly thought we would never see that again. These days, there is too much hate around, and I'm well aware of how much United are hated as much as loved up and down the country.

'But to see people react like that to George brought tears to my eyes. I believe that George's charm – the twinkle in his eyes – was as much a reason for that reaction from the public as his great skill.

'And though Roy Keane was captain during our most successful period, I could never feel the same way about him. Charm seems to be one thing he lacks. A United legend, no doubt. A wonderful footballer, no doubt. A United terrace hero, no doubt. I accept that most of my United mates don't share my opinion, but I wouldn't want to spend five minutes in his company, and I know he would certainly feel the same way about me. He hasn't got time for people. He doesn't seem to like people. I visited The Cliff a few times as a teenager, and Georgie and Denis not only signed autographs, they stopped to chat too. And they were charm personified. But to people like Keano, fans are just know-nothings. Prawn-sandwich brigade. What a shameful comment. I shared his disappointment that Old Trafford was no longer the cauldron that was worth a goal start for the team, and yes, I have tried to rouse some of my colleagues in the North Stand to start singing, but to humiliate your own fans like that was reprehensible.

'A captain isn't someone who hits out in all directions, blaming everyone around him when things go wrong. Keano's reported MUTV criticisms this season are not the first time he has blamed everyone else. I remember his remarks in 2000 when we went out of Europe. Suddenly, the club had an air of gloom . . . and we won the League the next week! In a way, I don't think the club has rediscovered the feel-good factor since.

'However, though I hope the day is a very long way off yet, I'm sure Keano would get a good send-off in the Republic. He's still a hero to many there, although no doubt there's plenty who will never forgive the World Cup walk-out. The funny thing is, though Keano was never my favourite United player, like every other United fan I'd stick up for him if anyone else had a pop. Keano over Mick McCarthy every time, and certainly over no-classers like Jason McAteer.'

Keano would have to appear in a top ten of United greats, wouldn't he?

'Yes, of course. He was a fantastic player for United and a big factor in why the team won so much in the 1990s. Up until injury slowed him down, Keano was just about the best box-to-box player in the business. For Eric, Kanchelskis, Giggs and Beckham and the others to work their magic, they first needed to get the ball. And Keano was the ultimate ball-winner. He truly dominated the midfield week in and week out, and maybe he was Fergie's eyes and ears on and off the pitch.

'It was just the level of apparent malevolence – to friend and foe alike – that I found so charmless. He would say, "Just look at the record and it justifies everything." Fair enough. I was as grateful for the success as any other United fan. Maybe every successful team needs a Keano. It's just that, to me, Keano would have fitted in more with Leeds under Don Revie!

'Eric Cantona was my 1990s favourite. Another true United legend. My best-ever United team would have Eric playing just off the Law-man, with Besty on the wing, Bobby Charlton behind, and Keano and Robbo to do the running. Now that lot would take some stopping. Player-wise, it's difficult to separate Keano and Robbo. Certainly, Keano had more success, but Robbo was carrying a poorer side. Robbo to me was a real Captain Marvel, though he probably got away with some crunching tackles that Keano would never have because he was captain of England!'

Journalist Andy Bucklow is also a big United fan. His debut was in 1967 when he witnessed George Best scoring the Reds' goal in the 3–1 defeat by Nottingham Forest at the City Ground. Andy was then aged just nine and went with his dad to the game.

I asked him where Keane would come on a list of United modern greats – before Charlton, Law or Best? Andy said, 'There's no doubt he would have got into any United side, period, and his influence as one man in a winning team could be said to be more than either of the three parts of that great triumvirate.

'To some extent, they fed off each other but also, at times, competed with each other, particularly in the case of Best and Charlton, who only became real friends long after each had retired. But United fans gorge on entertainment and excitement, and for sheer thrills and individual skills, it would be hard to make out a case for Roy against either Bobby, George or Denis. He was an amalgam of both Nobby Stiles and Paddy Crerand, two key underrated members of Busby's exciting '60s team. More recently, there's been Robson, of course, and Cantona. It's easy to forget now how intimidating the United team of the '90s must have been to opposing teams. They'd play you off the park and take no prisoners.

'From Peter Schmeichel, through Bruce, then Paul Ince and Roy Keane up to Mark Hughes and Cantona. Even the notorious Leeds team of the '70s would have baulked before kicking the likes of them. But the catalyst to success for the modern United was Cantona. Keane apart, the others were in situ and without a championship before Eric arrived.

'Roy was the icing on the cake when he was signed from Forest in the summer of '93 when the champagne was still fizzing following United's first title success in 26 years.

'The bottom line is that without Eric's influence there would have been no title in '93. And that most likely would have been the case if Roy had been signed before Eric. Eric provided the belief, and the young bucks like Keane, Giggs, Beckham, Scholes *et al.* bought into that belief. From not getting past first base, no mountain was too high.

'So for skill and excitement, Best was head and shoulders above anyone. For one man making a difference, you can't look too far past Eric. But there is no doubt that in the remarkable history of United, Roy would be in the top ten for his all-round contribution. His like don't come around very often, which is why the club will take years, if ever, before they adequately replace him.'

But do you think Roy is held in the same emotional esteem as the likes of Best? Would there be the same sort of mourning if Roy passed away?

'[They are] United legends and heroes both, and adored by supporters at Old Trafford. Yet it would be hard to imagine the Cork man getting the same adoring send-off as that accorded to wee Georgie. Whereas Best transcended club loyalties, Keane's confrontational style and abrasiveness, both on and off the pitch, polarised opinion. Support in Ireland was also split, even more so since

Keane's infamous World Cup walk-out in 2002.

'One could easily imagine thousands lining the streets for Roy but with flowers being strewn on the coffin from one side of the road and bricks being lobbed from the other.'

Andy's face broke into a mischievous grin when I mentioned that Keane had had talks with Everton over a possible move. He said, 'Well, one man who certainly wouldn't appreciate the Second Coming of Roy would be Philip Neville. The former youth team star at United was deemed surplus to requirements by Sir Alex in the summer but had done well for his new club Everton. But this was the same Neville who had spent the best part of a decade on the fringes on the United first team – and on the wrong side of constant public ear-bashings from Keane. So news that Roy had been in talks with Everton must have sent him running for the Andrex.

'Neville was building up something of a reputation as the new blue midfield enforcer, but Keane's arrival would have had him begging Sir Alex to return to United's bench.'

OK, Andy . . . Robson or Keane?

'They are the two most influential midfielders of the modern era (Gerrard doesn't compare with these two at their best). Their careers dovetailed briefly when Robbo was at the end of an outstanding, yet relatively unrewarding, career at OT and Keane was the new young buck who, however briefly, found himself playing second fiddle to Paul Ince. Three into two didn't go, and first Robson, then dramatically Ince, were purged from the playground for the new king of the hill.

'Three players stand out as icons in the Fergie era; without any one of them, United would not have had such an enviable recent history – Cantona, Schmeichel, Keane.'

Fair enough, but if it came to the crunch, would you pick Robson or Keane?

'It seems almost unthinkable to leave out either. Keane is

out on his own in the "show us yer medals" stakes. And the second of Robbo's two title medals was won with him as a declining influence. But for the best part of a decade, Robbo was the *only* world-class performer at Old Trafford. Hughes would later become one, and injury and other activities meant Whiteside never matured to become the player he could have been. Keane was part of arguably the best post-war United team, the '94–'95 side, even accounting for the sides which won the European Cup in '68 and '99. But for the foreigners restriction, which forced Fergie to leave out Schmeichel in a 4–0 thrashing at Barcelona, that team could have brought ultimate Euro success back to OT four years earlier.

'But there is no doubt the '99 Barcelona triumph would never have happened without Roy's selfless performance in Turin when he was booked early and knew he'd be suspended for the final but still carried the team over the line, starting with the comeback goal at 2–0 down.

'By contrast, at his peak Robson won a mere three FA Cups. But without him, in the attractive but erratic Big Ron days, they'd have won precisely nothing. The man virtually carried a team of underachievers and dilettantes to treat the fans to a day out at Wembley every few years, when Cup final success was an inadequate aspirin to the Liverpool-induced headache.

'He was injury prone. Just like Roy. The team was not the same without him. Just like Roy. He never gave less than 100 per cent. But Robbo was sent off just once (at Sunderland in an FA Cup tie) compared to the *eleven* for Roy – whose indiscretions have cost more than a few vital points over the years and could have lost momentum for the Treble if Schmeichel's penalty save and Giggsy's wonder goal hadn't rescued United against Arsenal after Roy had been sent off in the FA Cup semi-final replay at Villa Park. Plus, one of Roy's long injury absences, the cruciate ligaments of '97–'98, came Gazza-style after his infamous lunge on Haaland at Elland Road.

'An interesting intellectual exercise would be to consider how Robbo and Roy would have coped in each other's teams. There's no doubt that Robbo at his peak would have been a major player in the 1999 European Cup team. But how would Roy – and his temperament – have coped as the sergeant-major in Big Ron's cavalier army? Not too well, I would venture to suggest.

'Keano would have admired the bloodied Kevin Moran, who put his head where others' boots feared to tread. But if poor old Neville junior thought he had it bad from Keano in a winning team, what price the lackadaisical Peter Barnes or Jesper Olsen? That's not even to mention the likes of John Sivabeck, Colin Gibson and Graeme Hogg.

'And, given the permanent all-day drinking licence afforded by Ron to his pet players (including, it has to be said, Robbo), it hardly bears thinking about how much trouble Roy would have got into on a longer leash.

'Having said all this, I feel Roy was marginally the better player. But Robbo in the same era would have, on balance, been just as, if not more, effective.'

Other fans had no doubt about it: Best was the best, full stop. Born on 22 May 1946, he grew up on the Cregagh estate, joining United as an amateur in 1961. George made his professional debut for the club as a 17 year old against West Bromwich Albion in September 1963. He was a vital member of the Manchester United sides that won the League Championship in 1965 and 1967, and the European Cup in 1968, when he was voted both English and European Footballer of the Year.

Sometimes nicknamed 'the fifth Beatle', George had it tougher than Keane or any of them when it came to the press and public acclaim. He was the first pop-star footballer, receiving thousands of fan letters a week and regularly finding himself the focus of intense media attention. As his rock 'n' roll lifestyle began to take its toll, however, his football career deteriorated during the 1970s.

Here are just a few tributes from United fans – showing just why they rated George above Keane *et al.*:

> Bev Watson: George Best was a wonderful footballer who never stopped being a real person. He was part of my childhood and my adult life. I am very sorry he is gone.
>
> Lawrence Jenkins: I saw George play several times. In one particular game at Highbury in 1968–69, which I believe ended 2–2, there was one magic moment when Best ran at the Arsenal defence straight down the middle heading for goal. Then at least five Arsenal players converged on him just outside the penalty area, and yet out of that almost tangled mêlée of players, George found the tiniest gap and unleashed a shot which left the Arsenal keeper stranded as the ball thudded against the crossbar, and I swear the whole ground felt that vibration. The crowd gasped in absolute admiration – it really did take your breath away.
>
> Neil Summers: I saw George play for Fulham against Peterborough United in the League Cup. He received the ball on the corner of the penalty area, with a number of defenders in front of him and the keeper a yard or two off the line. He flicked the ball up and in one movement volleyed it over the keeper and just under the bar for an outstanding goal.
>
> Rod Aries: There's a comparison between boxing and football when Ali was considered the greatest because he had the 'complete package', but most agreed Sugar Ray Robinson was the greatest boxer. I think the same is said for George Best, who may not

have been the greatest footballer, but he possessed all the greatest attributes at the highest level.

As far as the players go, Tottenham midfielder Edgar Davids admitted he was a big fan of Keane's, and that he would have loved to have teamed up with him. The Dutchman said he almost joined United in the '90s but ended up staying at AC Milan. Asked how close he came to making the move, Davids said, 'Close? Very. It was the best conversation I have ever had with a manager. I won't go into detail but we spoke about general things.'

But the 32 year old said he had no regrets: 'Regrets? No, because I didn't do so bad in my career. But every team looks up to Manchester United. Chelsea can go on and have a great history, but United have been successful over the years. If you ask any team, they would take that history. What I like most about them is that they play with big hearts. In the big games, it is always there. I've always had that desire, and it is in Manchester United. Roy Keane has this spirit, and when you have that around every day, it can become second nature.'

United striker Ruud van Nistelrooy also paid tribute to Keane's deserved place in the United hall of fame, claiming he was better than Best, Cantona or Robson. Van Nistelrooy said, 'Roy will always be remembered as the greatest player who's played for the club. His leadership and quality of play and his character will always be within us, because I worked with him and trained with him for four and a half years, and he was the best player I ever played with, and it's just a shame it stops now.

'It was a sad day to hear it [that he had gone] and I needed time to deal with it and get over it, which is impossible in such a short time, but you have to forget a little bit and focus on the next game. It made such an impact on all of us, really.'

Managerial legend Sir Bobby Robson leaned towards his namesake Bryan in any comparison with Keane. He said Bryan was 'the bravest, most committed and the strongest player I ever had'. Football writer Brian Glanville also went for Bryan, calling him 'the most complete midfielder since Johan Neeskens'. David Beckham loved Keane but also acknowledged his debt to Robson, as a great midfielder and *the* inspiration for him when he started out. TV pundit Alan Hansen had no doubts, saying Keane 'was in a class of his own at his peak' and 'the best player the Premiership has seen'.

Maybe we should leave the final words about Keane's influence at United to the man who started our debate: Georgie Best. In 1999, he gave an interview to the *Irish Examiner*, in which he spelled out his beliefs that Keane was irreplaceable at United at a time when the player was involved in a contractual dispute with the club. Keane was seeking a £40,000-a-week deal, but United's board were determined not to budge on their offer of £28,000, even though Keane could have left on a free transfer next summer.

Best said, 'The situation's quite simple. If the club think he's asking for too much, they make the decisions and there will be only one outcome. At the same time, if someone else comes in and offers more money, then he could take it.

'I believe players are massively overpaid, but you can't blame them for taking what they're offered. I'm sure clubs will be queuing up to sign Roy, because he is such a terrific player. At the moment, there is no one in England who can replace Keane . . .'.

And there you have it: during his heyday, there was no one who could have replaced Keano – and, of course, you could say the same of the Belfast boy and Eric the King.

Lionhearts.

Champions of their eras.

True legends all – even if each was flawed in his own precious way.

BIBLIOGRAPHY

Clough, Brian, *Cloughie: Walking on Water – My Life*, Headline, 2002

Ferguson, Alex, *Managing My Life: My Autobiography*, Hodder & Stoughton, 1999

Flynn, Alex and Kevin Whitcher, *The Glorious Game: Extra Time – Arsène Wenger and the Quest For Success*, Orion, 2004

Hildred, Stafford and Tim Ewbank, *Roy Keane: Captain Fantastic*, Blake Publishing, 2001

Keane, Roy, with Eamon Dunphy, *Keane: The Autobiography*, Penguin, 2003

Quinn, Niall, *Niall Quinn: The Autobiography*, Headline, 2003

Taylor, Daniel, *Deep into The Forest*, Parrs Wood Press, 2005

Unknown Fan, *The Little Book of Keane*, New Island, 2002

NEWSPAPERS

Daily Mail (particular thanks to Lee Clayton and Paul Hayward)

Daily Mirror (particular thanks to Peter Willis)

Daily Record (particular thanks to editor Bruce Waddell)

Daily Telegraph
The Guardian (particular thanks to Daniel Taylor)
Mail on Sunday (particular thanks to Andy Bucklow)
News of the World (particular thanks to Andy Coulson, Neil Wallis and Nick Jones)
The Observer (particular thanks to Paul Wilson)
The People (particular thanks to Matt Clark)
The Sun (particular thanks to Jonathan Worsnop and Neil Rowlands, Steve Waring, Neil Custis, Alan Feltham and the boys on Sun Sport and Nick Chapman ICF)
Sunday Mirror (particular thanks to David Walker)
Sunday Telegraph (particular thanks to Patrick Barclay)
Sunday Times (particular thanks to Alan Hunter, Derek Clements and Hugh McIlvanney)
The Times (particular thanks to Craig Tregurtha)

MAGAZINES

England magazine (particular thanks to Sir Bobby Robson)
FourFourTwo (particular thanks to editor Hugh Sleight)
Red Issue
Red News
United magazine
United We Stand (particular thanks to Andy Mitten)

ONLINE

BBC Sport: http://news.bbc.co.uk/sport
Guardian Unlimited: www.guardian.co.uk
Manchester United FC: www.manutd.com
Sky Sports: www.skysports.com
Soccerbase: www.soccerbase.com
Talking Reds: www.manutd.com/talkingreds